THE SWORD
OF THE
PROPHET

THE SWORD
OF THE PROPHET

Islam
History, Theology, Impact
On the World

Serge Trifkovic

Regina Orthodox Press, Inc.
2002

ISBN 1-928653-11-1

Regina Orthodox Press, Inc.
Boston, MA
www.reginaorthodoxpress.com

TABLE OF CONTENTS

FOREWORD

Our political leaders tell us that Muslims are a peace-loving and hospitable people. We are admonished not to condemn Islam because of the acts of a tiny and fanatical minority. As a people, we are conditioned to be fair-minded and tolerant. We pride ourselves on our acceptance of diversity and the reality of a multicultural society. Many of us have children or grandchildren who go to school with Muslim children. This does not intimidate us; on the contrary, many of us look upon it as the way of the future. Yet, at the same time, we are uneasy.

We are uneasy because of an intuitive sense that many of the adherents of this religion seem out of step with the modern world. The beheading of apostates, the chopping-off of the hands and feet of convicted criminals, the stoning to death of women accused of adultery, including those who have been raped—such barbaric practices disturb us. When a Muslim cleric broadcasts a television message to Palestinians, exhorting them to martyr themselves for Allah's sake and urging them to annihilate Jews, we are rightly concerned. These acts seem more indicative of a seriously dysfunctional society than the characteristics of a benevolent and merciful religion.

We are also uneasy because we cannot ignore the dreadful events of September 11 in New York and Washington. We cannot understand the murder, in the name of God, of Israeli innocents by self-destructing Islamic fanatics—some of whom are teenage girls. We are disturbed and angry by the images on our television screens of screaming mobs in Cairo, Islamabad, and Tehran, celebrating the death of thousands of Americans blasted away by young Muslim men—"martyrs" in the name of Allah. We ask ourselves why is this happening, and why is it being done in the name of religion? What can be done about it?

Other facts suggest something is wrong in the Muslim world. With all of their oil wealth, why are there no Muslim countries among the top 30 of the world's richest nations? Why is it that two-thirds of the world's poorest people live in Muslim countries? Why, in the last 20 years, have over 2 million people died in conflicts involving Muslim communities? Why are democracy and the rule of law nonexistent in most Muslim states? Why do Muslims carry out so many of the worst acts of terrorism?

3

This book provides some of the answers to these questions. It does not do so by giving us yet another academic and "objective" treatise about Islam. It does so by asking us to look at the historical record of Islam and to examine closely some of the major tenets of a faith that on the record has contained—and continues today to contain within it—strong elements of intolerance and aggression. The book is a hard-hitting frontal assault on militant Islam. It pulls no punches in identifying the rise of Islamic fundamentalism as the greatest danger to "Western" values since the end of the Cold War.

The core of the problem is that under Islam there can be no separation of church and state. Islam is a way of life, and the faithful must accept and affirm their surrender to Allah, and live as members of the total Islamic community. This calls into question if a true Muslim can give political loyalty to a non-Muslim state. With over 20 million Muslims now living in the countries of Western Europe, and from three to five million in the United States, the question of loyalty to the country of one's citizenship becomes important.

Amir Taheri, the Iranian author, has pointed out that "The current consensus among Muslim jurists is that Muslims can live in lands ruled by non-Muslims, provided they use their presence to further the cause of Islam." Mr. Taheri quotes the medieval Egyptian theologian Muhammed Ghazzali, who said that *Muslims could live under non-Muslim rule as long as they do not forget that they are Allah's missionaries and, if needed, His soldiers.* Mr. Taheri reminds us that Bin Laden is more specific and believes that Muslims should only live in non-Muslim countries to further the cause of Islam and speed up the end of the infidel's rule.

Does our tolerant and democratic way of life contain within itself the seeds of its own destruction? Should organized intolerance be tolerated? Our society is inclined to see both sides of every question, and the current trend of political correctness reinforces this tendency. But how far should tolerance extend? Tolerance of those who wish to eradicate our way of life can be self-destructive. If through migration and current demographic trends Muslims become a majority in a Western country, how quickly will Islamic law be proclaimed? Can we expect then to be treated as equals?

This book leaves no doubt about the answer to this question. It is not optimistic about the possibility of a reformation that might lead to the ascendancy of a more liberal and moderate Islam that accepts the need to

4

separate church and state. Islamist militancy will not only continue, but will intensify. This book chastises the "opinion-forming elite" for its role in pretending that Islam does not present a serious problem.

The author points out that the most virulent form of Muslim extremism owes its growth to shortsighted United States foreign policy. United States military support to the Mujahedeen in the struggle to defeat the Soviet Union in Afghanistan was only the beginning. After the Soviet withdrawal from Afghanistan, American oil interests were courting the Taliban to secure a pipeline across Afghanistan to exploit the vast oil and gas reserves in Central Asia and the Caspian Sea. By allowing Pakistan and Saudi Arabia a free hand in Afghanistan, the United States guaranteed the military success of the Taliban forces.

It is common knowledge that Saudi Arabia is the most extremist of the Muslim States. It finances the infamous Madrassas that preach a litany of hate and turn out thousands of fanatical Islamic zealots. It indirectly provides the funding and its citizens provide most of the fighters for Bin Laden's Al-Qaeda organization. It supports, financially and by other means, the Palestinian terrorists and other Muslim anti-Western groups throughout the world. Yet the United States does not identify Saudi Arabia as an enemy. It was not even asked, as were other Muslim states, by Secretary of Defense Donald Rumsfeld to freeze the assets of people linked to Bin Laden. It is this double standard and hypocrisy that this book so deplores in pointing out the shortcomings of the United States' war against terror as conceived at present.

This is a book that deals with what many consider to be the major issue of our time—the question of whether the Western and Muslim civilizations can live together in peace. It outlines in carefully measured terms what must be done to ensure that this can happen. It does so in a fearless and straightforward fashion that is not inhibited by trying to strike a balance between the two civilizations. The reader is left in no doubt on whose side the author is on. Unfortunately, the reader is also left with the uneasy feeling that, just as the Western democracies refused to acknowledge the danger inherent in the rise of Nazi and Communist ideologies, our refusal to confront militant Islam may cost us dearly.

Ottawa, Summer 2002   *Ambassador James Bissett*

INTRODUCTION

The tragedy of September 11, 2001, and its aftermath have shown, yet again, that *beliefs have consequences;* the centrality of Islam to the attacks is impossible to deny. Our opinion-formers, inflexible in their secular-liberal ideological assumptions, deny it nevertheless. They do not take religion seriously. Instead of pondering the complex problem of the relationship between Islam, the West, and the rest, they assure us that no "religious" problem exists. Some of them at least seem to believe their own assurances, so that the most outspoken character witnesses for the hastily nicknamed "Religion of Peace and Tolerance" were non-Muslims: Sunday-morning popular entertainers, academicians steeped in political correctitude, and politicians. Their claims about the supposed distinction between "real Islam" and its violent aberrations were crudely ideological, based on their simple conviction that all faiths—having equal legal privileges—must in some sense be equally good, "true," and, hence, capable of celebrating all others in the spirit of tolerance.

Such assertions cannot change reality. A problem *does* exist. Islam is not only a religious doctrine; it is also a self-contained world outlook, and a way of life that claims the primary allegiance of all those calling themselves "Muslim."

Islam is also a detailed legal and political set of teachings and beliefs. There is "Christianity," and there used to be "Christendom," but in Islam such a distinction is impossible. To whatever political entity a Muslim believer may belong—to the Arab world of North Africa and the Middle East, to the nation-states of Iran or Central Asia, to the hybrid entities of Pakistan and Indonesia, to the international protectorates of Bosnia and Kosovo, or to the liberal democracies of the West—he is first and foremost the citizen of Islam, and belongs morally, spiritually, and intellectually, and in principle totally, to the world of belief of which Muhammad is the Prophet, and Mecca is the capital.

This is not, of course, true for every Muslim but it is true of every *true* Muslim: it is the central worldly demand of Islam. The purpose of this book is to outline its origins, its basic tenets, its historical record, and to explore its implications for the rest of us.

Before its self-destructive civil war of 1914–1918, the Christian world was as sharply defined as the Muslim world. Both were perfectly capable of defining themselves against each other in a cultural sense, and keeping their tolerations and rejections in useful order. What secularism has done, since replacing Christianity as the guiding light of "the West," is to cast aside any idea of a distinctly "Western" social, geographic, and cultural space that should be protected. This was obvious in Europe by the early 1960s, and for the past quarter-century, at least. it has become obvious in the United States. Patriotism rekindled after September 11 is a reminder that at the grass-roots level the capacity for instinctive self-definition is still alive, but it cannot be sustained if the dominant outlook is that of cultural relativism and anti-historicism.

The only way we can meaningfully judge the present and plan the future is by the example of the past. The problem of collective historical ignorance—or even deliberately induced amnesia—is the main difficulty in addressing the history of Islam in today's English-speaking world, where claims about far-away lands and cultures are made on the basis of domestic multiculturalist assumptions rather than on evidence. The absence of historical memory has taken too many well-meaning Westerners interested in Islam right through the looking glass into the virtual-reality world of superficial reportage, ideological treatises, and agenda-driven academic research that ignores the reality of what Islam actually is, and what it does to its adherents.

It is necessary to correct this trend of public commentary that tends, systematically, not to *understand* Islam but to construct a propagandistic version of it. That the worst culprits are the titled "experts" in the field is unsurprising. This author is not an Islamicist, but to be a non-specialist is almost a prerequisite for setting out an account of Islam that is free from wriggling apologetics, self-censoring fears, and self-denigrating deference to "the Other." He regards Islam with a mixture of feelings, but conceives his lack of *a priori* admiration to be no greater obstacle to understanding Islam and expounding its meaning than it would be to discussing yesterday's Marxism or seventeenth century New England Puritanism. The key to understanding is not sympathy and respect for any belief; it is curiosity, intellectual engagement, and a respect for truth.

Even if all history—as a philosopher argued—is in some measure contemporary history, it need not be dominated by the obsessions of the day. This work is presented, not in order to praise, condemn, or justify an important monotheistic faith, but in the conviction that the cause of peace

8

and tolerance, in the West and elsewhere, cannot be advanced by misrepresentation or by the sentimental lapse of seriousness.

Chicago, Summer, 2002   *Serge Trifkovic*

CHAPTER ONE

Muhammad

What we think we know about Muhammad, the founder of Islam, is more than we really know about the historical man. There are no reliable written Muslim sources on Islam that go beyond around A.D. 800, over two centuries after his birth, and the texts that we have after that date should not be read as a factual record of past events.

The narratives known as the *sunna* claim to provide first-hand accounts of Muhammad's words and actions as preserved in authentic *hadiths,* traditions about the prophet. They are an indispensable source for the study of early Islam, but they are not history. They addressed the political, legal, and spiritual needs of later times and tell us more about the mindset and agenda of the Arab rulers of their neighbors' conquered lands—in Baghdad, Damascus, or Persia, many generations after Muhammad's death—than about the man himself.[1]

The hadiths' claim to authenticity is based on supposedly complete and proper chains of sources—*isnads*—attesting to their genuineness, but the light of critical scholarship has long established a negative correlation between an outwardly impressive chain supporting a story and its reliability.[2] Not unlike the modern spinners of urban legends, the compilers of hadiths sought to make their yarns more credible by providing detailed yet unverifiable information on names, places, and dates.

There are, nevertheless, salient themes and key elements in the tradition that overlap. They are almost certain to contain historical facts, only partly blurred by the authors' desire to present Muhammad as a holy man of noble descent in their account of his life and works. The development of that account parallels the development of the faith itself, and both finally coalesced, more or less in their present form, around the turn of the second millennium A.D., and many hundreds of miles away from the Prophet's native city.

Ernest Renan's famous assertion that Islam was "born in the full light of history" is therefore incorrect. On closer scrutiny, it transpires that "the

---

[1] Cf. John Wansbrough, *Kuranic Studies,* Oxford, 1977.
[2] Joseph Schacht, "A Revaluation of Islamic Tradition," *Journal of the Royal Asiatic Society*, 1949, p. 147.

full light" is but the reflected glimmer of medieval Muslim scholars, men who were believers and, therefore, of necessity, apologists.

This is a complex and highly technical subject riddled with controversy, not least because the claim of contemporary Muslim scholars, that the surviving early literature accurately conveys the story of Muhammad's life, has been accepted by many of their Western colleagues more or less at face value, lest the believers' susceptibilities be disturbed. The way in which political correctitude has impeded science is ironic: 150 years ago Renan, true to his secular convictions, advocated the study of the life of Christ that would be "as free of dogmatic shackles" as that of Muhammad had been in the Western world. If he were with us today, he would have to reverse his demand: Jesus Christ is freely "deconstructed" and "contextualized" in the same Western institutions of higher learning— and often by the same people—who defer uncritically to Muslim sensibilities and obsessions.

The experts will continue their quest for the "historical" Muhammad.[3] Others will dwell on the problem of what are "sources" and what is "history," in Islam or in any other record of past human endeavor. Without passing judgment on whether and to what extent the Tradition is telling the truth, we shall limit our account of Muhammad's works and the tenets of his faith to what most Muslims through thirteen centuries have regarded— and still regard—as factually accurate and dogmatically correct sources: the Kuran, the Traditions, and the Consensus. That account has not changed for almost a millennium, and as such it has shaped the minds and lives of billions of people. That is ultimately what matters more than the authenticity of the sources.

THE SETTING

The birthplace of Islam was Arabia, where Muhammad, "the Praised One," the prophet and the founder of the faith, was born in the city of Mecca, in or around A.D. 570. Mecca lay in the region of Hijaz, at the western edge of an immense, arid plateau, over a thousand miles long and almost as wide, sloping gently eastward. Mountain walls, peaking at close

---

[3] For a valuable survey, see Ibn Warraq (Ed.), *The Quest for the Historical Muhammad,* New York, 2000.

to 10,000 feet, envelop on three sides "the land of terror and thirst" separated from the mellowing winds of the ocean by a rocky barrier that stops the rain clouds as effectively as it deters invaders. Some parts of Utah or Nevada come to mind in this landscape, with its wild yet mournful aspect. There are no intricacies of scenery known to those of us who dwell in areas touched for millennia by human hand. It is as if the highest of the Rockies have been submerged leaving just their barren peaks visible, with nothing but the desert in between, a glittering plain of naked rocks or a sea of sand interrupted by the massive dunes. The summer heat regularly reaches 130 degrees Fahrenheit, and 10-year droughts are not uncommon, while what rain there is often comes in massive torrents, causing flash floods in the *wadis*.

Outside an air-conditioned SUV, to an unseasoned outsider this looks like the domain of death, threatening burns by day and frost by night, fit only for its many horned vipers and desert cobras, lizards, and scorpions. The effect of wind bottled up in the gullies creates an eerie sound from the dunes, whose hum adds to the melancholy aspect of the place. Topsoil does not exist for the best part, having long been blown away by the wind, broken up by heat and cold, and condemned to barren nothingness.

Arabia is singularly devoid of trees, so much so that the standard Arabic word for tree, *shajar,* is ordinarily used by the Bedouin to denote desert bushes that furnish grazing for his camels, his sheep and goats (collectively known as *ghanam*), and firewood for his tent. What vegetation there is only succeeds in the oasis, where nourishment for date palms can be obtained from water in the subsoil, and—more recently—in irrigated, fertilized fields that supply the costliest corn and produce in the world.

But if we leave the wind-swept plateau and cross the mountain range enclosing it, a more hospitable coastal strip never more than 50 miles wide lies ahead. The wells do not dry up, the plants bear fruit all year round, and the pastures support all kinds and numbers of hoofed beasts. The mention of Arab tribes, under the various forms of *Arabi, Arubu*, or *Aribi*, appears often in the Assyrian inscriptions as early as the ninth century B.C., and their country is spoken of as "seldom or never traversed by any conqueror," and as inhabited by wild and independent tribes. It is slightly to the east of the transitional strip between the foreboding desert and the welcoming sea that the cities of Mecca and Medina lay, the scene of events surrounding the life and times of the extraordinary man who was to become the prophet of Islam.

That scene was divided by the Greek and Roman writers into *Arabia Deserta* (desert), *Felix* (happy), and *Petraea* (stony). The division was arbitrary, and unknown to the Arabs themselves. Early European information concerning Arabia was based mainly on Herodotus, Strabo, Pliny, and Ptolemy. It was meager and unsatisfactory. The references to Arabia found in the Old Testament were even more so. Many Arabs believed that they were descended from Ishmael, the son of Abraham; they were known as Moaddites. Muhammad's ancestors belonged to this group. Others claimed their ancestry to the uplands of the southwestern corner of the Arabian Peninsula, in today's Yemen. It has been suggested that they are descended from another Old Testament patriarch, Joktan,[4] and that there is in fact a local tradition of an ancestor named Qahtan.

The Old Testament references to Arabia are scanty. The term *Arab* itself, as the name of a particular country and nation, is found only in later Old Testament writings (e.g., not earlier than Jeremias in the sixth century B.C.). In older writings, the term *Arab* is used only as an appellative, meaning "desert," or "people of the desert," or "nomad" in general. The name for Arabia in the earliest Old Testament writings is either Ismael or Madian as in the twenty-fifth chapter of Genesis, which is a significant indication of the relative antiquity of that remarkable chapter.[5] The meaning of the term *Arab* was either that of "nomad," or "the Land of the Setting Sun" (i.e., the West, it being situated to the west of Babylonia, which was considered to be the biblical record of Genesis 11, as the traditional starting point of the earliest Semitic migrations). By the ancient Hebrews, however, the land of Arabia was called "the Country of the East," and the Arabs themselves were "the Children of the East," as the Arabian peninsula lay to the east of Palestine.

Until modern times, almost every Arab tribe still claimed to be descended from one of these two stocks, although there is no firm evidence that this legendary lineage corresponded to historical reality. Contrary to the theory that Arabia was the birthplace and homeland of the Semitic nations, the people of Arabia have been ethnically related to different

---

[4] Gen. 10:25–26.
[5] Cf. *The Catholic Encyclopaedia* (1908), "Arabia."

groups whose homelands are outside the Peninsula, and modern DNA research confirms that they do not belong to a single "race."

Before Muhammad's birth, the two traditional branches appear to have entertained some distaste for each other, the fact partly explicable by the universal rivalry between the settled farmer—the way of life prevalent among the Yemenites—and the nomad or merchant, more prevalent among the Moaddites. The latters' lifestyle was dictated by nature: a flock or a herd will soon consume all the scant grazing in an area, whereupon the owners had to move camp to another area. The settled communities in central and northern parts were limited to the springs or wells, and their denizens lived either by growing date palms or acting as middlemen, trading in frankincense and other perfumes, buying camels, sheep, wool, or animal oil from the tribes, and exporting them to the neighboring lands. Muhammad was born into a society of men ruthlessly active in pursuit of their simple needs, patient of the hardships inherent in their abode, and reconciled to their fate without futile grumbles.

Needless to say, there was no such thing as an "Arab nation" before Muhammad, either in the sense of a centralized political structure or of the shared ideals, collective memories, and cultural traits. Only after the rise of Islam, and the emergence of the Arabian Muslims as the founders of a mighty empire, the name *Arab* came to be used by those Muslims themselves, and by the nations encountering them, to describe all people of Arabian origin. "Arabia" itself—the vast land of *Jazirat al-Arab*—also did not come to denote the entire Arabian Peninsula until much later. There was no "nation," but a complex mosaic of warring or cooperating tribes, of shifting allegiances and broken coalitions.

A number of Red Sea kingdoms emerged in the southern part of the peninsula. The two most important were the Mineans (the *m'dbzm* of the Old Testament) and the Sabeans, whence the Queen of Saba came to pay her homage of respect and admiration to King Solomon. A third kingdom was that of Kataban, a fourth, Hadramaut, as well as those of Lihyan, Raidan, Habashah, and others. For the most part, they were not much more than tribal alliances based on common commercial interests.

Central and northern Arabia fell short even of nominal statehood, but some tribes were more prominent and powerful than others and exercised authority over others. The significant Thamud tribe inhabited northern Hejaz, and its influence, albeit not control, extended far into the central regions. The Lihyanites, probably a branch of Thamud, lived along the Red Sea coast. The Lakhmids of today's Jordan were to gain some prominence through their association with outside powers.

Until the third century A.D., the whole northern region was much influenced by two groups on the northern outskirts of Arabia, the Nabataeans and Palmyrenes, Hellenized and certainly civilized, who exercised some authority along the major caravan routes. After the fall of Palmyra (A.D. 273), the Romans entrusted the maintenance of order in the Syrian Desert to the Lakhmids, and some fifty years later the Persians installed one of their princes as "the King of all Arabs." He was more successful in obtaining the recognition of his title from foreign courts than from his reluctant subjects, however, and his successors preferred the security offered by Persian overlordship to the risky attempt to enforce their titular claims. The one lasting effect of this brief experiment in nation-building was the adoption of Arabic as the official language by the Lakhmids instead of Aramaic, a Semitic language akin to both Hebrew and Arabic and widely used throughout the Middle East. The fully developed Arabic language of pre-Islamic poetry and the development of the Arabic script based on Aramaic was their major legacy.

To the northwest, Syria and Palestine were ruled by Byzantine emperors from Constantinople; the coast of the Persian Gulf and eastern Mesopotamia fell under the sway of Persian kings, while parts of the Red Sea Littoral were temporarily conquered by the Ethiopian Christian kingdom. None of these distant empires ever attempted a full conquest of the hinterland of the vast peninsula, however. Shortly before the Christian Era, Antigonus and Ptolemy had, in vain, attempted to gain a footing in Arabia; and Pompey himself, victorious elsewhere, was checked on its frontiers. During the reign of Augustus, Aelius Gallus, the Roman Prefect of Egypt, with an army of 10,000 Roman infantry, 500 Jews, and 100 Nabataeans, undertook an expedition against the province of Yemen. He advanced as far as Marib, the capital of Yemen, but his force was unaccustomed to the heat, and he was forced to retreat to Egypt without accomplishing any permanent and effective conquest. Later attempts to conquer the country were made by Roman governors and generals under Trajan and Severus, but these were mostly restricted to the neighborhood of the Syrian frontiers.

16

In subsequent centuries no further attempt was made to penetrate the desert, much less to establish passable roads protected by permanent military outposts, free for tax collectors, administrators, and missionaries to pass: the effort simply did not seem worth it. "What is there to be found in your country?" a Persian king supposedly asked an Arab chieftain who sought the help of the king's soldiers in return for a province. "Sheep and camels! I am not going to risk my armies in your deserts for such a trifle."

Lack of central authority bred a somewhat Hobbesian mindset. The possession of arms and the scant regard for human life, especially if it infringed on one's honor, or claim to pastures, camels, women, or some other earthly good, was the mark of manhood. Robbery and murder outside the protective confines of one's clan were not deemed bad *per se*, they were judged by the results as a means to an end. The respect for one's neighbor was strictly contingent on his power and his means. Familiarity with violence and death did not necessarily breed contempt for one's earthly demise, but its prospect did not strike terror into the hearts of real men, either. "Never has a lord of our race died in bed," boasts an Arab poet of old. "We have risen," says another "and our arrows have flown, and the blood that stains our garments scents us more sweetly than the odor of musk."[6]

The sturdy women of the desert were perforce but a supporting cast to the proceedings, but the admiration leading to love that manly virtues inspired were to be coveted and actively sought: "Courage, they chant, defenders of women. Strike with the edge of your swords. We are the daughters of the morning star, our feet tread upon soft cushions, our necks are decked with pearls, our hair is perfumed with musk. The brave who face the enemy, we pressed them in our arms; the base who flee, we cast them off and deny them our love." But those words betray that Arab women before Islam were persons, free to give or deny love. They were masters of their own bodies and owners of their property, as free to dispose of their belongings as they were to choose their husbands, and to divorce them, if they so wished.

Many events from Muhammad's later life and teachings are easier to understand in the context of the pagan Araby, the land in which life was, if

---

[6] Andre Servier, *Islam and the Psychology of the Musulman*, New York, 1924, pp. 20–21.

not altogether nasty, then certainly brutish and often short. It barely could be sustained outside the supportive context of an extended family that was the basis of social organization. Belonging to a tribe, with all the attending loyalties and protection, was the key to survival, and its members regarded each other as brothers by virtue of their supposed common ancestor. "Love your tribe," an Arab poet says, "For you are bound to it by ties stronger than any between husband and wife."

In the vast land, left to its own devices, generations succeeded each other, leaving "no more trace than the camel tracks on the sand of the desert dunes." The neighbor was the fellow tribesman and relation, with the shared pride of ancestry, and faithfulness to the pledged word, honesty, and ethical code only operated within the context of such links. The possession of things material did not entitle the owner to public esteem, unless personal qualities attendant upon true men accompanied it. In any event, riches were seen as impermanent, expressed in heads of camel and sheep, in slaves, women, or pieces of gold and silver that one had to carry on one's person—and therefore subject to robbery, rape, and plunder. Even if such misfortune befell one, however, it was not the end of the world: revenge and loot was a two-way street, open to all.

This society appreciated the value of assured delights, and the limit of most aspirations was reached in the soft cushions, savory dishes, cool springs, and dewy-lipped women. Pre-Islamic poetry, elaborate and elegiac in its warning of the brevity of our earthly existence, is full of rhapsodies celebrating the Arab's forsaken dwelling, the charms of his lost beloved, the sensual pleasures and their transience, the beauty of his horse or camel, and the pride in his ancestry and tribe. Manly virtues, endurance, and absence of undue compassion were highly valued, and morality was a function of necessity, confined to the social horizon of the tribe.

Islamic tradition is at pains to assert the existence of tension and spiritual crisis among the Arabs that were resolved by the emergence of Islam, but offers no proof and no clear indication of a religious void that longed to be filled: "A god is an imaginary being who can do good or harm; and everything goes to show that the Arabs who had not seen the great world were firmly convinced that their gods or goddesses could do both."[7] In so far as religious sentiment required personal gratification, there

---

[7] D.S. Margoliuth, *Mohammed and the Rise of Islam,* London, 1905, p. 24.

is no reason to suppose that the Arabs' pre-Islamic beliefs failed to provide it.

It was silly of Renan to claim that there had never existed "a spectacle more gracious, more attractive, more lively than that offered by the Arab way of life before Islam" with its "unlimited liberty of the individual, complete absence of law and power, an exalted sense of honor," etc., but for the past four centuries Westerners have been all too willing to romanticize the noble savage. This was a truly barbarian society, not in the judgmental sense implying superiority of others but in the value-neutral sense of a culture as yet free of any urge to reflect upon itself.

PRE-ISLAMIC BELIEFS

In the late fifth century A.D., the way of life and outlook of the people of Arabia had changed little for generations, but great changes were taking place in the lands surrounding their heartland. The center of gravity in the Roman Empire had moved to Constantinople and increasingly acquired a Greek character. It eventually came to be known as Byzantium, by the original name of its new capital city. After Constantine the Empire was Christianized, but in its eastern parts many faithful followed a variety of sects that were to be deemed heretical by the Church. The Monophysites, who upheld a single nature in Christ, were particularly strong in Armenia, Syria, and Egypt. The Nestorians, who asserted Christ's essential humanity, prevailed in Mesopotamia.

At the same time, the Christian outlook redefined the basis of loyalty to the imperial crown by the subject peoples—from *pax Romana* that was indifferent to its subjects' beliefs unless they were perceived as a threat to the established order, to the polity aspiring to *civitas Dei*. This shift, while aspiring to religious uniformity, also allowed for the development of greater diversity of local cultural idiom than would have been the case under Alexander's Hellenizing successors, or under Rome in its zenith. Bishops also provided a strong focal point to their communities not paralleled by imperial officials, while revered old men, predecessors of the Russian *starets*, popularized the faith and provided it with social relevance.

To the East of Byzantium was Persia, an ancient civilization holding sway over huge lands ruled by long dynasties. The Sassanians, who gave their name to the Empire, followed Zoroastranism, a form of monotheism that postulated the world as the scene of permanent warfare between good and evil under the watchful but nonintervening one God, in which the eventual triumph of good was assured but needed to be facilitated by virtuous men. A dualist variety known as Mazdaism was the Sassanide state religion that legitimized the secular order.

In both empires substantial Jewish communities were to be found, and lively cultural interaction between those lands was interrupted only during a series of intermittent wars that the Byzantines and Sassanians fought from A.D. 540 to 629, when much of Syria, Palestine, and today's Iraq was a battlefield at one time or another, additionally decimated by plague. In the end the border was reestablished on the Euphrates, but both states were greatly weakened by the endeavor, and the economic and administrative structure of the devastated and depopulated Byzantine provinces never was to be completely rebuilt.

The area known as the "Fertile Crescent," which extended from the Mediterranean and across Syria to Mesopotamia, was attractive for settlement to many Arabian nomads, who found the climate and soil far friendlier than their native desert. They were mostly Christianized in their new abode, but preserved many of their social customs and traditions. According to the majority of the Fathers and historians of the Church, the origin of Christianity among them is to be traced back to the Apostle Paul, who in his Epistle to the Galatians, speaking of the period of time immediately following his conversion, says: "Neither went I up to Jerusalem to them which were apostles before me; but I went to Arabia, and returned to Damascus" (Gal. 1:17). What particular region of Arabia was visited by the Apostle is unknown, but it is unlikely that he would have ventured much further south than the edge of the desert heartland.

The neighboring empires established a network of allies among Arab chieftains in the borderlands, who eventually turned into semi-independent vassals. Their subjects were open to civilizing influences and acted as the transition of those influences into the Arab heartland.

The Kingdom of Ghassan, bordering Syria, was comprised of many Arab tribes whose first migrations there must have taken place as early as the time of Alexander the Great. Toward the third and fourth centuries of the Christian Era, the Romans formed alliances with them to counterbalance the influence of the Mesopotamian Arabs of Hira, who were under Persian rule. Their capital city was Balka, then Petra. Although living a nomadic life and practically independent, with "no dwelling but the tent, no entrenchment but the sword, no law but the traditionary song of their bards," these Arabs were under the nominal but quite effective control of the Romans as early as the time of Pompey.[8] Such Syrian Arabs always looked upon the Romans as their best and most powerful defenders and protectors against the Sassanian dynasty of Persia, by which they were constantly oppressed.

The Romans replaced the Lakhmids as the guardians of the Syrian Desert and installed in their place the Quda'ah, a tribal alliance inhabiting the northeastern part of the peninsula. Around A.D. 490, one of their chieftains, Qusay ibn Kalib of the Quraysh tribe, became the prince of the city of Mecca and the guardian of its *haram,* the sacred enclave and temple, the *Kaaba.* As its guardians, the Quraysh came to enjoy special respect among the tribes.

From the remotest times Mecca had been a place of pagan pilgrimage. Arabs came to bow down in the temple of *Kaaba* ("cube") before a certain black stone, probably a meteorite said to have been brought down from heaven. The use of meteorites was a perennial pagan favorite; Acts 19:35 mentions "that which was sent down from Zeus," probably a meteorite. As part of the pagan ritual, they were required to run around it seven times and to kiss it, before running a mile to the nearby dry well of Wadi Mina "to throw stones at the devil."

Black stones were worshipped in various parts of the Semitic world, and the generic terms for the Kaaba and similar structures were *betyl.* Betyls, *bait-ili,* "homes of the god," were sometimes used as sacrificial altars for votive offerings. Elsewhere, notably at Byblos (where the stone was conical), large stones served as cult objects in place of statues. The Black Stone of Kaaba enjoyed special preeminence, and the temple also eventually housed hundreds of idols that were revered by different Arabian tribes. When away from Mecca, they turned in its direction in prayer.

Each tribe had its chief deity, and many had a sanctuary devoted to it, a *haram,* that was exempt from tribal conflict and cared for by a family under the protection of a neighboring tribe.[9] Their divinities often personified the heavenly bodies or natural phenomena, including the sun

---

[8] *The Catholic Encyclopaedia,* op. cit.
[9] Albert Hourani, *A History of the Arab Peoples,* New York, 1991, p. 11.

(Shams), stars, and especially the moon. But unlike the pagan civilizations of the Mediterranean and the Asian subcontinent, there was no developed mythology among the Arabs; their deities did not have a past or distinctive character. One liked or feared them or placated them by ritual, but did not know them. A god, or the male or female *jinns*—spiritual beings that could be benevolent or demonic—resided in a stone or a tree, often but not always in human form; animals in particular were believed to host good and evil spirits.

The best-known idol was Hubal, while the other two whose names were recorded in Islamic tradition were Isaf and Na'ilah, lovers who were turned into stone as punishment for fornication in the temple. They were placed on two little hills near Mecca, Safa and Marwa, while Hubal was in the Kaaba.

The dominant deity was the moon god in several variations, whose title was *al-ilah*—the chief among all gods—shortened by frequency of usage to *Allah*. The evidence of those pagan times is scant as Muslims were loath to preserve any remnants of pre-Islamic pagan traditions, with the notable exception of those shrines and artifacts that had been co-opted by Muhammad. Nevertheless, the frequency with which the crescent moon appears in pre-Islamic archaeological artifacts throughout Arabia attests to its special status. The Sabeans in the south of Arabia had developed a lunar calendar by which they followed their rites, including a month of fasting that started with the appearance of the crescent moon and continued until its reappearance. The moon god, and his spouse, the sun goddess, produced three deities known as the Daughters of Allah, al-Lat, al-Uzza, and Manat, who enjoyed particular favor with the Meccans.

"Allah" was clearly an Arabic word—albeit borrowed from Aramaic—denoting an Arabic deity.[10] It corresponded to Babylonian *Baal* or *Bel*, although in one form or another the root is found in other Semitic languages as a designation of the divinity. Some authors maintain that Allah was in fact the moon god Hubal, the latter being his proper name that was less commonly used. Whether it was originally a proper name, pointing to a primitive monotheism, or was from the beginning an appellative, is uncertain.

---

[10] Jeffery, Arthur (ed.), *Islam, Muhammad and His Religion*, New York, 1958, p. 85.

Allah's most frequently used title, *ar-Rahman* (the Merciful) also was known in South Arabia well before the advent of Islam, and signified a moon god as well. The deity seemed to have served a similar position as Allah did in Mecca. The pagan Arabs used the theophorous "Allah," as well as its feminine form, "Allat," in the names of their children with some frequency.[11] (This is also testified by the names of Muhammad's father and his uncle.)

Muslim tradition claims that just as the essence of God is unchangeable, so is His name, and that Allah has ever been the name of the Eternal Being. In reality,

> Allah may be an Arabic rendering of the Hebrew *El,* and the unused root *Ul,* "to be strong," or from *Eloah,* the singular form of Elohim. Another word very frequently used for the Almighty in the Qur'an is *Rabb,* which is generally translated in English versions of the Qur'an as "Lord." It seems to stand in the relative position of the Jehovah of the Old Testament and the *kyrios* of the New Testament.[12]

While the tribesmen of the desert were disinclined to the elaboration of multiple meanings, ambiguities, and theological complexities that gripped the Greek, Persian, and Jewish mind, their more developed neighbors' influences were nevertheless felt in their increased proneness to a monotheistic outlook that emerged simultaneously throughout Arabia in the late fifth and early sixth century A.D.

In southern Arabia, the stellar pantheon of moon gods served by priests in temples gave way in the fifth century to "the Lord of Heaven and Earth." Three generations later, a similar impulse drove a king fascinated by Judaism to destroy a vibrant Christian community in Yemen, but subsequent Ethiopian incursions brought back a degree of Christian presence. Further north, the Meccan merchants settled for the overall principle of one God, Allah, as the pinnacle of all others.

Without knowing it, the generations immediately preceding Muhammad were clearing the way for his mission: Muhammad's tribe of Quraysh became known as the People of Allah, or the Protected Neighbors

---

[11] Ibid.
[12] T.P. Hughes in the *Dictionary of Islam.*

of Allah. The word was well familiar to Muhammad's contemporaries, denoting a pagan deity that his tribe revered as superior to all others, rather than the Supreme Being, creator and sustainer of the universe. He did not need to invent a completely new word but eventually redefined the uniquely Arab "Allah" on his own terms.

Muhammad was born into a pagan society, but by the end of the sixth century it was different from paganism as commonly understood in its proto-monotheistic tendencies.[13] Some individuals, known as *hunafa,* had given up paganism without converting to Christianity or Judaism. Muhammad later referred to Patriarch Abraham as a *hanif,* because he was neither Jew nor Christian.[14] He claimed that the Arabs' knowledge of Allah was transmitted by word of mouth for over 2,500 years from the time of Hagar and Ishmael to Muhammad. It was briefly suppressed by idol worship prior to the coming of Muhammad, but was upheld by the hanifs, who had kept the faith in the God of Abraham.

Mecca was close to the seaport of Jeddah and about halfway between Yemen and Syria, which enabled it to develop as an important trading center connecting the caravans from India and Persia with those from the West. The Meccans ventured as far as Syria to the north and Aden to the south. Caravans moved freely, thanks to the agreements between the Quraysh and their neighbors, Byzantium, Persia, Yemen, and Ethiopia. Thus, both religion and commerce made Mecca an important center that brought great prosperity—certainly by the standards of the land—and aroused the envy of the have-nots further inland. The Quraysh were accepted as arbiters in tribal disputes, and the tribe's noble house of Abd Manaf collected tax to feed the pilgrims.

Affluence seems to have diminished the fighting spirit of the Meccans and engendered the longing for order and security. They preached the sanctity of private property and organized defense of caravans that were occasionally held up for ransom by robber bands and by the conflicts between the tribes. The Meccans succeeded in getting the tribes to agree to temporary truces, the most widely respected of which was that of the Holy Month. Their prominent status also enabled them to appeal to what in modern times would be recognized as the spirit of patriotism, especially

---

[13] The term is W. Montgomery Watt's.

[14] Kuran 2:135.

when it came to expelling the Abyssinian invaders in the late sixth century. In addition, their exalted status was reflected in the Meccans' insistence that theirs was the one true dialect of Arab language. The singers of epics were drafted in this effort, and their verses provided the pool of words that became the standard from which the Arab language was eventually formed.

NOT A PROPHET IN HIS NATIVE CITY

According to Muslim legend, miraculous signs accompanied Muhammad's birth. He was born clean, circumcised, with his navel cord cut, and immediately fell to the ground, took a handful of dust, and gazed to heaven, proclaiming, "God is Great."[15] But his recently widowed mother Amina—his father Abd'Allah having died before Muhammad's birth—faced hardship. Compared to the successful merchants of Mecca, the family of infant Abu'l-Qasim—the Banu Hashim branch of the house of Abd Manaf—was poor.

He was an only child, and at the age of six he lost his mother, a gentle sickly woman prone to hallucinations. Following her death Muhammad passed to the care of his grandfather, Abdel-Mottaleb, but this respected and influential man died himself three years later (A.D. 579). A nine-year-old Muhammad was then entrusted to the care of his uncle, Abu Taleb, a successful businessman who decided to make use of him as a camel driver in his commercial caravans. The boy grew up on the social margins of a society in which power and money were the defining currency of one's standing. Muhammad's later bitterness towards the establishment of his native city and its social and spiritual structure reflected the sense of powerlessness felt by a resentful young man.

In his early teens, Muhammad traveled to Syria and Palestine as a driver of his uncle's camels. By the desert campfire and in the markets of eastern Byzantium, he became acquainted with many Jews and Christians and acquired some knowledge of their religion and traditions. According to some sources, on one of those travels a monk taught him the basics of Christianity; however, this appears unlikely. From the inaccurate and sometimes greatly distorted accounts of the Christian faith that Muhammad provides in the Kuran, it appears more likely that he received the outline of

---

[15] Cf. Geisler and Saleeb, pp. 68–69.

25

the Christian teaching by the adherents of various heterodox Christian sects in Arabia itself.

A Syrian monk by the name of Buhaira figures in another traditional tale, recognizing the mark of prophethood in the youth and warning Muhammad's uncle to guard the boy against the Jews, who would harm him if they found out the truth.[16] This did not disrupt what otherwise seems to have been a normal and uneventful childhood.

An important moment in Muhammad's early life came in A.D. 595, when the Ethiopians threatened Mecca from their coastal base and were repelled by a coalition assembled by his influential uncle. It appears that Muhammad could not bear the sight of the battlefield and ran away, which exposed him to contempt and ostracism. To make ends meet, at the age of 25 he became a shepherd—the lowliest position in that culture—and soon gladly accepted the offer to become an assistant to a traveling cloth merchant. His new work took him to Hayacha, a market town south of Mecca, on one of his journeys. There he met a wealthy widow, Khadija, 15 years his senior, and entered her service as a camel driver at first, eventually rising to become a supervisor and her partner.

Muhammad executed his duties with diligence and was grateful to have escaped his destitution, while Khadija soon found that, in spite of her advanced age by the standards of the time, passion was still alive in her heart. Muhammad agreed to marry her, and one can only speculate about the extent to which the feeling of gratitude and the logic of personal interest impacted his decision. Either way, from that point on his future seemed assured and, for a decade, Muhammad focused his hitherto unrevealed talents and energy to the development of Khadija's business interests. His commercial savvy and flare for communication made him an affluent man, self-educated by travel and meetings with fellow men of different backgrounds, increasingly confident of his stature in life and his powers.

By his late thirties, Muhammad lived a life of material comfort but free from excess. The old sense of alienation from the Meccan establishment did not abate, however. It was reciprocated in the envy of his fellow tribesmen, who observed his rise from rags to comfort based on a matrimonial scheme regarded as unworthy of a real man in a land where

---

[16] Ibn Ishaq, *The Life of Muhammad* (translated by A. Guillaume), New York, OUP, 1980, p. 81.

manly pride demands young and sturdy brides ready for frequent childbirth and heavy toil.

Muhammad's detachment from Meccan society and from the life of the Quraysh tribe seems to have prompted the development of his dreamy and contemplative side. He would often wander in the hills around Mecca meditating in solitude, and during the holy month of Ramadan he was known to spend weeks on end in the caves of mount Hira.

Solitude produces strange effects even in the sturdiest and most stable of people, as the experience of solitary confinement may testify. Solitude of the desert, with its extremes of temperature, its strange sounds, and its mournful aspect, had a strong effect on Muhammad. One day, coming out of one of his meditative trances, he confided to his wife a strange experience. It was in the year A.D. 610, when Muhammad was 40 years of age, that he told her he was visited by a majestic being—whom he later identified as the angel Gabriel—with a call to prophecy: "You are the Messenger of God." According to the earliest of Muhammad's biographers, the angel came to him while he was asleep, holding a piece of silk cloth covered with written characters. The earliest biography of Muhammad describes this event as follows:

> When it was the night on which God honored him with his mission and showed mercy on His servants thereby, Gabriel brought him the command of God. "He came to me," said the apostle of God, "while I was asleep, with a coverlet of brocade whereon was some writing, and said, 'Read!' I said, 'What shall I read?' He pressed me with it so tightly that I thought it was death; then he let me go and said, 'Read!' I said, 'What shall I read?' He pressed me with it again so that I thought it was death; then he let me go and said 'Read!' I said, 'What shall I read?' He pressed me with it the third time so that I thought it was death and said 'Read!' I said, 'What then shall I read?'—and this I said only to deliver myself from him, lest he should do the same to me again. He said: 'Read in the name of thy Lord who created, Who created man of blood coagulated. Read! Thy Lord is the most beneficent, Who taught by the pen, taught that which they knew not unto men.' So I read it, and he departed from me. And I awoke from

my sleep, and it was as though these words were written on my heart."[17]

This event, the Night of Power, or Destiny, marked the beginning of his career as messenger of God—*rasul Allah*—or Prophet, *nabi*. From that time on, at increasingly frequent intervals until his death, Muhammad received "revelations," verbal messages that he believed came directly from God. In his later experiences of receiving messages there was normally no vision. Occasionally there were physical symptoms that accompanied revelations, such as hearing the sound of bells, perspiring on a cold day, and losing consciousness, and these later gave rise to the suggestion that he was an epileptic. The essence of such experiences was his claim that he found a verbal message in his "heart," that is, in his conscious mind. Sometimes Muhammad and his followers kept these messages in memory, and sometimes they were written down. About A.D. 650 they were supposedly collected and written in the Kuran, the sacred scriptures of Islam, and eventually codified in the form that has endured till today. Muslims believe the Kuran is divine revelation, written in the very words of God himself.

At first Muhammad appears to have been reluctant to accept the apparition's claims at face value and feared demonic possession, but his wife Khadija provided him with assurance and support: "Rejoice, O son of my uncle, and be of good heart! By Him in whose hand is Khadija's soul, I hope that thou wilt be the Prophet of His people." She told him that a virtuous man such as he could not be a victim of demonic delusions but should accept the call with humility and gladness. She was indeed the first convert to what was becoming a new faith.

With the help of Khadijah's cousin Waraqah b. Naufal, a hanif who had read Christian scripture and eventually became a Christian, Muhammad came to interpret these messages as similar to those sent by God through Moses and other prophets to Jews and Christians. He became convinced that by the first great vision and by the receipt of the messages he was commissioned to communicate them to his fellow citizens and other Arabs. The proclamation of the messages was accompanied by their explanation and exposition in his own words.

---

[17] Ibid, p. 106.

This development did not occur overnight. No new messages followed the first grand revelation for about three years, prompting a long bout of depression in Muhammad. He was gripped by the sense of abandonment by his Creator and worthlessness of life. At the end of this period, however, he started receiving regular messages, and started preaching in secret, to friends and family. About A.D. 613, he decided to go public with his revelations. His teaching was simple, focused on the submission to one transcendent Allah; on the end of the world and the Day of Judgment, when all will be brought to life; on the subsequent delights of paradise for the virtuous and torments of hell for the sinners; and on the practice of charity. In the early days, it was delivered in the tone of warning rather than doctrinally defined rules: "Thus have We sent by inspiration to thee an Arabic Qur'an; that thou mayest warn the Mother of Cities and all around her."[18] He saw his task as "to admonish the unjust, and as Glad Tidings to those who do right."[19]

The beginning of Muhammad's ministry, received with indifference or derision by most Meccans, was slow. The first two converts after his wife were Muhammad's slave and adopted son, Zaid, and his cousin Ali, the son of Abu Taleb—sixteen years old, enthusiastic, adventurous, and blindly devoted to Muhammad. His close friend and life-long companion Abu-Bakr was next. A few mostly young men joined them; by the time their number reached 39, they spent their days together in the house of a young man called al-Arqam, joining Muhammad in his acts of worship and prayers. These culminated in an act of prostration in which they touched the ground with their foreheads in acknowledgment of God's majesty. The names of seventy converts are recorded by the time there was sustained opposition to the new religion in Mecca.

The converts were few, but their faith was strong. Not many Meccans were touched by Muhammad's charisma and the eloquence of his lively and earnest recitations, but those who did respond, such as Umar, were dumbfounded. Muhammad's success was in part due to his undoubted mastery of the Arab language, and those Westerners who find the Kuran a tedious read are well advised to remember that the eloquent turn of phrase

---

[18] 42:7.
[19] 46:12.

29

of its author appealed to an audience that placed form above content and style above composition.

The leaders of the Meccan establishment, indifferent to Muhammad's claims and endeavors at first, started reacting against them after he had rebuffed their attempts to appease him by giving him lucrative trading contracts. They sneered at the audacity of a common man with tarnished standing and no natural claim to authority or prestige, who blithely invited obedience of his betters. His insistence on the Day of Judgment, when the sinners would pay for their lax ways, was seen as criticism of the Meccan way of life, a seditious ploy designed to undermine established social patterns and a threat to the order of things.

The Meccans' rejection of Muhammad's claims concerning eschatology, which they found not only disturbing but also subversive, was reinforced by commercial self-interest. His attack on the divinity of old idols could deny the Quraysh tribe its hefty profits derived from the guardianship of the temple of the Kaaba, although Muhammad's rejection of the idols did not include an attack on the shrine itself. This implied consequence of Muhammad's claims, when its implications were finally grasped, was taken as yet another proof of his disregard for interests of his community and his obligations to the tribe. The initial humorous contempt for Muhammad's claims to prophethood turned to indignation.

Hoping for an impressive gesture that would finally sway his fellow citizens, Muhammad presented the key tenets of his early teaching to a gathering of most prominent members of his tribe. The worship of idols is a lie, he said, and the images of deities at Kaaba were nothing but worthless heaps of wood and stone, devoid of spirit or power. There is only one God, Muhammad went on, the creator of heaven and earth and men, and he—Muhammad—was his prophet and messenger. That, in brief, is the true faith, and everything else a lie. Muhammad ended by inviting his fellow tribesmen to accept his teaching, in which case he assured them of their salvation, the alternative to which was the everlasting agony in the flames of Gehenna.

Attempting to sway the doubters by theological compromise, Muhammad went so far as to allow for the possibility that three particularly well-liked Meccan deities—the moon god's daughters al-Lat, al-Uzza, and Manat—were divine beings, capable of interceding with Allah on behalf of the faithful:

Do not revile the idols which they invoke besides Allah, lest in their ignorance they revile Allah with rancor. Thus have We made the actions of all men seem pleasing to themselves. To their Lord they shall return, and We will declare to them all that they have done.[20]

Muhammad then refrained from cursing the Meccan idols but called them all by the same name, "Allah," thus merging 300-odd deities at the Kaaba into one, and calling all of them by the same name.[21] He subsequently abrogated this section of the original Kuran, claiming that this was an interpolation of Satan—hence the "Satanic verses." (Some contemporary Muslims reject the story; but medieval Islamic scholars regarded it as authentic. It is inconceivable that orthodox Muslim chroniclers would have invented this story, which in any event underlined Muhammad's humanity.[22])

Muhammad's attempts at appeasement did not work, however. The Meccans made great fun of the pretensions of the son of Abd'Allah, of this once ragged lad who owed his fortune to a decrepit widow, and who wept like a woman at the least provocation. A prophet, this former shepherd? A messenger from God? This coward who had fled from the battlefield? Nonsense![23] Hurtful, cruel mockery soon turned into open persecution.

The harshness of that persecution, which started in A.D. 615, is overstated in Islamic tradition. Some of Muhammad's followers were certainly harassed, but not one was killed. (One cannot but wonder if in Saudi Arabia today a local Meccan were to suggest the official cult of the Kaaba was defective in any way, and to insist that it be reformed to suit his "revelation," offending not only established sensibilities but also the modern *hajj* business—would his likely fate be harsher or more gentle than that "suffered" by Muhammad?) Several escaped to the Christian kingdom of Abyssinia, but their move may have been prompted by commercial opportunities, as some remained there well after Muhammad's power base in Medina was fully developed.

---

[20] 6:108.
[21] Guillaume, *The Life of Muhammad*, p. 162.
[22] Cf. W. Montgomery Watt (1953).
[23] Servier, p. 53.

His opponents, led by one Abu Jahl, suspected Muhammad of harboring political ambitions and seeking the position of leadership in the city. A mob raged against Muhammad, the "divider" who wanted to tell real men what they can and cannot do, calling him a blasphemous unbeliever. There was little physical violence, and Muhammad's own life was safe, thanks to his influential uncle Abu Taleb. He retreated into the caves of Mount Hira and spread his word among the occasional passersby with time on their hands. In the meantime, Muhammad's uncle—who genuinely believed that his nephew was insane—tried to convince his fellow citizens that this was indeed so, and that he should be pitied rather than persecuted. In A.D. 616, however, they orchestrated a boycott of the clan of Hashim by other clans, accusing its members of failure to curb Muhammad's activities.

Far from being curbed, Muhammad's claims had grown more extravagant. In A.D. 619, his "journey into heaven" took place, when one night the angel Gabriel supposedly took him from Mecca to Jerusalem on the back of a white mule-like beast with a human head, where he prayed two *rakkahs* at the "Furtherest Mosque" before proceeding on a trip through "the seven heavens." There he encountered all the previous prophets, including Adam, Jesus, Moses, and Abraham, before being taken into the presence of God to be instructed in proper worship: "Glory to (Allah) Who did take His Servant for a Journey by night from the Sacred Mosque to the Farthest Mosque (*Masjid al-Aqsa*), whose precincts We did bless, in order that We might show him some of Our Signs: for He is the One Who heareth and seeth all things."[24] Muhammad was apparently unaware that the first Jerusalem Temple was destroyed by Nebuchadnezzar's Babylonian armies in 587 B.C., while Titus and his Roman soldiers leveled the Second Temple in A.D. 70, more than five centuries earlier. These facts were not unknown to some of his traveled Quraysh contemporaries, however. (The Temple site that eventually became the Dome of the Rock, the Furtherest Mosque, *Masjid al-Aqsa,* was built in A.D. 691.)

Having failed to convince his fellow citizens and tribesmen of his prophetic calling, Muhammad increasingly turned to strangers. He may have expected to be accepted by the Jews and Christians as a prophet, and

---

[24] 17:1.

his Meccan revelations contain positive statements about them. Do not argue with "the People of the Book," he told his followers, "but say, 'We believe in the Revelation which has come down to us and in that which came down to you.'"[25] At that time he allowed for the possibility that Jews and Christians could attain salvation. They, and his own followers, "any who believe in God and the Last Day and work righteousness shall have their reward with their Lord: on them shall be no fear, nor shall they grieve."[26] It was only later, in Medina, when Muhammad's prophetic claims were rejected by Jews and Christians, that his position underwent complete change to uncompromising hostility and justification of violence.

HIJRAH

The Quraysh took a dim view of Muhammad's contacts with outsiders, which further alienated him from the rest of the tribe, who came to see him as a renegade. In A.D. 619 his protective uncle Abu Taleb died, and Muhammad's faithful wife, Khadija, followed only months later. His situation was growing precarious, as the leadership of the clan of Hashim passed to another uncle, Abu Lahab, who was closer to the Meccan establishment and under its pressure withdrew the clan's protection from Muhammad. Having already been disappointed in the negus of Ethiopia, whence he received discouraging reports from his followers, he left for the town of al-Taif, Mecca's neighboring city to the southeast, but did not manage to establish a base there. Having obtained the pledge of protection from the head of another clan, Muhammad returned to Mecca, this time as a despised and unwanted outcast.

His subsequent attempts to gain support of other tribes were unsuccessful. His fortunes changed in the summer of 621, however, when he gained the trust of twelve visitors from the oasis settlement of Yathrib, some 200 miles to the north of Mecca, who came to the city for the annual pilgrimage to the Kaaba. They revealed themselves as Muslims to Muhammad and returned to Yathrib, promising to propagate his message.

There had existed some antagonism between these two places, reflecting the old quarrel between the farmer and the nomad, the

---

[25] 29:46.
[26] 2:62.

33

homesteader and the shepherd. Yathrib was smaller, but it had a better climate than Mecca, more water, more fertile lands—and a less exciting social life. It also had a large Jewish and Christian colony, with the former proclaiming, as ever, the imminent arrival of a messenger from God, and the latter injecting a note of restraint and humility, with their advocacy of forgiveness of injuries. But while the settled farmers of Yathrib were ready for the concept of a one and only God, in Mecca the notion was hampered by Muhammad's poor standing. He was not to be a prophet in his own city.

In June 622, during pilgrimage, a group of 75 people from Yathrib came to Muhammad, professing Islam and pledging to defend Muhammad as if he were one of their own kin. Following "the Two Pledges of al-'Aqaba," Muhammad encouraged his Meccan followers to leave the city in small groups and make their way north. His decision to flee to Yathrib may have been prompted by the news that a council of tribal elders was being assembled for the purpose of his trial. His life was in danger, not because of his prophetic claims as such, but because he was perceived as a traitor: his position was akin to that of an Athenian who not only denies the divinity of the gods but also denounces his native polis and pledges allegiance to Sparta.

In his escape from Mecca, Muhammad was joined by a small group of refugees—seventy *muhajirun* in all—that included Zaid, Ali, Abu-Bakr, his new father-in-law, Othman, his son-in-law, and Omar. They were all intensely loyal to Muhammad personally, and their readiness to sever the links of birthplace and clan association is a testimony to the prophet's personal charisma and leadership ability. This was the *hijrah,* and Muhammad's arrival in Yathrib on September 24, 622, marked the beginning of the history of Islam. From that time, Yathrib became the city of the Prophet, Medinnet el Nebi, which has been shortened to Medina. Significantly, just prior to leaving for Medina—where he knew that he would finally have armed men at his disposal—Muhammad received his first revelations allowing him to fight the Meccans.[27]

His hosts' acceptance of his prophetic claims was partly rooted in their political problems. Medina was the home of indigenous Arab clans, of Jewish settlers who prospered from agriculture and trade, and more recent Arab immigrants of the tribes of al-Aws and al-Khazraj. The quarrels

---

[27] 22:39–41, 2:193.

34

among the three groups escalated to bloodshed in about A.D. 618, but in subsequent years stability seemed elusive, which prompted the hope that a wise and just outsider could arbitrate and establish order. Muhammad obliged. The resulting "Constitution of Medina," an agreement regulating relations among eight Arab clans and Muhammad's followers from Mecca as the ninth group, stated that disputes would be submitted to "Muhammad the Prophet," but otherwise gave him no position of political authority in the traditional sense. As the Jews were reluctant to sign a document that accepted Muhammad's prophetic claims, they were not a direct party to the agreement but were only mentioned as one of the groups subject to its provisions.

It took Muhammad a year and a half, and a victory in battle, to fully establish his power base, and another three years to become *de facto* absolute ruler of Medina, but the outcome seemed uncertain at first. He was given a plot of land and had a house built for him where his followers gathered to pray, but he was short of money. His seventy *muhajirun* were slow to adapt to the need for gainful employment, and his most zealous disciples, Ali, Zaid, Abu-Bekr, Omar, and Othman were itching for action of a different kind. Only fighting the despised Meccans would satisfy the desire for revenge of true believers who were slighted and persecuted by the haughty merchants. Muhammad thereupon approved of *razzias* ("ghazawat"), armed raids against Meccan caravans passing near Medina on their way to Syria. Such raids, once customary, had become rare in preceding years, and security on Arabian roads had improved, thanks to the Meccan diplomacy and power.

Muhammad's three initial attempts, which he led in 623, all ended in failure, possibly because his plans had been revealed to the Meccans in advance. In early 624, the Muslims had their first successful raid, when they followed sealed orders given to them by Muhammad before leaving Medina. They ambushed a caravan from Yemen at Nakhlah, near Mecca, killing one man, taking two prisoners—for whose ransom Muhammad later received eighty ounces of silver—and carrying much loot back to Medina.

The success of the raiders was partly due to the complete surprise of their victims: the attack took place in the holy month of Ramadan, the time of truce generally respected even by the most pugnacious of brigands until that time. This did not present a problem to Muhammad, however, who had just received a revelation allowing warfare even during Ramadan:

35

"Warring therein is grievous; but to obstruct the way of God and to deny Him, to hinder men from the holy temple, and to expel His people thence, that is more grievous than slaughter."[28] From that point revelations suitable to the needs of the moment, helping Muhammad augment his political and legal authority (or even helping him keep his quarrelsome wives in check), had become frequent and surprisingly specific in the way Allah obliged in addressing the daily needs of his prophet.

Emboldened by this success, two months later Muhammad led over 300 of his men in what was his most ambitious action until that time, against a large Meccan caravan making its way home from Syria. The caravan, ably led by Abu Sufyan, the leader of the Umayyah clan, eluded the attackers for days. Muhammad's old foe, Abu Jahl, learning of Muhammad's intent, led a superior protective force of between 600 and 800 men. He decided not to follow the caravan to safety, however, but turned back to fight and eliminate the Muslim threat once and for all.

The battle, which took place near Badr on March 15, 624, turned into an unexpected victory for Muhammad: over 40 Meccans were killed, including Abu Jahl, and over 60 taken prisoner, to the loss of only 14 of his followers. It was interpreted as a "miracle" that had eluded Muhammad in his daily life, a glorious victory scored with the help of Allah and a thousand angels. It greatly increased his prestige and power in Medina.

It was most unusual for an Arab to go so far in his estrangement from his tribe as Muhammad had done even before Badr; to take arms against his kinsmen was indeed unprecedented, but "Islam hath rent all bonds asunder." The Muslims' resentment and anger at the Meccans notwithstanding, divine justification was required for so radical a step as ambushing and murdering one's own kin. Allah's messages, conveyed by Muhammad, grew accordingly more bellicose: "I will instill terror into the hearts of the unbelievers, smite ye above their necks and smite all their finger tips of them."[29]

At the same time—and perhaps as importantly to his followers—the prospect of booty and ransom was made lawful and good: "You desire the lure of this world and Allah desires for you the hereafter and Allah is Mighty, Wise. Now enjoy what you have won as lawful and good and keep

---

[28] 2:217.
[29] 8:12.

36

your duty to Allah."[30] For the fallen, paradise awaits immediately: "Allah guarantees that He will admit the Mujahid in His Cause into Paradise if he is killed, otherwise He will return him to his home safely with rewards and war booty."[31] The promise was reiterated in other verses: "Allah promiseth you much booty that ye will capture, and hath given you this in advance, and hath withheld men's hands from you, that it may be a token for the believers, and that He may guide you on a right path. And other [gain], which ye have not been able to achieve, Allah will compass it."[32] As for the division of the spoils, every man was allowed to retain the plunder of those whom he had slain with his own hand, with the rest thrown into a common stock. A dispute arose about its division, forcing Muhammad to resolve it with a message from Heaven—and to take possession of the whole booty: It was God who had given the victory, and to God all the spoils belonged. From the proceeds one-fifth was Muhammad's: "They ask thee concerning the Prey. Say, the Prey is God's and his Prophet's. . . . And know that whatever ye take as spoils of war, lo! a fifth thereof is for Allah, and for the messenger and for the kinsman."[33]

MUHAMMAD UNLEASHED

The triumph at Badr was one of the most decisive moments in Muhammad's life. A new side of his personality came to the fore, and a new man was presented to the world, as the severed head of Abu Jahl was thrown before him. The simple preacher and warner of Mecca turned into a vengeful warlord who jubilantly exclaimed that the spectacle pleased him better than "the choicest camel in Arabia." "Otba! Shaiba! Omeyya! Abu Jahl!" exclaimed he, as one by one the corpses were, without ceremony, cast into the common grave:

"Have ye now found that which your Lord promised you true?
What my Lord promised me, that verily have I found to be true.
Woe unto this people! Ye have rejected me, your Prophet! Ye

---

[30] 69:30–37.
[31] Al-Bukhari, Volume 4, Book 52, Number 46.
[32] 48:20–21.
[33] 8:41

cast me forth, and others gave me refuge; ye fought against me, and others came to my help!"[34]

The prisoners were brought up before Muhammad. As he scrutinized each, his eye fell fiercely on al-Nadr, whom he had never forgiven, captivating the Meccans with more entertaining tales. On more than one occasion, as Muhammad was delineating the life of the patriarchs and prophets and giving examples of divine retribution that had fallen on impious nations, al-Nadr would speak after him and say: "Listen now to things which are as good as those with which Muhammad has entertained you." He would then relate the marvelous exploits of the Persian heroes Rustam and Isfendiar, and finally ask his enchanted audience: "Are the stories of Muhammad more beautiful than mine? He is spouting ancient legends that he has gathered from the mouths of men more learned than he."

On the day after Badr, it was time for Muhammad to settle the score. Realizing that his fate was sealed, al-Nadr bitterly complained that had the Quraysh taken Muslims prisoner, they would never have killed them. "Even were it so," Muhammad scornfully replied, "I am not as thou and Islam hath rent all bounds asunder." Al-Nadr was beheaded by Ali.

Another condemned pleaded for his life, asking who would take care of his little girl. "Hell-fire," Muhammad replied, and, as the victim was slain, he added, "I give thanks unto the Lord that hath slain thee, and comforted mine eyes thereby!"[35] The Kuran contains the accompanying revelation from on high: "It is not for any Prophet to have captives until he hath made slaughter in the land."[36] Fresh revelations described the unbelievers as "the worst animals."[37] The Prophet was now the "enemy of infidels."[38] Killing or, in the case of Jews and Christians, enslaving and robbing them, was not only divinely sanctioned but mandated.

Muhammad returned to Medina in triumph and proceeded to settle scores with his detractors there. An atmosphere of fear descended on the city; informers passed all disrespectful or merely careless remarks to the prophet, who followed them up with "proceedings that were sometimes

---

[34] Muir, p. 114.
[35] Ibid, p. 117.
[36] 8:68.
[37] 8:55.
[38] 2:90.

both cruel and unscrupulous."[39] Medina was turned into an early exercise in the total blending of religion and self-referential political ideology, of mosque and state. The options for all Medinans were reduced to conversion, expulsion, or death. His first victim was Asma bint Marwan, a poetess who disliked both Muhammad personally and the religion he preached. In one poem, she urged her fellow-tribesmen not to obey a stranger who did not belong among them. Anticipating Henry II's outburst, Muhammad exclaimed, "Will no one rid me of this daughter of Marwan?" One of his followers by the name of Umayr duly did, that same night, stabbing her as she nursed her youngest child. After she was murdered, Muhammad praised the killer and assured him that "two goats won't butt their head about her"—which presumably excluded her children and her family. The following day, they all converted to Islam.

The prophet of Islam took a dim view of poets generally, but especially those who dared mock him in verse. Allah accordingly conveyed the verdict that poets are inspired by Satan and have gone astray.[40] They are possessed.[41] They are no better than soothsayers.[42] This seems almost like an obsession with Muhammad. He never mastered the complicated canon of Arab poetry; that he could not respond to his eloquent detractors in kind must have pained him greatly, since it had to be explained away by none other than Allah: "We have not taught versification to our prophet."[43] Muhammad had other means at his disposal, however, and that was the undoing not only of Asma but also of one Abu Afak, supposedly over a hundred years old, who protested previous murders by the Muslims. Abu Afak also mocked Muhammad in verse, and especially his desire to control people's lives: "Saying 'Permitted,' 'Forbidden,' of all sorts of things." The apostle simply commented, "Who will deal with this rascal for me?"—and one of his "weepers" did.[44] That a person of so advanced an age should be murdered for a verbal slight would have been inconceivable to the pre-Islamic Arab custom.

---

[39] Ibn Warraq, 1995.
[40] 26:224.
[41] 37:35–36.
[42] 52:29.
[43] 36:68–69.
[44] Ibn Ishaq, p. 675.

(Music did not fare any better with Muhammad than poetry. That mainstream Islam has no music, and that there is no singing at the mosque may be related to Muhammad's view that "None raised up his voice with a song but Allah sent him two devils upon his shoulders who beat his chest with their heels till he stopped."[45] He once heard the sound of a flute and put his fingers into his ears and turned to go another way.[46])

Another doomed poet was a Jew by the name of Ka'b bin al-Ashraf, who bewailed the defeat of the Meccans at Badr and made up some unsavory poems about Muslim women. That was his undoing, with the prophet simply saying, "O Lord, rid me of the son of Ashfar, however You wish." Characteristically, Muhammad approved of subterfuge in arranging his murder, and the assassins achieved their goal by pretending to be friendly to the victim until they got him away from his family and out of his house.[47] The modern Muslim justification of the murder, directed at the non-Muslim, English-speaking audience, has an unsettling ring to it: "Ka'b had become a real danger to the state of peace and mutual trust which the Prophet was struggling to achieve in Madinah. He was dangerous and a public enemy to the nascent Muslim state. The Prophet was quite exasperated with him. . . . This was all part of the great process . . . which helped to make Islam spread and establish it on foundations of justice and piety."[48] The man's severed head was built into those foundations. Muhammad rejoiced at its sight, and his next step in establishing "peace and mutual trust" was to instruct his followers to kill any Jew who fell into their hands. One Muhayyisa bin Mas'ud, to prove his devotion, went to Ibn Sunayna, a Jewish merchant who had given him work in the past, and killed him without ado. His elder brother Huwayyisa, who was not a Muslim at that time, reproached him, saying, "You enemy of God, why did you kill him when much of the fat on your belly comes from his wealth?" According to early Islamic chroniclers, Muhayyisa answered,

> "Had the one who ordered me to kill him ordered me to kill you, I would have cut your head off." He said that this was the beginning of Huwayyisa's acceptance of Islam. The other replied,

---

[45] *Al Hadis*, Book 2, Chapter 12, No. 283.
[46] *Al Hadis*, Book 2, Chap. 12, No. 20.
[47] Bukhari, vol 5, #369.
[48] www.islam101.com/people/companions/maslamah.html.

"By God, *if Muhammad had ordered you to kill me, would you have killed me?"* He said, "Yes, by God, had he ordered me to cut off your head, I would have done so." He exclaimed, "By God, *a religion which can bring you to this is marvelous!"* and he became a Muslim.[49]

This was the true meaning of Islamic *iman,* usually translated as "personal faith," but different from the Western understanding of that word. It can be described as "sanctuary" or place of safe refuge. In Arabia, an outlaw would seek iman after being expelled from his tribe. Muhammad trusted the Medinans to protect him as one of their own. For an early Arab believer in Muhammad's faith, this meant nothing less than a complete change of identity. He did not belong any longer to his blood-tribe but to the Islamic *umma,* and would seek protection from Allah and his prophet. Those who did so and changed their minds were doomed, like the apostates from the tribe of Ukl whose hands and feet were cut off, their eyes pulled out, and who were left to die in the sun.[50]

Following Ibn Sunayna's killing, a group of Muhammad's followers from the Khazraj tribe plotted the murder of an elderly Jewish merchant by the name of Abu Rafi. He had never done any harm to the Muslims, but his prominence made him a suitable target. Six men went to kill him with the Prophet's blessing, broke into Abu Rafi's house in the middle of the night, and slashed him with their swords as he slept. When they returned to Muhammad there was a dispute among them as to who had actually killed the man. At this Muhammad smiled and started checking their swords. He decided that the man who owned the sword that still had traces of food on the blade was the winner. Apparently Abu Rafi—one of at least 27 people murdered on Muhammad's orders—had just finished his dinner before falling asleep, and Muhammad judged that the sword that had slashed through his stomach ended his life, spilling its contents. After this his followers reveled that "there was not a Jew there who did not fear for his life." Their fears were justified, as Muhammad had determined that it was time to dispense with individual murders and to deal with that stubborn community collectively.

---

[49] Ibn Ishaq, *Sirat Rasul Allah* (translated by A. Guillaume), *The Life of Muhammad*, p. 369.
[50] Sahih Al-Bukhari, Vol. 7, Bk. 71, No. 590.

In Mecca, Muhammad had hoped to be accepted as God's messenger by the Jews and to win them over by ordering his followers to turn in the direction of Jerusalem during prayer, and adopting the Jewish Day of Atonement, Ashura, as the Muslim holy day. He seems to have underestimated the Jewish tribes' allegiance to their scriptures and the effect that the many irreconcilable discrepancies between his own Kuranic pronouncements and the Jewish tradition would have on them. His superficial, second-hand knowledge of the holy texts made it impossible for him to argue on par with the learned merchants of Medina steeped in their Tradition. The result of their unsurprising refusal to give it up in favor of the claims of a poorly educated refugee was that Muhammad's earlier, favorable pronouncements about the Jews evolved into an implacably hostile position. The perceived slight, as was customary with him, turned into rage. The result is summarized in a chillingly euphemistic account by a contemporary Muslim scholar:

> As soon as these tribes realized that Islam was being firmly established and gaining power, they adopted an actively hostile attitude, and the final result of the struggle was the disappearance of these Jewish communities from Arabia proper.[51]

This "disappearance" was not a spontaneous phenomenon, but the result of what would be known in our own time as ethnic cleansing and genocide. The first stage consisted of individual murders of Jews; the second entailed the expulsion of two tribes from Medina; the third was completed with the slaughter of one remaining tribe. After the defeat at Uhud, Muhammad realized the danger of repeated engagements against the Meccans, who were better fighters than the farmers of Medina. And yet he needed a success to atone for the setback, and turned the swords of his followers against a far softer target. He first received a divine warning that the Jewish tribe of Banu Nadir plotted his death, and promptly ordered them to leave Medina within ten days. At first they refused; but after a siege of several weeks, they surrendered and were expelled. All of their considerable belongings and land were distributed among Muhammad's faithful. (They were slaughtered two years later in their new abode.) His

---

[51] W.N. Arafat, "New light on the story of Banu Qurayza and the Jews of Medina," *Journal of the Royal Asiatic Society of Great Britain and Ireland*, 1976, pp. 100–107.

own royal fifth finally made him a wealthy man. The visible and very tangible benefits of being Muslim acted as a powerful inducement for the remaining doubters to embrace Islam, even if they remained unconvinced by Muhammad's preaching.

In the attack against the tribe of Banu-'l-Mustaliq in 626, Muhammad's followers slaughtered many tribesmen and looted thousands of their camels and sheep; they also kidnapped some of their "excellent women." The night after the battle, Muhammad and his followers staged an orgy of rape. As one Abu Sa'id al-Khadri remembered, a problem needed to be resolved first: In order to obtain ransom from the surviving tribesmen, the Muslims had pledged not to violate their captives.

> We . . . desired them, for we were suffering from the absence of our wives, but at the same time we also desired ransom for them. So we decided to have sexual intercourse with them but by observing 'azl [coitus interruptus]. But we said: We are doing an act whereas Allah's Messenger is amongst us; why not ask him? So we asked Allah's Messenger (may peace be upon him), and he said: It does not matter if you do not do it, for every soul that is to be born up to the Day of Resurrection will be born.[52]

In telling his companions to go ahead and rape their captive married women without practicing al-'azl, the only contentious issue was whether the victims' ransom value would be diminished or lost completely if they were returned pregnant to their husbands. Muhammad's revelations had already sanctioned the rape of captive women, and the above hadith explicitly references Kuran:

> And all married women are forbidden unto you except those captives whom your right hand possesses. It is a decree of Allah for you. Lawful unto you are all beyond those mentioned, so that you seek them with your wealth in honest wedlock, not debauchery.[53]

Alarmed by the apparent consolidation of Muhammad's position, the Meccans decided to deal a crushing blow once and for all to the traitor who dared disrupt their commerce. In early 627, an army huge by Arabian

---

[52] Sahih Muslim, Book 8, Number 3371.
[53] 4:24.

standards—some 10,000 men led by Abu Sufyan—advanced against Medina. Muhammad had prepared reserves of food, however, and ordered a ditch to be dug, protecting the exposed approaches to the city. After a siege of only two weeks, during which Muhammad undermined the attackers' unity by sending envoys to different tribes comprising the Meccan coalition, they gave up and withdrew.

In the flush of victory, he proceeded to attack the last Jewish tribe in Medina, Banu Qurayzah, which he accused of disloyalty and complicity with the Meccans. This time, mere expulsion and robbery would no longer do. Muhammad offered the men conversion to Islam as an alternative to death; upon their refusal, up to 900 were decapitated at the ditch, in front of their women and children. Torches were lit so that the slaughter could be accomplished in one day. "Truly the judgment of Allah was pronounced on high" was Muhammad's comment. Allah added a few words of his own: "And He has caused to descend from their strongholds the Jews that assisted them. And he struck terror into their hearts. Some you slaughtered, and some you took prisoner."[54]

The women were subsequently raped; Muhammad chose as his concubine one Raihana bint Amr, whose father and husband were both slaughtered before her eyes only hours earlier; such treatment had already been sanctioned by prophetic revelation. As for the captured husbands, fathers, sons, or brothers, the messages now grew ever harsher: "Take him and fetter him and expose him to hell fire. And then insert him in a chain whereof the length is seventy cubits."[55] Those are the lucky ones; others "will be killed or crucified, or have their hands and feet on alternate sides cut off."[56] In this world, for the captured infidel, "we have prepared chains, yokes and a blazing fire."[57] In the hereafter, things get even worse: "But as for those who disbelieve, garments of fire will be cut out for them, boiling fluid will be poured down their heads. Whereby that which is in their bellies, and their skins too, will be melted. . . . And for them are hooked rods of iron. Whenever, in their anguish, they would go forth from thence

---

[54] 33:25.
[55] 69:30–37.
[56] 5:33–34.
[57] 76:4.

44

they are driven back therein and (it is said unto them): Taste the doom of burning."[58]

By the summer of 627, Muhammad's prestige and authority were truly unassailable. He had transformed himself imperceptibly into an absolute ruler even before the siege, and the attendant change of his personality did not escape the notice of his contemporaries. "That man aspires to dominate the Arabs," said the Taiyite chief Zarr ibn Sadus. The shrewd politician Abu Sufyan was to make the same observation: "Prophetism is finished, the empire is beginning":

> In the secret depths of Muhammad's conscience there surged more and more precise aspirations toward domination and sovereignty, or *al-mulk* as the Arabs say. He felt he had been born to govern his contemporaries, and in this he was not mistaken. In the past, he had enumerated in the Kuran (3:12) the series of temptations which could enslave human beings: *The passion for women, the desire for male children, the thirst for gold and silver, spirited horses, and the possession of cattle and land, in fact all the pleasures of life on earth.* Now the Prophet wanted to possess them. In Mecca he had continually stated the purity of his intentions and his unselfishness. This claim he put, for his own account, into the mouths of the prophets, his predecessors. Did this misunderstood innovator himself fail to recognize where his ambition was to bring him, and how he was to be seduced by riches, *the greatest that any leader in Central Arabia had ever possessed* (Caetani)? After a painful period of tentative efforts, success had come. This was a difficult test! Was it to leave him with the strength to resist?[59]

It was not. Muhammad admitted that two things in the world, women and perfume, attracted him—so much so that, flushed with success, he departed from his own laws and claimed his privilege as a prophet in pursuit of the former. He reddened his hair with henna[60] and took to

---

[58] 22:19–22.

[59] Henri Lammens: "Fatima and the Daughters of Muhammad," as quoted in Ibn Warraq (Ed.), *The Quest for the Historical Muhammad,* New York, 2000, pp. 248–249.

[60] Bukhari, vol. 1, no. 167.

wearing a veil. (This did not save him from lice, however.[61]) Contrary to his regulations, he had at least fifteen wives, some claim up to twenty-five. The youngest of them was Aisha, who was seven years old "and with the dolls" when Muhammad—44 years her senior—married her, and two years later consummated the marriage. Marriage relationships were used by Muhammad to cement the links with his followers. Aisha was the daughter of Abu Bakr, who was to be the first caliph, and after Badr he also married Hafsah, daughter of Umar (second caliph), whose husband was killed in battle. Of Muhammad's daughters, Fatimah was married to Ali (later fourth caliph) and Umm Kulthum to Uthman (third caliph).

Muhammad was a vain and jealous man, and his possessiveness was reflected in the Kuranic verse forbidding his wives to remarry after his death. Their jealousy of him—fed by his inordinate sensuality—at times presented him with a problem. An Egyptian slave woman by the name of Maryah, and a Christian at that, aroused Muhammad's passion for nights on end, which provoked a rebellion in the harem. Divine assistance was in the end needed to restore order in the household, with the Kuranic verse approvingly telling Muhammad not to restrain himself from "that which Allah has made lawful to you," only for the sake of pleasing his wives.[62] Thus authorized, Muhammad repudiated his disobedient wives for a month and dedicated himself to Maryah. In the end the seditious wives were admitted back into his presence, but not before Allah admonished the ring-leaders, Hafsa and Aisha, with another verse: "If ye two turn in repentance to Him, your hearts are indeed so inclined; but if you help one another against him, then verily, Allah is his Protector, and Jibrael and the righteous among the believers, and furthermore, the angels are his helpers. It may be if he divorced you (all) that his Lord will give him instead of you, wives better than you."[63] With Allah, Gabriel, the angels and the faithful thus aligned, the two women took their lot in stride.

Potentially more scandalous for the prophet's standing within the community was the case of Zeinab, the only wife of Zayd, Muhammad's adopted son. One day Muhammad came to her house looking for Zayd, who was away, and noticing the youthful beauty of his daughter-in-law's scantily clad body, he exclaimed, "Praised be Allah, who changes men's

---

[61] Bukhari, vol 9, no. 130.
[62] 66:1–3.
[63] 66:4.

hearts!" Zeinab reported the incident in detail to Zayd, who saw the writing on the wall and duly divorced her—much to the feigned chagrin of his adopted father—thus enabling Muhammad to take her as one of his many wives. The deal was soon sanctioned by Allah's revelation: "So when Zaid had accomplished what he would of her, then We gave her in marriage to thee, so that there should not be any fault in the believers, touching the wives of their adopted sons, when they have accomplished what they would of them; and God's commandment must be performed."[64] We do not know of Zayd's true feelings as he was instructed by Muhammad to notify his recently divorced spouse of the prophet's intention to wed her: "Rejoice, O Zeinab, for the Messenger of God has betrothed you to himself." Zeinab subsequently boasted to Muhammad's other wives that their fathers had given them to him in marriage, but it was Allah himself who gave her in marriage to his prophet.

PROPHET VICTORIOUS

The sight of a victorious leader, resolute in battle and merciless with the defeated infidel, generous to his followers and feared by his foes, worked wonders for the man who on his own could not do miracles. At the same time, Mecca was in crisis after the failure of its campaign against Muhammad. In March 628, Muhammad determined to test the Meccans' resolve by seeking access to the holy pilgrimage sites for himself and a band of his followers. The Meccans stopped them but negotiated a treaty with Muhammad, allowing the Muslims to come in the following year. This was the Treaty of al-Hudaybiyah, in which Muhammad agreed to temporarily discard his title of "prophet of Allah" for immediate political benefit of gaining a foothold in his native city.

Muhammad rewarded his followers for their orderly conduct during the protracted and sometimes tense proceedings by leading them against the Jewish settlement of Khaybar, north of Medina. It was inhabited in part by the relocated tribes he had expelled from Medina in earlier years; now they were forced to give one-half of their harvest of dates to the Muslims. At the same time, in Mecca the morale was declining, and a few prominent citizens left for Medina to declare their allegiance to Muhammad. When

---

[64] 36:37.

the Prophet of Islam came to Mecca as a pilgrim in 629, even his old foe Abu Sufyan became reconciled to the city's eventual submission. The immediate cause came in November of that year, when a skirmish between some Meccan allies and Muhammad's followers prompted him to abrogate the treaty and start preparing a campaign against Mecca.

There was to be no war, however: as Muhammad marched on his native city at the head of an army of 10,000, Abu Sufyan and other leading citizens came out to meet him and formally submitted to his authority. Muhammad's triumph was complete, and the human cost to the faithful was slight: in all 82 recorded battles and skirmishes during the lifetime of Muhammad, only 259 Muslims lost their lives.[65]

"Upon what meat has this our Caesar fed that he has grown so great?" wondered Shakespeare's Romans, and the Meccans may have asked the same on January 12, A.D. 630, when the victorious Muslims rode into their streets. The city of the prophet's birth observed in numb silence the destruction of 360 divinities worshiped by as many Arabian tribes in the temple of Kaaba. There was no doubt in either side's mind that this was occupation, not liberation. The choice facing the vanquished was clear from the dilemma faced by Abu-Sufyan when he was brought to Muhammad:

> Muhammad told him: "Woe to you, Abu Sufyan. Is it not time for you to realize that there is no God but the only God?" Abu Sufyan answered: "I do believe that." Muhammad then said to him: "Woe to you, Abu Sufyan. Is it not time for you to know that I am the apostle of God?" Abu Sufyan answered: "By God, O Muhammad, of this there is doubt in my soul." The 'Abbas who was present with Muhammad told Abu Sufyan: "Woe to you! Accept Islam and testify that Muhammad is the apostle of God before your neck is cut off by the sword." Thus he professed the faith of Islam and became a Muslim.[66]

Anticipating consternation of uninitiated Western readers to Muhammad's approach, who may be squeamish to the notion of faith imposed by the threat of beheading, contemporary Muslim commentators

---

[65] Sahih Muslim III, p. 491.
[66] Cf. Ibn Hisham, part 4 of his *Biography of the Prophet*.

explain that the modest demand for "the surrender of the tongue"—as opposed to the insistence on "heartfelt faith," which would assuredly come later—was a sign of tolerant disposition, more humane than the choice between sincere submission and death. The notion that the threat of death, the one constant in both scenarios, is at odds with the claim that "there is no compulsion in faith" is calmly disregarded.

As it happens, Muhammad's pragmatism in demanding only verbal submission to start with was a very useful device in spreading Islam throughout the conquered lands, from Bosnia to India. St. Paul's "Let each be fully convinced in his own mind" could not apply to the conquering faith that depended on the power of the sword, not that of the word. In the longer term, as it turned out, the formal submission of the first generation of converts inevitably led to the irreversible change of identity and belief system of those that followed. Lingering suppressed guilt at the original act of betrayal turned Muslim converts of the Balkans, in particular, into zealous oppressors of their Christian kinsmen who had retained their identity.

In return for formal submission of the leaders Muhammad decided against allowing some of his zealous followers to take revenge on Mecca and settle old scores. In a gesture certain to encounter approval of the Quraysh, he proclaimed the Kaaba—now cleansed of idols—to be the temple of Allah. He shrewdly judged that under the circumstances, forgiveness was not to be taken for weakness but for strength and virtue. By insisting on conciliation in the conquered city of Mecca, Muhammad was able to persuade the tribes and clans to accept the idea that from now on Islam, rather than tribal affiliation, was to be the unifying principle of society. By providing for considerable continuity between old beliefs and new religion, he facilitated the conversion of the remaining skeptics within, and pagan tribes without.

In A.D. 632, when Muhammad performed a solemn pilgrimage, over 40,000 believers accompanied him. The triumph of Islam in the Arab lands, and possibly beyond, was assured. The progression from a moral preacher to a warrior-prophet and eminently successful politician, unifier of Arabia, and finally the Seal of the Prophets, was complete.

Soon after his return to Medina, Muhammad died of a violent fever at the age of 63, the eleventh year of the Hejira, and the year 632 of the Christian Era.

MASTER OF LIFE?

The change of Muhammad's status from a marginalized outsider to a revered and feared master of life and death produced a remarkable transformation of his personality in the last twelve years of his life. With Khadija's moderating influence no longer present to help keep his passions in check, Allah was invoked as *deus ex machina*, providing revelations relevant not to the Prophet's daily political objectives, but also to his personal needs. Nowhere was this more obvious than when it came to his exaggerated sensuality.

That Muhammad's actions and words, as immortalized in the Kuran and recorded in the Traditions, are frankly shocking by the standards of our time—and punishable by its laws, that range from war crimes and murder to rape and child molestation—almost goes without saying.

There are contemporary Western authors, however, who argue that we must not extend the judgmental yardstick of our own culture to the members of other cultures who have lived in other eras. In response, it should be pointed out that even in the context of seventh century Arabia, Muhammad had to resort to divine revelations as a means of suppressing the prevalent moral code of his own milieu. Attacking caravans in the month of Ramadan, taking up arms against his own kinsmen, murdering people without provocation, and indulging with considerable abandon one's sensual passions was so fundamentally at odds with the moral standards of his own Arab contemporaries that only the ultimate authority could, and did, sanction it. As an Edwardian author put it in the blunt language still allowed in his time, the problem with Muhammad's behavior is not that he was a Bedouin, but that he was a morally degenerate Bedouin.[67]

The word *genocide* was not even coined when Allah declared, and Muhammad conveyed: "When we decide to destroy a population, we send a definite order to them who have the good things in life and yet transgress; so that Allah's word is proved true against them: then we destroy them utterly."[68] Disobedient people "we utterly destroyed because of their inequities, setting up in their place other peoples."[69] But no material benefit

---

[67] Servier, op. cit. p. 43.
[68] 17:16–17.
[69] 21:11.

could be derived from corpses, so the lives of the unconverted conquered could be spared if they agreed to pay a tribute to the Muslims. In his own lifetime, Muhammad established the model for subsequent relations between Islamic conquerors and their Christian or Jewish subjects: "Fight those who do not profess the true faith (Islam) till they pay the *jizya* (poll tax) with the hand of humility."[70] That Islam sees the world as an open-ended conflict between the Land of Peace (*Dar al-Islam*) and the Land of War (*Dar al-Harb*) is the most important legacy of Muhammad. Ever since his time, Islam has been a permanent challenge to all non-Muslim polities around it. The Kuranic dictum to fight Jews and Christians until "they pay the Jizya with willing submission," denied the possibility of any permanent peaceful co-existence.

Muhammad's practice and constant encouragement of bloodshed are unique in the history of religions. Murder, pillage, rape, and more murder are in the Kuran and in the Traditions "seem to have impressed his followers with a profound belief in the value of bloodshed as opening the gates of Paradise" and prompted countless Muslim governors, caliphs, and viziers to refer to Muhammad's example to justify their mass killings, looting, and destruction.[71] "Kill, kill the unbelievers wherever you find them" is an injunction both unambiguous and powerful.

The option of conversion was always available to its surviving victims, of course, and to be on the right side of Allah—and of history, as it seemed for a long time—was not too demanding. God, the creator and sustainer of the world, rewarded all those who expressed their worship in prayer, almsgiving, and self-purification, and above all in unquestioning obedience to Muhammad, his messenger. That "Allah is great, and that there is no God but Allah, and Muhammad is his messenger" was easily grasped by the nomadic tribes of the desert and, later, of the steppe, especially when the celestial reward was preceded by the tangible loot divinely sanctioned. The results were phenomenal.

Did Muhammad genuinely believe that his own revelations, enabling him to act literally as he pleased, really came from Heaven? A contemporary author deems the question irrelevant:

---

[70] 9:29.
[71] Ibn Warraq (1995), p. 349.

A vast amount of useless ink has been spilled on the question of Muhammad's sincerity. Was he a knowing fraud, or did he sincerely believe that all the "revelations" that constitute the Kuran were direct communications from God? Even if we allow Muhammad total sincerity, I do not see how it can possibly matter to our moral judgment of his character. One can sincerely hold beliefs that are false. More important, one can sincerely hold beliefs that are immoral or not worthy of respect. Certain racists sincerely believe that Jews should be exterminated. How does their sincerity affect our moral condemnation of their beliefs? It seems that "sincerity" plays a similar role to the "insanity plea" made in modem courtrooms, by lawyers wishing to exonerate their villainous clients.[72]

Ibn Warraq goes on to say that the least that Muhammad can get away with is self-deception, something that even his admirer W. Montgomery Watt accepted when he wrote that "the alleged fact that the revelations fitted in with Muhammad's desires and pandered to his selfish pleasure would not prove him insincere; it would merely show him to be capable of self-deception." But it is hardly a "defense" of Muhammad to state that if he was sincere, then he was also incredibly self-deluded; and if not, then he was an impostor:

Apologists who have argued that Muhammad was an astute politician, a realist, a brilliant statesman, a great judge of character, a wise lawgiver and superb diplomat, perfectly sober, and not given to epileptic fits, cannot now suddenly plead that Muhammad was also capable of extraordinary self-deception. Thus the conclusion forces itself upon us that in later life, he consciously fabricated "revelations," often for his own convenience, to sort out his domestic problems.[73]

On the Prophet's own admission, Islam stands or falls with the person of Muhammad, a deeply flawed man by the standards of his own society, as well as those of the Old and New Testaments, both of which he acknowledged as divine revelation; and even by the new law of which he

---

[72] Ibn Warraq (1995), p. 347.
[73] Ibid.

claimed to be the divinely appointed medium and custodian. The problem of Islam, and the problem of the rest of the world ,with Islam, is not the remarkable career of Muhammad *per se*, undoubtedly a great man in terms of his impact on human history. It is the religion's claim that the words and acts of its prophet provide the universally valid standard of morality as such, for all time and all men.

CHAPTER TWO

The Teaching

Islam is not a "mere" religion; it is a complete way of life, an all-embracing social, political and legal system that breeds a worldview peculiar to itself. It is traditionally divided into dogma, faith (*iman*), and practice (*din*). The most important article of faith is expressed in the formula "There is no God but Allah, and Mohammed is His Prophet." In addition to *tawheed*, the unity of Allah, and *risallah*, the recognition of Muhammad's prophethood thus stated, the obligatory tenets include belief in the authority and sufficiency of the Kuran; in angels, genii, and the devil; in the immortality of the soul; the resurrection; the Day of Judgment; and in Allah's absolute, eternal decree for good and evil.

To separate the untrustworthy "hypocrites" from the true faithful, in Medina Muhammad introduced the "five pillars" of Islam that are the basis of its practice: recital of the original formula of belief *(shahada)*, prayer with ablution *(salat)*, fasting *(sayam)*, almsgiving *(zakat)*, and the pilgrimage to Mecca *(hajj)*. The participation in the holy war was added later. A *bona fide* Muslim has to follow them all.

All of these pillars are rooted in pre-Islamic ideas, beliefs, and practices. This is most obvious in the rituals connected with pilgrimage that are to this day virtually unchanged from pre-Islamic times. Pilgrimage to Mecca once in a lifetime is a duty incumbent on every free Muslim of sufficient means and bodily strength. The ceremonies repeat strictly those performed by Muhammad himself. They are the same as in pagan days, including the circumambulation around the Kaaba, the kissing of the Black Stone, visits to Safa and Marwa—including the run between the two hills—the throwing of stones against a stone pillar symbolizing Iblis (the devil) in Wadi Mina, and the slaughtering of sacrificial animals at Mina.

These practices are seemingly at odds with the recent claim that Islam is a uniquely "rational" religion. Even in its earliest days, the *hajj* did not make sense to the initiates of Islam. To the considerable surprise of his aggressively anti-pagan followers, Muhammad did not abolish this practice, but rather he himself performed it and commanded his followers to do so, in spite of their objection. The anecdote about Muhammad's faithful follower, son-in-law, and second successor, Umar, kissing the stone demonstrates the confusion of the early Muslims caused by a compromise with pagan practice. He kissed it and said, "I know that you are a stone that does not hurt or benefit. If I had not seen the prophet kiss you, I would have not kissed you."[1]

Fasting during the month of Ramadan combined the traditions of brief Jewish fasting during Yom Kippur (the Day of Atonement) and the Sabeans' month of fasting that had been adopted in Mecca some time before Muhammad's birth. Still hoping to be accepted by the Jews, in his first year in Medina Muhammad kept Yom Kippur and did not sacrifice animals the Meccan way. Had he continued on a friendly footing with the Jews, it is probable that he would have maintained the practice. In the following year he combined the Jewish ritual with the ceremonies of the Kaaba. Muhammad performed the double sacrifice apparently founded on the practice of the Jewish high priest, when he sacrificed first for his own sins and then for the people's:

> The ceremony was repeated by Muhammad every year when present at Medina, and it is still observed throughout the Muslim world at the time when the sacrificial rite is being performed at Mina, which closes the Greater pilgrimage.[2]

To this day the Jewish Day of Atonement (Yom Kippur) almost coincides with the Muslim Eid-u'l Adha, at which sacrifices are being slaughtered, although the biblical meaning and purpose have been altered beyond recognition: the Muslim sacrificial altar is the Kaaba, and, according to the Kuran, "the sacrificial camels we made for you as among the symbols from Allah."[3]

Fasting is commended at all seasons in Islam, and mandated in the month of Ramadan from sunrise to sunset. At its end comes the great feast-day, *Bayram* or *Fitr*, the "Breaking of the Fast." The distribution of alms to the poor was also in existence in Mecca when Muhammad was born. Almsgiving is highly commended at all times, and on Bayram obligatory, but the beneficiaries have to be Muslims only.

The daily prayers are five in number: before sunrise, at midday, at four in the afternoon, at sunset, and shortly before midnight. All prayers

---

[1] Sahih of Al-Bukhari, part 2, p. 183.
[2] W. Muir. *The Life of Muhammad*, pp. 194–195.
[3] 22:33–37.

56

originally faced Jerusalem, but after Muhammad's break with the Jews this was changed toward Mecca. They must be preceded by washing, neglect of which renders them ineffective. *Salat* is meant to provide disciplinary practice, spiritual nourishment, and motivation. Precisely regulated units of ritual, *Rak'ah*, accompany the recitation of the five daily prayers in Arabic. It is a devotional act consisting of standing, bowing down, standing up, then going down in prostration to the ground, sitting and prostrating again. In practice, the recitation of a prescribed formula in a language foreign to many Muslims means that *salat* is often reduced to purely formal observance. Public prayers are performed on Friday in the mosque, led by an imam and attended by men only. The *salat* required prayers twice a day at first, at dawn and dusk, but the later demand for five reflected the more advanced prayer rituals of Judaism and the five daily prayers of Zoroastrianism.

There are also obligatory prohibitions against usury, wine, swearing false oaths by Allah, calling on Allah's testimony against another man, defrauding or scoffing at another Muslim, making accusations against a chaste woman, spreading gossip and slander, considering oneself safe from Allah's wrath, giving preference to this world over the hereafter, lying, seizing property of orphans, ignoring pleas, cursing etc. They are elaborated in the body of Islamic law, the *Shari'a*. The opposite of Islam is *shirk*. Its original meaning was to commit the ultimate sin of associating Allah with other gods. In a broader sense, "lesser" shirk applies to hypocrisy of nominal Muslims who fulfill their prayer obligation due to peer pressure, force of habit or compulsion, while "hidden" shirk refers to impure thoughts and feelings.

The principal tenets of Islam, its doctrine, law, and world outlook, are presented in the Kuran, the "recited Tradition." To help them understand and interpret their holy book, the Muslims have *sunnah,* "a well trodden path," translated as a normative way of conduct, practice, usage, rule, course, institution, and behavior. The "unrecited Tradition" of Muhammad's words and deeds is recorded in *hadiths,* the narration of the sayings, doings, and tacit approvals of the prophet. Sunnah is the rule of law thus conveyed, so that one hadith may contain many sunnahs.

There are six collections of hadiths regarded as authoritative by most Muslims: Sahih al-Bukhari (d. A.D. 870), Sahih Muslim (d. A.D. 875), Sunan Abu Dawud (d. A.D. 888), Sunan At-Tirmidhi (d. A.D. 892), Sunan

An-Nisa'i (d. A.D. 915), and Sunan Ibn Majah (d. A.D. 886). Their collections are known as "The Six Books" *(al-kutubu's-sitta)* and regarded as *de facto* holy books in addition to the Kuran. The collections of al-Bukhari and Muslim are most highly esteemed of all, and the incidents related are regarded as the most "sound" ("sahih"). They preserve in many volumes the details of the acts and sayings of Muhammad and provide the basis for elaboration of Islamic law and custom. The result is *ijma,* the consensus of the scholars of Islam represented by the prominent imams, the Kuranic commentators and the masters of Muslim jurisprudence. Their chief method is analogy, strict deduction from recognized principles admitted in the Kuran and in the Traditions. It has replaced *ijtihad*, or effort at individual thought, in the ninth century.

ESCHATOLOGY

Allah is allegedly the same as *Jahweh Elohim*, the God of Abraham, Isaac and Jacob: "our Allah and your Allah is One; and it is to Him we bow."[4] He is eternal, absolute, "He begetteth not nor is He begotten and there is none like unto Him." The absolute unity and sovereignty of Allah is the foundation of the entire edifice. His existence is proven in the Kuran by pointing out the order of nature and the order of life as "signs for those who believe," for those who use their reason, who reflect and understand, who see and hear, who know and who believe. The attributes of Allah are listed in his "99 most beautiful names," 72 of which are used in the Kuran 1,286 times. Ultimately, Allah's absolute transcendence means that he is everything and nothing. He cannot be grasped by the human mind and is greater than we can comprehend. Every thought about him is insufficient and false. He cannot be fathomed, only worshipped. The evidence of his mercy is his creation of the world and man.[5] By virtue of being infinite, he is inseparable from his creation, nearer to man than his jugular vein.[6]

For the believers who sin and genuinely repent, Allah is "compassionate," "merciful," and "forgiving." He is "loving," but that love is conditional: If you love Allah, follow me, Muhammad says, and he will

---

[4] 29:46.
[5] 6:12.
[6] 50:16.

love you and forgive your sins; but Allah "does not love the unbelievers."[7] Allah's absolute sovereignty means that his "closeness" to man does not imply a two-way relationship; man's experience of Allah is impossible. Any attempt to verbalize such a notion would imply heretical encroachment on his absolute transcendence. That transcendence is so absolute in its implication that Allah is Oneness in himself that we are led to conclude that Allah is the only being with real existence, and the rest of his creation has a contingent existence. Ultimately, it may be argued that Allah is All, which is the essence of pantheism.

From the act of creation of the world, Islam seeks grounding in datable events that are perceived as fundamental to the progress of history. (Just how long the act of creation lasted is unclear from the Kuran. It is six days in 32:4 and 50:38, but it is only two days in 41:12 and 41:9. The commentators are at pains to explain away this discrepancy, in view of the Kuran's supposed perfection and total coherence. The earth is flat and stationary, with the sun and the moon rotating around it on their fixed orbits.[8])

In addition to man, Allah has created the angels, other spiritual beings called *jinn*, or *genii*, creatures of fire, able to eat, drink, propagate, and die. Their creation preceded that of man, and they differ from man in that they are capable of freedom of choice.[9] Sometimes they materialize and can be seen by men, but mostly they remain invisible. They also can be converted to Islam, or be obedient to a biblical king, but their exact role remains unclear beyond the inevitable fact that both jinn and men were created to serve Allah.[10]

There is also the devil, known in the Kuran by two words, *Shaitan* (derived from Hebrew) or *Iblis* (derived from the Greek word *diabolos*). A Muslim has to believe in these creatures to be righteous.[11] Mohammedan angelology and demonology are almost wholly based on later Jewish and early Christian traditions. The angels are believed to be free from all sin; they neither eat nor drink; there is no distinction of sex among them. They

---

[7] 3:32.
[8] 36:38; 39:5; 13:2; 21:33; 35:41; 27:61; 31:10.
[9] 72:11.
[10] 51:56.
[11] 2:177.

are usually invisible, except to animals, although at times they appear in human form.

The most important of angelic beings is Gabriel, the bearer of divine revelation, whose appearance marked the beginning of Mohammad's prophecy. The Seraphs surround the throne of Allah, constantly chanting his praises; the Secretaries, who record the actions of men; the Observers, who spy on every word and deed of mankind; the Travelers, whose duty it is to traverse the whole earth in order to know whether, and when, men utter the name of Allah; the Angels who have charge of the eternal torment of hell; and a countless multitude of heavenly beings, who fill all space.

Satan is ambiguously defined in the Kuran, so that it is unclear if we are dealing with a fallen angel or the leader of a group of jinn disobedient to Allah.[12] His rebellion against God started with the creation of men. God created Adam from clay and breathed into him his spirit.[13] He fashioned him in due proportion and gave him the senses.[14] He ordered other previously created beings to prostrate themselves before Adam, but Satan refused—claiming creation from fire was superior to that of clay. Ever since, his chief role has been to deceive humankind and lead it astray from the straight path of Allah's will (35:5). The order of prostration is curious, since in Islam it is an act of worship due only to Allah. Islamic commentators have taken this to mean Allah's declaration to angels that man is superior in his capacity for learning and growth.

Allah may have "breathed his spirit into man," but that did not imbue man with godliness or likeness to his creator, and this is fundamentally a different concept of man's origin to that of Christian witness. There is no original sin in Islam, and man need only follow the straight and narrow of understanding God's will and obeying it to obtain salvation. He did forbid Adam and Eve to approach or taste of a certain tree, but Satan misled them into disobedience. This was not a catastrophic event; however, it was a mistake without lasting consequences that was forgiven upon repentance.

At its foundation, Islam has an unresolved theological contradiction. Attributing human characteristics to Allah is regarded as a sin, *tashbih,* but so is its opposite, *tatil,* which means divesting Allah of all attributes. The difficulty of dealing with the nature of the Creator in Islam arises from

---

[12] 18:50.
[13] 15:26.
[14] 15:26.

seemingly contradictory views in the Kuran, which describes Allah as unique, yet also refers to him as having eyes, ears, hands, and face. Tashbih is forbidden out of the fear that its practice will lead to paganism and idolatry; tatil is feared to lead to atheism and agnosticism. This is contrary to the Christian understanding of God, who does share his knowledge, felicity, and power with his creatures:

> [Islam] preserves a rigid unity in God but only at the expense of real personality. It clings to a rigid simplicity but only by sacrificing his relatability. In short, it leaves us with an empty and barren concept of deity. . . . For Muslims, God not only has unity but he has singularity. But these are not the same. It is possible to have unity without singularity. For there could be plurality within the unity. Indeed, this is precisely what the Trinity is, namely, a plurality of persons within the unity of one essence. Human analogies help to illustrate the point. My mind, my thoughts, and my words have a unity, but they are not a singularity, since they are all different. Likewise, Christ can be an expression of the same nature as God without being the same person as the Father. In this connection, Muslim monotheism sacrifices plurality in an attempt to avoid duality. In avoiding the one extreme of admitting any partners to God, Islam goes to the other extreme and denies any personal plurality in God.[15]

The stress on the importance of secondary causes distinguishes Christianity from Islam's exaggerated monotheism that ultimately leads either to pantheism or agnosticism.

SIN, REWARD, AND PUNISHMENT

The Christian belief in the Fall is inseparable from the concept of salvation and the yearning for the Savior. In Islam, by contrast, men are neither "fallen" nor "saved" and, therefore, can do no more than avoid disbelief in Allah to be granted everlasting life, if so be the will of Allah. In Islam sin is not treated extensively, and only one is utterly unpardonable, *shirk*, association of other divinities with Allah. This is an important point,

---

[15] Geisler and Saleeb, op. cit., p. 263.

because it has resulted in an explicitly nominalistic system of ethics. Nothing we do, say, or think is good or bad *as such* in Islam, nothing is right or wrong without specific reference to the revealed will of God or the traditions of his prophet.

One consequence of Allah's absolute transcendence and lordship is the impossibility of human free will. Islam not only postulates the absolute predestination of all that we think, say and do, it would regard as heretical any suggestion that man has any choice in the proceedings; all has been divinely preordained and willed by Allah and all is known to him in advance: nothing will ever befall us save what Allah has written for us.[16] This is implacable fatalism: Allah's divine will predetermines whatever has been or shall be in the world, whether good or bad.

Sinners are as predestined as the virtuous believers and will suffer eternally in Gehenna. "They have hearts with which they do not comprehend, they have eyes with which they do not see, they have ears with which they do not hear."[17] But even that lamentable state of "the heedless ones" has been willed by their creator, who had naturally had the capacity to make all virtuous, but "we have set a barrier in front of them and a barrier behind them" instead.[18] Had it been his will, he could have brought "every soul its guidance," but in the event he will "assuredly fill up the burning regions of Hell" with those whose destiny it is not to be so blessed.[19] The totality of all events, deeds, and thoughts is irrevocably fixed, preordained, and recorded from eternity, but nevertheless all men will have to rise from the dead and submit to the universal judgment. The Day of Resurrection and of Judgment will be preceded and accompanied by seventeen fearful signs in heaven and on earth, and eight lesser ones—some of which are identical with those mentioned in the New Testament. The Resurrection will be general and will extend to all creatures. Hell is divided into seven regions, for faithless Muslims, for the Jews, Christians, various kinds of pagans, and "hypocrites."

Allah keeps precise count of the good and bad deeds of every person and weighs all words and thoughts against each other to present an error-free account on that great Day of Judgment, the source of life-long anxiety

[16] 9:51.
[17] 7:178–179.
[18] 36:7.
[19] 32:13.

for every Muslim. No one knows why he leads some to paradise, or why hell is the destiny of others. A Muslim prostrates himself before Allah like a slave before his master, who does not know whether he will be apportioned life or death, grace or damnation.

The agony of the damned is graphically, almost lovingly, depicted in numerous Kuranic passages. They will languish amid pestilential winds and in scalding water, in the shadow of black smoke. Draughts of boiling water will be forced down their throats. They will be dragged by the scalp, flung into the fire, wrapped in garments of flame, and beaten with iron maces. When their skins are well burned, others will grow for fresh torture. While the damnation of all infidels will be hopeless and eternal, the Muslims, who, though holding the true religion, have been guilty of heinous sins, will be delivered from hell after expiating their crimes.

As for the virtuous, the joys and glories of paradise are tangible and eminently sensual. To the dwellers of hot and arid regions, the rivers and cool fountains are an important feature of the regions of bliss, some of them flowing with water, others with wine or honey, besides many other lesser springs and fountains, whose pebbles are rubies and emeralds, while their earth consists of camphor, their beds of musk, and their sides of saffron.

But the charms of resplendent and ravishing girls—*houris*—will eclipse all these glories. "But the pious shall be in a secure place, amid gardens and fountains, clothed in silk and richest robes, facing one another: Thus shall it be: and we will wed them to the virgins with large dark eyes."[20] The prophet's own priorities are perhaps reflected in his assurance that the tangible enjoyment of their charms will be the principal felicity of the faithful. These maidens are created not of clay, as in the case of mortal women, but of pure musk, and free from all natural impurities and defects. Their breasts are *kawa'eb*—swelling and firm, not sagging. To enjoy them in full, Allah will give each Muslim 72 *houris* and the manliness of a hundred mortals in this heaven of perpetual youth and copulation, "all that they desire."[21]

The righteous will be served also by boys, "pure as pearls," dressed in green garments of fine silk and heavy brocade, adorned with bracelets of

---

[20] 44, 51–54.
[21] 25:15–16.

silver, and used to drinking wine.[22] The presence of intoxicating youths in such a luxurious environment must have some unusual purpose. They do not seem to be ordinary servants, who would not need to be ever-young, breathtakingly beautiful, and adorned in sumptuous dresses and jewelry. According to some interpretations of the Tradition and in the considered opinion of a contemporary Islamic commentator, "The men in Paradise have sexual relations not only with the women [who come from this world] and with 'the black-eyed,' but also with the serving boys. . . . In Paradise, a believer's penis is eternally erect."[23] Even the most prestigious Islamic seat of learning gets involved in debating the minutiae of such issues:

> In 1992, Islamic assassins had gunned down . . . Farag Foda, a professor and columnist, a human rights activist, and an outspoken critic of the Islamic militants. . . . About two weeks before his murder, he mocked what passed for intellectual discourse among Islamists by citing a recent sermon by Egypt's most popular preacher . . . [who] had been telling his audience that Muslims who entered paradise would enjoy eternal erections and the company of young boys draped in earrings and necklaces. Some of the *ulema,* the religious scholars at al-Azhar University, the government's seat of Islamic learning, had disagreed. Yes, they said, men in paradise would have erections, but merely protracted, not perpetual. Other experts disputed the possibility of pederasty in paradise.[24]

At the moments of rest between those protracted periods, three hundred servants will bring to each blessed the same number of dishes of gold, containing each a different kind of food. The righteous will be clothed in the richest silks and brocades, and adorned with bracelets of gold and silver, and crowns set with pearls, and will make use of silken carpets, couches, and pillows, to be enjoyed in perpetual youth, beauty, and vigor.[25]

This was truly a Bedouin's paradise, tangible and easy to envisage, but its sensuous grip is visible today in the death announcements of suicide-bombers in the Palestinian press, which often take the form of wedding, not

---

[22] 76:21.

[23] Galal Al-Kushk, as quoted in *Al-Quds Al-Arabi,* London, May 11, 2001.

[24] Judith Miller, *God Has Ninety-Nine Names,* Simon & Schuster, 1996, pp. 25–26.

[25] See 47:15, 87:31–33, 56:35–37, 56:22–23, 36:55–56, 55:56, 37:41–49.

funeral, announcements. "With great pride, the Palestinian Islamic Jihad marries the member of its military wing . . . the martyr and hero Yasser Al-Adhami, to the black-eyed."[26] Sa'id Al-Hutari, who exploded himself and 23 Israeli teenagers at a Tel Aviv disco on June 1, 2001, wrote in his will: "Call out in joy, oh my mother; distribute sweets, oh my father and brothers; a wedding with 'the black-eyed' awaits your son in Paradise."[27] At the funeral of Izz Al-Din Al-Masri, who carried out the suicide bombing of the Sbarro pizzeria in Jerusalem on August 9, 2001, his family "distributed sweets and accepted their son as a bridegroom married to 'the black-eyed' in Heaven."

ALLAH'S WILL, THE ONLY FREEDOM

Allah alone is able to create good or evil at any time by decree, but his reward for the pious is pure kindness and his punishment of sinners is pure justice: he is touched by neither. Piety of believers and transgression of sinners do not affect him in the least; they are merely visible signs of his wish to punish some and to reward others. Good works are the result of his grace, and evil the result of his rejection; Allah creates people as well as their actions.[28] That is inevitable, as all that exists is his creation, in the past, present, and eternal future, to declare his oneness and glory. Declaring his glory and celebrating his praise is the sole purpose of existence of the universe and man.[29] The universe is divinely ordered, and every creative thing in it is endowed and at the same time limited by its defined nature, with all elements acting as a harmonious whole. Allah reveals only his will,

> and we have it in perfection in the Kuran. But Islam does not equate the Kuran with the nature or essence of God. It is the Word of God, the Commandment of God, the Will of God. But God does not reveal Himself to anyone. Christians talk about the revelation of God Himself—by God of God—but that is the great difference between Christianity and Islam. God is transcendent, and once you talk about self-revelation you have hierophancy and

---

[26] *Al-Istiqlal*, October 4, 2001.
[27] *Al Risala*, the Hamas organ, July 7, 2001.
[28] 37:94.
[29] 17:44.

immanence, and then the transcendence of God is compromised. You may not have complete transcendence and self-revelation at the same time.[30]

The entire world is by definition obedient to Allah and his laws. The whole creation must be in a state of Islam—submission to Allah—to be itself.

Islamic teaching on the ultimate question that has vexed all men in all cultures since time immemorial, that of the purpose of our existence, is accordingly simple and unambiguous. Allah has honored men by creating them, and our only purpose is to serve and glorify him—not because it makes any difference to Allah, who is utterly beyond our reach, but because that is our vocation. The Kuran implied that much when Muhammad tells us that "all people are born as true Muslims, innocent, and pure."[31] Those who profess Islam are "the best of peoples, evolved for mankind, enjoining what is right, forbidding what is wrong, and believing in Allah." The rest of creation is there to serve man's needs. While nature is subject to man, at all times Allah is the master and man is the slave.

In Islam, the familiar theological problems of predestination are present in acute form. All along, however, it remains unstated in the Kuran, and unexplained in the Tradition, why the merciful Allah creates legions of sinners predestined for eternal and unbearable suffering, sinners who have no personal choice in the outcome of their lives. Mainstream Christian traditions insist on the freedom of the sinner, on the small but vital element of free will in the drama of salvation. Many theological difficulties flow from this, and many post-Christians would secretly agree with the Muslims that man's willed impact on his destiny is no greater than that of a laboratory rat bred predestined for vivisection. Islamic predestination is particularly severe: it simplifies religion and so annihilates some theological difficulties, but at the price of a cruel fatalism.

The Mutazila sect in eighth-to-tenth century Baghdad, the first Muslims to use the categories and methods of Hellenistic philosophy to assert free will and responsibility for one's actions, dissented and claimed

---

[30] Kenneth Cragg, *Christian Mission and Islamic Da'wah: Proceedings of the Chambesy Dialogue Consultation*, Leicester, The Islamic Foundation, 1982, pp. 45-46.
[31] 30:30.

that Allah would be unjust if he predestined all human actions; but strict predestination prevailed and remains the mainstream Islamic view.

"Freedom" is incompatible with this relationship; in Islam any notion of freedom distinct from that implicit in the complete submission to the will of Allah is not an ideal, but a perilous trap.[32] To paraphrase Marx, freedom is the realized necessity of such submission. In the conventional, non-Islamic sense, it is both impossible and undesirable. Only Allah creates our acts and enables us to act, while we are but transmission belts with a preordained balance of debit or credit that determines our destiny in the hereafter. "He knoweth what appeareth to His creatures as before or after or behind them. Nor shall they compass aught of his knowledge except as he willeth."[33] Our only purpose is the service of Allah.[34] "Freedom" is no part of that purpose, not any more than to "know God" or to be more like God. Men can strive no higher than obeying Allah's will as revealed by his Prophet. There is no "revelation" in Islam, meaning revelation of God's nature, but only of his will and obedience to it. Human imperfection is not subject to improvement in the direction of God, and any such notion is blasphemous to a Muslim.

All this leaves an outsider baffled, wondering if there really is not more to it, a higher obligation. Even prayer is a payment of debt, not communication.[35] What hope do we have of placating a capricious Allah, who plots against men to destroy them by commanding them to commit abomination "and so the word of doom has its effect and we annihilate with complete annihilation"?[36] How can we serve a supreme being that is so transcendent as to be devoid of personality? For, "the unrelated, unrelatable, absolutely one could not be a person. There is no such thing as a person in the categorical singular."[37]

In the end, Allah, the unknowable and unpersonable, is served out of fear, obedience, "submission," and hope of bountiful heavenly reward. Islam explicitly rejects the notion that "he who has my commandments and

---

[32] Watt, *Islam and Christianity Today*, p. 127.

[33] 2:163–165.

[34] 51:56.

[35] 35:29–30.

[36] 17:16.

[37] Joseph Ratzinger, *Introduction to Christianity*, trans. J. R. Foster, New York, The Seabury Press, 1979, pp. 128–29.

keeps them, he is it who loves me."[38] The Kuran states the opposite: "Say, If ye love Allah, follow me; Allah will love you and forgive you your sins."[39] This "love" is merely a means of winning love and forgiveness. Ultimately, it is the love of the self, coupled with the hope of posthumous forgiveness as the reward for obedience.

This lack of genuine affection is mutual. The Kuran defines Allah's love of men in terms of his endorsement of the virtuous ones: "Spend your wealth for the cause of Allah and be not cast by your own hands to ruin; and do good. Lo! Allah loveth the beneficent.[40] Muhammad lists those loved at different places in the Kuran as the pure, kind, just and righteous believers, who do good, love Allah and fight for him in battle, and who do no mischief or exult in riches or cheat, do not violate Allah's laws, live not extravagantly in excess and waste, are not ungrateful or wicked, are not arrogant or vainglorious or boasters, and do no wrong. Allah's "love" is earned through good deeds—just as man's "love" for him is rooted in self-interest. This is a contractual relationship, very different from the God who seeks to reconcile man to himself.

"PEOPLE OF THE BOOK"

The purpose of prophets and messengers is to remind us of our imperfection, to bring us back to the right path, which remains our only purpose in life. The Tradition states that Allah has sent 124,000 prophets and 315 apostles, although their exact number is not stated in the Kuran.[41] Of the prophets, 22 are mentioned by name in the Muslim holy book, including Adam, Noah, Abraham, Moses, and Jesus. All of them were Muslim, including Jesus, and their religion was Islam. Even Abraham was "a Muslim and one pure of faith."[42] Those prophets are surprisingly alike in the Kuranic rendering of their deeds and words, with the exception of Jesus, and their purpose is to remind every people that they will be judged with justice.[43] All of them are claimed to have preached the same message

---

[38] John 14:21.
[39] 3:31.
[40] 2:135.
[41] 40:78.
[42] 3:60.
[43] 10:47.

and come from the same heavenly source.[44] They promised that they would tell their communities about the coming of Muhammad and instruct them to embrace his religion.[45] Muhammad is the last of them all, "with guidance and the Religion of Truth, to proclaim it over all religion."[46] The pagans may detest it; while Jewish rabbis and Christian monks debar men from the way of Allah, for which a painful doom awaits them.[47]

All prophets come from the same Allah, but traditions prior to Mohammad had distorted or falsified their teachings and led people astray. This was the fault of Jews and Christians, who have broken their covenant of God. It has now been entrusted only to the Muslims, "the best of peoples evolved from mankind."[48] Since the Kuran is the word of Allah himself, no part of it was derived from earlier revelations or from other religions, though it claims to conform with the original and uncorrupted teaching of the Law and Gospel.[49]

The widespread belief in the non-Muslim world that Islam accords respect to the Old Testament and the Gospels as steps in progression to Mohammad's revelation is mistaken. Modern Muslim commentators try to stress the supposed underlying similarities and compatibility of the three faiths, but this is not the view of "true" (i.e., "orthodox") Islam.[50] Muhammad's insistence that there is a heavenly proto-Scripture and that previous "books" are merely distorted and tainted copies sent to previous nations or communities—Jews and Christians—meant that their scriptures were the "barbarous Kuran" as opposed to the true, Arabic one.[51] The Tradition also regards the non-canonical Gospel of Barnabas, and not the New Testament, as the one that Jesus taught. The Kuran alone fulfills and, by doing so, sets aside all previous revelations, which have been incomplete, tainted, or tampered with.

While the influence of orthodox Christianity upon the Kuran has been slight, apocryphal and heretical Christian legends are the second most

---

[44] 43:4.

[45] 3:75.

[46] 9:33.

[47] 9:34.

[48] 3:110.

[49] 57:26

[50] 2:42, 3:71.

[51] 41:44.

important original source of Kuranic faith.[52] Experts will also detect influences of Sabaism, of Zoroastrianism, and of native ancient and contemporary Arabian heathen beliefs and practices, either alluded to or included in the Kuran, including the divine sanction for the practices of polygamy and slavery.[53] The reports in both the Kuran and the Hadith concerning Paradise, the houris and the silk-adorned youths, the jinn and the angel of death have been directly taken from the ancient books of the Zoroastrians.[54] The Persians have also originated the story that on the Day of Judgment all people will have to cross a bridge stretched across hell leading to paradise, on which the unbelievers will stumble and fall.

The biblical stories and versions of the Gospel had been passed on to Muhammad by way of the narratives, presumably from Jewish and Christian sources, but it is probable that he had never read the Old or the New Testament, nor—if he was indeed illiterate—had them read to him directly. Those narratives had deeply impressed him, but being incomplete and imprecise, they gave his imagination free rein. Of the books of the Old Testament he knew only of the Torah (Pentateuch) and the Psalms, while the Scriptures he treats collectively as "the Gospels." Muhammad took these narratives as they were given to him, and their use in the Kuran amounted to random, approximate and often badly misunderstood reproduction of the Talmudic traditions and the Apocrypha.[55] They are devoid of the spiritual message of the original, however.

Some Kuranic stories have no basis in the Old Testament or the Gospels, and several are distinctly folkloristic, such as Surra 27:17–19, which narrates the advance of Solomon's army of the jinn, men, and birds through the Valley of the Ants, calling on them to enter their dwellings, lest they be crushed. Later on, the winds are made to obey Solomon's orders, while demons had to dive deep in the sea to bring him treasures of precious stones.[56] In the *Chapter of the Jinn,* we learn that one morning, as Muhammad was reciting verses beside a palm tree, a group of the demonic jinn heard him, repented, professed belief, and pledged never to worship

---

[52] See Muir, op. cit. infra, 66-239; Tisdall, *The Original Sources of the Kuran,* London, 1905, pp. 55–211.

[53] Wellhausen, "Reste des arabischen Heidentums," Berlin, 1897.

[54] W. St. Clair Tisdall, *Sources of Islam.*

[55] Renan, *Muhammad and the Origins of Islam.*

[56] 21:81–82.

Satan again.[57] They were so moved by Muhammad's words that their conversion was instant.[58] Elsewhere, swarms of flying creatures pelt elephants with stones of baked clay. Alexander the Great—a righteous monotheist, he!—located the sun's setting place.[59] Seven young men enter a cave and sleep for three hundred and nine years.[60] (This appears to be a garbled version of the Seven Sleepers of Ephesus.[61]) Allah disagrees with Moses, who claimed that he was the most knowledgeable of men, and instructs him to find one Khadr with the help of a whale; the latter proceeds to kill a boy allegedly predestined to become a disbeliever, and thus proves his superior wisdom.[62] (The Tradition insists that it is right and proper to pre-empt anticipated evil by murder.[63]) Allah transforms Jews into apes in some chapters, swine in others.[64] He sends two angels to tempt people into learning magic. A murdered boy is hit with a body part of a cow, rises up to name the killers, and immediately drops dead again.[65]

Many Old Testament stories are changed beyond recognition and can be treated as Muhammad's "source" only in the most general sense. Abraham did not offer Isaac, but Ishmael, as a sacrifice. "Haman" was pharaoh's chief minister, even though the Haman known to Jews lived in Babylon one thousand years later. Moses was picked from the river not by his sister but by his mother.[66] A Samaritan was the one who molded the golden calf for the children of Israel and misguided them, even though Samarians arrived only after the Babylonian exile.[67] The accounts of Moses' life are sketchy and say nothing of his character, descent, the time he was sent as a prophet, the purpose of his mission, and where, how, and why he appointed Aaron as his deputy. It does not relate the argument between them and the people of Israel, which is crucial to the story. Moses' encounter with God in the burning bush is told differently on three

---

[57] 17:1.
[58] Sahih of Al-Bukhari, part 6, p. 200.
[59] 18:83–98.
[60] 18:9–25.
[61] www.oca.org/pages/orth_chri/Feasts-and-Saints/August/Aug-04.html#seven.
[62] 18:60–82.
[63] Bukhari, part 6, pp. 111–112.
[64] 7:163–166 and 5:60.
[65] 2:67–73.
[66] 28:6–8.
[67] 20:85–88.

occasions. In 27:8 he was greeted with, "Blessed is he who is in the fire, and he who is about it," but in the next Sura the voice said, "Moses, I am God, the Lord of all being" (28:30), and finally in 20:11-12, God says "Moses, I am thy Lord; put off thy shoes; thou art in the holy valley, Towa." The story of Noah reflected Muhammad's dilemmas and difficulties rather than Noah's mission, and even the names of the idols that Noah warns against are Arabic. [68]

The Kuran makes reference to Jesus, Mary, and events related to them, but with a critical distinction. It explicitly denies that Jesus was crucified: Allah made the Jews so confused that they crucified somebody else instead who had the likeness of Christ: "They slew him not nor crucified, but it appeared so unto them."[69] Muslims claim that an impostor by the name of Shabih was crucified, and he resembled Jesus in his face only. It seems illogical to those who count "proud" as one of the "99 most beautiful names of Allah" that Jesus, who was capable of raising the dead and of healing the blind and the leper, willingly submitted to the cross and failed to destroy the Jews who intended to hurt him.

Islam rejects the whole concept of the cross, claiming that it is against reason to assume that Allah would not forgive man's sins without the cross: to say so is to limit his power: "He forgives whom he will, and he chastises whom he will."[70] Salvation in Islam is based on a continuous effort to obtain Allah's favor, which will be rewarded in heaven if he so wills. Good deeds in Islam are a requirement for obtaining that reward, not the fruit of love and faith. The denial of the Trinity is also explicit: Allah begets not (i.e., he is no Father) and was not begotten, that is, he is no Son; and no one is like him, which means he is no Holy Spirit.[71] "They are infidels who say, Allah is the third of three."[72] But "Isa" is not the Son of Allah, only a special prophet, and the Christians' contrary claim shows how they are perverted.[73]

---

[68] 71:1–28.
[69] 4:15.
[70] 5:18.
[71] 112.
[72] 4:171 and 5:73.
[73] 9:29–30.

In many places Mary is mentioned in the Kuran as the sister of Moses and Aaron[74] and the daughter of Imran.[75] Muhammad had evidently confused the mother of Jesus with her namesake of more than a thousand years before. The Tradition resolves the problem by claiming that the maternal grandfather of Jesus was named "Imran," which may also have been the name of the father of Moses, while Mary is addressed as "sister of Aaron" in the ancestral sense. Mary gave birth to "Isa" under the shade of a palm tree, not in a manger.[76] The Christians are guilty of blasphemy because of their belief in the "trinity" of Allah, Mary, and Jesus. The "real" Jesus was a righteous prophet and a good Muslim who paved the way for the final prophet, Muhammad himself.

Any discrepancies between his revelations and earlier scriptures did not seem to bother Mohammad in his earlier, Meccan period, which is puzzling if he seriously expected to be recognized as a prophet by the Jews and Christians. His eventual failure to achieve this decided not only his treatment of those groups, justified by the late Surras in Medina, it has also left a permanent mark on the attitude of Islam to all outside groups and in all periods. While Jews and Christians, "People of the Book" (*ahl al-kitab*), are treated mildly in the early Meccan Surras, it is only the later, infinitely harsh Medinan verses that retain their validity due to the Islamic doctrine of "progressive revelation," which postulates that Allah substituted certain pronouncements for "something better or similar."[77] The objection that "no change can there be in the Words of Allah" (10:64) is easily resolved: the only exception applies to Allah himself making the change. Furthermore, Allah reserves the right to withdraw all revelation: "If it were Our will, we could take away that which we have sent thee by inspiration: then wouldst thou find none to plead thy affair in the matter as against Us."[78]

Of all the "people of the book," only Muslims can attain salvation. Jews and Christians may be distinguished from pagans and elevated to somewhat higher status, but their refusal to acknowledge Muhammad as the messenger of God dooms them to unbelief and eternal suffering after

---

[74] 19:28.
[75] 66:12, 3:35.
[76] 19:23.
[77] 2:106.
[78] 17:86.

73

death.[79] Christians are mortal sinners because of their belief in the divinity of Christ; and their condemnation is irrevocable: "God will forbid him the garden and the fire will be his abode."[80] Muhammad's confused understanding of the Trinity is evident from the Kuran, however: "They blaspheme who say: Allah is one of three in a trinity; for there is no god except One Allah. Christ the son of Mary was no more than an apostle; many were the apostles that passed away before him. His mother was a woman of truth, they had both to eat their (daily) food."[81] His reference to physical needs makes it clear that a misunderstanding of the "trinity"—God the Father, Mary, and Jesus—is at the root of Muhammad's view of Christianity.

The one crucial difference between the Bible as a whole and the Kuran is God's love and His desire to redeem sinners by way of sacrifice. Without sacrifice there is no forgiveness, no atonement and no reconciliation that gives meaning to life and creation.

THE KURAN

In Islam there are different categories of revelation: *wahi*, the lower granted to artists and saints, and the higher, *inzal,* the "sent down" revelation of Allah's will. The latter is contained in the holy book of Islam, the Kuran. This "Recited Revelation" is to the Muslims the eternally existent word of Allah himself, sent down through his chosen (*mustafa*) apostle and prophet, Muhammad. The notion of descent is important: since Allah transcends his own creation, the Kuran could only "come down" from whoever sends it.

As Allah's direct and unadulterated word, to a Muslim the Kuran cannot be subjected to textual analysis and critical evaluation. It is a collection of Muhammad's sayings, derived from his conscious mind in moments of alleged inspiration, dictated to his followers, and written down or memorized by them. Through this medium, Muhammad instructed his followers what to believe, how to worship, what to do, and what to avoid. It also contains a mix of moral, historical, and legendary lessons taken from

---

[79] 5:72–73.
[80] 5:75.
[81] 5:72-75.

the canonical but mostly apocryphal Christian and Jewish Scriptures, and from contemporary and ancient Arabian heathenism. As such,

> The Qur'an is a faithful mirror of the life and character of its author. It breathes the air of the desert, it enables us to hear the battle-cries of the Prophet's followers as they rushed to the onset, it reveals the working of Muhammad's own mind, and shows the gradual declension of his character as he passed from the earnest and sincere though visionary enthusiast into the conscious impostor and open sensualist.[82]

While it is uncertain whether Mohammad was literate or not, he did not write down his revelations but gave them orally. After Muhammad's death his followers determined that Allah's revelation was complete and the task of putting together his word in a single book became necessary. Contrary to the statements of the Kuran's compilers, as related in the most reliable of hadiths, the orthodox Muslim view maintains that its original is preserved in heaven for all eternity. The Tradition claims that about a year after Muhammad's death the first attempt to put the holy book together in a collected whole was made at the command of Abu Bakr.[83] Many of the reciters of the Surras had fallen in a battle, and it was feared that some parts of it would be lost. The *Fatihah* was placed first as a sort of introduction to the book, as it was even then widely used as a prayer, and so was better known than any other. The other chapters (Surras) were arranged on the principle of putting the longest first and the shortest at the end of the book.

The version of the Kuran that we have today, as finally approved at the time of Caliph Uthman, is divided into 114 Surras—86 of which had been revealed in Mecca, and 28, mostly longer ones, covering a third of the book, in Medina.[84] Most chapters are named after a significant word or

---

[82] W. St. Clair Tisdall, *The Original Sources of the Qur'an,* London, 1905.

[83] Bukhari.

[84] Chronologically, Noeldeke divides them into the first period in Mecca: 96, 74, 111, 106, 108, 104, 107, 102, 105, 92, 90, 94, 93, 97, 86, 91, 80, 68, 87, 95, 103, 85, 73, 101, 99, 82, 81, 53, 84, 100, 79, 77, 78, 88, 89, 75, 83, 69, 51, 52, 56, 70, 55, 112, 109, 113, 114, 1; the middle period in Mecca: 54, 37, 71, 76, 44, 50, 20, 26, 15, 19, 38, 36, 43, 72, 67, 23, 21, 25, 17, 27, 18; the latter period in Mecca: 32, 41, 45, 16, 30, 11, 14, 12, 40, 28, 39, 29, 31, 42, 10, 34, 35, 7, 46, 6, 13; and Medina: 2, 98, 64, 62, 8, 47, 3, 61, 57, 4, 65, 59, 33, 63, 24, 58, 22, 48, 66, 60, 110, 49, 9, 5.

theme, but some chapters have names with no apparent meaning.[85] All but one start with "In the name of God, most gracious, most merciful." The verses are called *aya,* "signs," but their numbering is not uniform. The book is subdivided into 30 parts, each of these meant to be read on one day during the fasting month of Ramadan.

From the earliest days of Islam, it was held that the book is not only the final revelation but also the only totally authentic one, untainted by human intervention. Some caliphs declared that the Kuran itself is eternal, like Allah, and decreed the death penalty for anyone claiming that the word of Allah is created. Even today, any suggestion that the Kuran has been tainted or in any way corrupted by human use is not only offensive, but heretical, to Islam. Yet Caliph Umar was frank about the limitations of the effort to collect and standardize it: "Let no one of you say that he has acquired the entire Qur'an, for how does he know that it is all? Much of the Qur'an has been lost."[86] Muhammad's widow A'isha complained that one Surra was reduced from two hundred verses to only 73 in Uthman's edition. She also stated that some verses were lost when a domestic animal got into the house during preparations for Muhammad's funeral and ate them. In tradition we frequently encounter reference to "the verse of the stoning" that was lost because no two witnesses could be found who had memorized it identically. Several early caliphs and Muhammad's companions talked of lost or changed verses, including 'Ali, Abu Bakr, Ibn Mas'ud, and Ibn 'Abbas. Some disagreed on the number of chapters and their verses, others on the order of the chapters. The accusation that he had changed the Kuran was an excuse invoked for Uthman's murder. Even though it was not the real motive, the fact that it could be advanced at all indicates that the issue of the Kuran's authenticity was highly controversial among early Muslims. In spite of Uthman's standardization, after his death the Kuran continued to be read in the "seven dialects," which produced limited but clear ambiguities of meaning—and there is no scholarly Muslim consensus about which dialect the book was supposedly given in to Muhammad.

The Kuran comes in the form of Arabic verse and has remarkable resemblance to the religiously inspired poetry of Umayya ibn Abi's-Salt, a

---

[85] These chapters are: 20, 36, 38, 50, and 68. No one knows what *Taha, Yasin, Sad, Qaf,* or *Nun* mean.

[86] Suyuti: *Itqan,* part 3, p. 72.

hanif and Muhammad's contemporary who obviously relied on the same sources as Muhammad. Its language soon became the standard by which other Arabic literary compositions had to be judged; the word of Allah could not be wrong or imperfect.[87] It is inadmissible for the Kuran to be read during prayers in languages other than Arabic, lest the inimitability of the book is lost. It is also claimed that it cannot be translated, and all translations (including Persian, Urdu, Bengali, and Indonesian used by hundreds of millions of faithful) only have the status of retellings. So does the word of Allah belong to the Arabs only? Muhammad was not far from saying so: "Love the Arabs for three things: Because I am an Arab, the Kuran is in Arabic, and the language of the people of the paradise is Arabic."

Some two dozen grammatical errors in the Kuran, including a few wrong cases, have been a source of embarrassment and difficulty to the Tradition. The scholars either had to claim that the book itself sets the true standard, and the received usage at variance with it was wrong, or else the claim that Gabriel dictated it in "perfect Arabic" is spurious.[88] There are additional oddities, including many foreign words, contrary to the claim in the Kuran itself.[89] They perplexed the Companions.[90] Some commentators explained that Muhammad alone spoke "perfect Arabic" (i.e., "nobody can have a comprehensive knowledge of the language except a prophet").[91] But Allah's purpose remains mysterious indeed if his word is so inscrutable that it baffled even Muhammad's companions and relatives. The difficulty was partly due to the fact that its original text was without diacritical points or vocalization, and some letters are omitted:

> In Arabic the meanings of the words require the use of diacritical points above or below the letters, otherwise it becomes very difficult (if not impossible) to comprehend their meanings. Vocalization also is very significant in the field of desinential inflection, along with writing all the letters of the word without omitting any of them. . . . The meaning differs from one word to

---

[87] References to Arabic language of the Kuran: 14:4; 29:192–195; 13:37; 42 7; 39:28, and 43:3.

[88] 2:177; 3:39; 4:162; 5:69; 7:16; 20:63; 21:3; 22:19; 49:9, 63:10.

[89] 16:103; 41:44.

[90] In "The Itqan" (part 2, pp. 108–119), Suyuti lists 118 non-Arabic words.

[91] Abd El Schafi, *Behind the Veil,* Pioneer Books, 1996, p. 187.

another, depending on the place of these diacritical points. Many of the Arabic alphabets require the presence of the diacritical point to differentiate between one alphabet and another and hence between one word and another.[92]

Vocalization and diacritical points were invented and applied to the Kuran many years after Muhammad's death. As for the meaningless words, some of them "no one knoweth how to explain save God," so anyone who attempted to divine their meaning, or that of the obscured verses, was liable to punishment. When one Sabigh asked such questions, Caliph 'Umar nearly beat him to death day after day.[93]

As for the inconsistencies, in Al-Sayda: 5 the length of the day of resurrection is one thousand years, while Ma'arij: 4 changes it to 50 thousand years. (Ibn 'Abbas frankly admits, "These are two days which God—may He be exalted—has mentioned in His book, and God knows best.") In the Day of Judgment, we are told infidels will attempt to conceal their sins from Allah.[94] In another, we are told that they will not conceal anything.[95] The Tradition explains that what their tongues conceal, their hands and their limbs will admit. Heaven was created after the Earth in many verses, but in one verse the Earth was created after the heavens. God does not swear in Mecca (90:1), but then does it nevertheless (95:3). The phrase, "O which of your Lord's bounties will you deny?" is repeated thirty-one times in a chapter of 78 verses, the story of Noah is repeated in 12 chapters, that of Abraham in 8 chapters, Moses' in 7 chapters, and Adam's in 4 chapters. Moses' conversation with pharaoh is repeated 12 times.

There is considerable difference in style and substance between the Meccan and Medinan verses. The early revelations are more imaginative, rhapsodic, and emotional. The earliest Surras have Mohammad in the guise of "warner" who calls on men to rectify their morals because they will have to answer for their deeds to their creator. His sole purpose is to bring his hearers to a belief in the one, only Allah, by appealing to their feelings rather than their reason. The focus is on the imminence of judgment

---

[92] Ibid, pp. 189–190.
[93] Ibid, p. 196.
[94] 6:22–23.
[95] 4:42.

followed by detailed descriptions of the torments of Hell and the joys of Paradise. The oneness, majesty, and complete transcendence of Allah are presented in a series of short verses with considerable poetic power and imagination.

As the Meccan society rejected his claims and scorned his messages, Muhammad's compositions became longer and more argumentative, asserting his prophethood and engaging in polemics with those who rejected him. In the second period of the Meccan Surras, Muhammad cuts himself off completely from the idolatry of his compatriots. He refers to Allah as Ar-Rahman, "the merciful one," which the Meccans seem to have taken for the names of separate deities, and the name is abandoned in the later chapters. We first find the long, distorted stories of the preceding prophets. In this middle period, when Muhammad was attacked as an imposter, he emphasized the continuity between himself and the preceding prophets, stressing the punishment that fell upon their disbelieving contemporaries. The moral is always the same: Muhammad is God's prophet, and any denial of the truth of his mission would bring on his fellows the same retribution. Medinan revelations, in turn, seek to secure his own position and influence and justify his actions. They also show the transition stage between the intense and poetical enthusiasm of the early Meccan chapters and the more prosaically didactic later ones.[96]

As he progressed from a moral teacher to the secular ruler and master of people's destinies, Muhammad's style and message changed considerably in Medina. He becomes the model for humanity, to be obeyed along with God; he is "a mercy for all creatures," and God calls blessings on him. Islam was fast becoming an institutionalized state religion, and this is felt in the Surras dealing with ethics and law. They denounce *Munafiqun*, hypocrites who converted from fear or compulsion. The late Surras also signify the final break with the Jews and Christians, who are fiercely denounced. The Muslims must be merciless to the unbelievers but kind to each other.[97] "Whoso of you makes them his friends is one of them."[98] War, not friendship, is mandatory until Islam reigns everywhere.[99] Muslims are

---

[96] Muir, *The Kuran in "Sacred Books of the East,"* I, Oxford, 1880, pp. LXI, LXII, and LXIII.

[97] 48:29.

[98] 5:55.

[99] 8:39 and 2:193.

ordered to fight the unbelievers "and let them find harshness in you."[100] They must kill the unbelievers "wherever you find them."[101] The punishment for resistance is execution or the cutting off of hands and feet from opposite sides.[102] Muhammad was no longer trying to convert his hearers by examples, promises, and warnings; he addresses them as their master and sovereign, praising them or blaming them for their conduct, giving laws and precepts as needed.

The long Surras from this last period are less poetically inspired. In them Mohammad presents Allah as a repetitive polemicist and adjudicator of occasionally quite trivial disputes. Nevertheless, for all its unevenness of style, the claim of the absolute perfection of the language of the Kuran is not open to doubt or even discussion to a Muslim. When Muhammad addresses the faithful on an issue of daily significance, his own words are preceded by the command "Say," implying that his delivery is by divine authority. We are repeatedly reminded that it is none other but Allah who is speaking to us through his prophet, whose revelations are all kept in a heavenly "mother of a book," where the Kuran is inscribed in a tablet.[103] Allah even throws a challenge at the reader: If ye are in doubt as to what has been revealed to Muhammad, then produce a Surra like thereunto; "but if ye cannot—and of a surety ye cannot—then fear the fire whose fuel is men and stones which is prepared for those who reject Faith."[104] The alleged linguistic perfection and sublime sophistication thus "established" are then advanced as the sufficient proof of the book's divine origin: the book "is not such as can be produced by other than Allah."[105]

The Tradition disapprovingly notes that the infidels used to say, "Muhammad utters something today and abolishes it tomorrow." Most Islamic scholars consider even his everyday words to be actual revelations, for the Kuran ordains that he "is not astray, neither errs, nor speaks he out of caprice. This is nothing but a revelation revealed."[106] But since "sometimes the revelation used to descend on the prophet during the night

---

[100] 9:123.
[101] 9:5.
[102] 5:33.
[103] 85:21–22.
[104] 2:23–24.
[105] 10:37.
[106] 53:2–4.

and then he forgot it during daytime," verse 2:106 was needed. Similarly troubling was the predicament of two men who had learned a Surra Muhammad had taught them, but then forgot it. Muhammad could not remember it either, but explained that this was because "it is one of those which have been abrogated, thus, forget about it."[107] The scholars have little room for maneuver here: Allah changes his ordinances to fit the change of time and circumstances, although these remain apparently static to a mortal eye—even if the abrogation takes place from the beginning of a Surra until its end! When "Fear Allah as He should be feared"[108] caused consternation among the faithful, it was soon abrogated and replaced with "fear Allah as much as you are able to do so."[109] It became very hard for them to do so, the Tradition explains, so Allah agreed to lighten the people's burden.[110]

The fact that Muhammad got away with it all testifies to the faith, or some other quality, of his faithful followers. The detractors claimed that "whenever he forgot what he related to his followers, he spared himself the embarrassment by claiming that God had abrogated what he conveyed to them before;" the ever-faithful Aisha related how the prophet heard a man reciting in the mosque and said, "May God have mercy on him, he has reminded me of such and such verses which I dropped from Surra so and so." The companions had to remind Muhammad of the forgotten verses at times, but when they were not available they had to be abrogated.[111]

Unlike the Christian faith in God revealing Himself through Christ, the Kuran is not a *revelation of Allah*—a heretical concept in Islam—but the direct revelation *of his commandments* and the communication *of his law*. Unlike the Muslim, who sees the Kuran as the "perfected Gospel," the Christian sees the "perfected Gospel" in Christ, the Word Incarnate. This is a somewhat tenuous metaphor, however, not a valid parallel: the Christian God "comes down" and seeks man because of His fatherly love. The Fall cast a shadow; the Incarnation makes reconciliation possible. Allah, by contrast, is cold, haughty, unpredictable, unknowable, capricious, distant, and so purely transcendent that no "relationship" is possible. He reveals only his will, not himself. Allah is "everywhere," and therefore nowhere

---

[107] Ibid, p. 220.
[108] 3:102.
[109] 64:16.
[110] El Schafi, op. cit., p. 223.
[111] 2:106.

relevant to us. He remains uninterested in making our acquaintance, let alone in being near to us because of love. We still are utterly unable to grasp his purposes, and all we can do is what we have to do—to obey his commands. That the Kuran provides divine guidance for life is accepted not only as an intellectual dogma, but as a daily and life-long reality for faithful Muslims.[112] To them it "must have the last word, not archaeology and archaeologists," as it "has been revealed by Him who knows the secret in the heavens and earth."[113]

It is impossible to pass a value-neutral verdict on the subject. Non-Muslim commentators fail to see in what way the Kuran is an improvement over, or advancement on, the moral teaching, language, style, or coherence of the Old and New Testament. It looks, feels, and sounds like a construct entirely human in origin and intent, clear in its earthly sources of inspiration and the fulfillment of the daily needs, personal and political, of its author.

Perhaps the failure of a non-Muslim to appreciate the alleged superiority of the Kuran can only reflect Allah's decision, already announced in the book, to render the condemned imperceptive. But the revelation that non-Muslims are not allowed to understand the Kuran—"and we put coverings over their hearts and minds, lest they should understand the Kuran, and we put deafness in their ears"[114]—sits oddly with Allah's command regarding the unbelievers: "strike off their heads; then when you have made wide slaughter among them, carefully tie up the remaining captives."[115] If a non-Muslim cannot understand the holy book by divine decree, he can convert to Islam only "by the mouth," that is, by force.

The Kuran is to be recited, as its name says, not subjected to analytical study by a reasoning mind: "Whoever so interprets the Quran according to his opinion, let him seek his abode in the fire."[116] In Muhammad's own words, "Dispute about the Quran is infidelity." (Contrast that to St. Paul's injunction, "Study to show thyself approved unto God, a workman that needeth not to be ashamed, rightly dividing the word of truth.") When

---

[112] Geisler and Saleeb, p. 102.

[113] Sayed Qutb, introduction to *Under the Wings of the Qur'an.*

[114] 17:46–47.

[115] 47:4.

[116] *Al Hadis*, Bk. 1, Sec 3, Chap. 4, no. 55 and 57.

Samuel Zwemmer visited the Mosque of Omar in Jerusalem, he and the attendant Sheik spent several hours studying the Bible, but the Sheik could not do this with the Kuran at peril of Hell fire.

If the eloquence of style, the refinement of thinking, and the emotional power indicate divine origins of a text, it could be argued that Homer, Virgil, Dante, Shakespeare, or Goethe also had Allah whispering in their ear, and for the best part with considerably greater vigor.

ECUMENICAL JIHAD?

Of all major religions known to man, the teaching of Islam makes it the least amenable to dialogue with other faiths. Among non-Muslims it seeks converts or obedient subjects, not partners in a dialogue. Nevertheless, among some contemporary Western social conservatives, there exists an *a priori* desire to forge an alliance of believers against the moral and spiritual "decay" of a sinful world—an "ecumenical jihad," a war of all religions against none:

> If we will work and fight and love in action side by side with our Protestant and Catholic and Orthodox and Jewish and Muslim neighbors, we will come to perceive something we did not understand before. . . . If we did not balk at having Stalin's followers as our allies against Hitler, we should not balk at having Muhammad's followers as our allies against Stalin.[117]

Exactly the same sentiment drives President Bush's advisor on Islam, a professor at Cleveland-Marshall College of Law, David Forte. He speaks no Arabic and readily admits that he merely "dabbles" in Islamic jurisprudence. Nevertheless, his conviction that Islamic terrorists and Muslim aggressors are, by definition, heretics and not "real" Muslims has been fully internalized by the president, whose speeches seem to pluck whole phrases from Forte's writings. The problem is that Forte also subscribes to the theory of "ecumenical jihad," which is admittedly very different in intent from the usual liberal Islamophilia, but perhaps even more pernicious in its consequences:

---

[117] Peter Kreeft, "Ecumenical Jihad," in *Reclaiming the Great Tradition,* InterVarsity Press, 1997, p. 24.

Forte doesn't just want to redeem Islam from its critics. As a Catholic conservative who serves on a Vatican task force on strengthening family, he wants to redeem religious orthodoxy itself—or, at least, cleanse it of the extremist stain. "Nothing this evil could be religious," he is fond of saying. It's a bromide that jibes perfectly with Bush's own unabashed fondness for religiosity of all stripes.[118]

He wrote in his 1999 book on Islamic law that "though radicals often create an effigy of the West as a 'devil,' their real animus is against traditional Islam." Today's extremists, he claims, are a theologically marginal tradition "that Islam early on rejected as opposed to the universal message of its Prophet." In a remarkable twist of reality, Forte accuses the secularized media establishment of negative stereotyping of Islam because it is a religion: "When they talk about Islam, they talk about jihad. They patronizingly assume that violence is an essential part of Islam." This view, however erroneous, boils down to the conviction that believers, no matter their denomination, are better people than nonbelievers, and that a religious outlook—*any* religious outlook—is preferable to the nihilistic wastelands of postmodern secularism.

Some post-Christian promoters of "Ecumenical Jihad" readily sacrifice the doctrine of Grace, Incarnation, and Trinity on the altar of an open-ended interfaith dialogue that should finally lead to ultimate deist unity, "a genuine religious pluralism," in which "Islam is recognized as a different but equally valid response to God, created by a different revelatory moment, namely Mohammad's reception of the Qur'an."[119]

By giving up any pretense of doctrinal conviction and rootedness in their presumed tradition, these people cease to represent anything at all. By still claiming to be Christian, they encourage their Muslim interlocutors in the belief that there is no need to engage in any dialogue—odious from the Islamic theological standpoint anyway—since such evident lack of faith and conviction on the Christian side encourages them to expect imminent and speedy embrace of Allah and his prophet as the only logical outcome. What "dialogue" there is, therefore, starts on the Muslim side with the

---

[118] Franklin Foer: "Blind Faith." *The New Republic*, October 22, 2001.

[119] Cf. John Hick: "Islam and Christian Monotheism," in Dan Cohn-Sherbok (ed.), *Islam in a World of Diverse Faiths,* New York, St. Martin's Press, 1991.

assumption that a clear and frank restatement of Islamic dogma will prompt others to see the light.

An example of the Muslim attitude to interfaith dialogue was provided by the 1980 conference of the Society for the Study of Theology in Oxford. The delegates were told that one Abdus-Samad Sharafuddin of King Abdul-Aziz University in Jeddah, while unable to attend in person, requested the organizers to distribute his paper, entitled *About the Myth of God Incarnate: An Impartial Survey of Its Main Topics*. The author explained that his work was of monumental importance, as "it shatters age-long darkness like a bolt from the blue; like a rational, God-sent lightning it strikes the London horizon to explode an age-long blunder in Christian thought."[120]

(The notion that Islam has a wonderfully clear simplicity compared to the cluttered complexity of Christianity is not new. This was answered decades ago by C. S. Lewis: "If Christianity was something we were making up, of course we could make it easier. But it is not. We cannot compete, in simplicity, with people who are inventing religions. How could we? We are dealing with Fact. Of course anyone can be simple if he has no facts to bother about."[121])

Sharafuddin started his study by declaring that the Christian worship of Jesus as Lord is an act of open idolatry. He concluded it by explaining that the true understanding of Jesus is given in the Kuranic verse: "The Messiah, Son of Mary, was nothing but a messenger. Messengers have passed away before him." The concept of Trinity was "refuted" with another Kuranic quote!

The proponents of an "Ecumenical Jihad," from President George W. Bush and Professor Forte to a Christian conservative like Peter Kreeft, share two fallacies. Their faulty understanding of Islamic theology leads them to imagine that "Allah" is more or less interchangeable with the "God" of other monotheists. Their incomplete understanding of the phenomenon of secular globalization leads them to seek an equally monolithic counterweight on the side of faith. In reality, the only effective resistance to secularism will come from old identities revitalized and

---

[120] Dan Cohn-Sherbok, "Incarnation and Trialogue," in Dan Cohn-Sherbok (ed.), op.cit.

[121] C. S. Lewis, *Mere Christianity,* New York, The Macmillan Company, 1943, p. 145.

reaffirmed, not blurred and compromised. To survive, Christians need to rediscover theological firmness and doctrinal clarity.

CHAPTER THREE
Jihad Without End

Our flowers are the sword and the dagger;
Narcissus and myrtle are naught.
Our drink is the blood of our foeman;
Our goblet his skull, when we've fought.

-Ali ibn Abi Talib

Muhammad described the three most important works a man could perform as faith, war in the path of Allah, and a blameless pilgrimage. Muhammad's successors did not need convincing; they were prone to war by custom and required no excuses to wage it. They were simple fighting men, accustomed to living by pillage and the exploitation of settled populations, and heaping loot and jizya was the only means of making a living known to them. Theirs was an "expansionism denuded of any concrete objective, brutal, and born of a necessity in its past."[1]

Islam provided an additional motive for wars of conquest that probably would have occurred anyway, and an ideological justification for those wars that was inherently global and totalitarian. The view of modern Islamic activists, that "Islam must rule the world and until Islam does rule the world we will continue to sacrifice our lives,"[2] is neither extreme nor even remarkable from the standpoint of traditional Islam. It has been divinely sanctioned from the moment Muhammad had established a safe power base in Medina: "O Prophet! Rouse the Believers to the fight," the Kuran orders, and promises that twenty Muslims, "patient and persevering," would vanquish two hundred unbelievers; if a hundred, they will vanquish a thousand.[3] Allah further orders the faithful to fight the unbelievers, and be firm with them.[4] "And slay them wherever ye catch them, and turn them out from where they have turned you out; for tumult

---

[1] Ibn Warraq, 1995, p. 219.
[2] Al-Badr spokesman Mustaq Aksari, CNN, September 19, 2001.
[3] 8:65.
[4] 9:123.

and oppression are worse than slaughter."[5] The end of the fight is possible only when "there prevail justice and faith in Allah."[6]

There are dozens of "solid" hadithic quotes with Muhammad's assurances that Allah guarantees to all *jihadi* warriors instant paradise in case of martyrdom, or "reward or booty he has earned." To be a Muslim was rewarding in the hereafter, and profitable in this life:

> Jihad is the best method of earning, both spiritual and temporal. If victory is won, there is enormous booty and conquest of a country, which cannot be equaled to any other source of earning. If there is defeat or death, there is everlasting Paradise and a great spiritual benefit. This sort of Jihad is conditional upon pure motive (i.e., for establishing the kingdom of Allah on earth).[7]

Both "Islam" and "jihad" were originally secular concepts, denoting a sublime virtue in the eyes of the Arab: defiance of death, bravery, and struggle. The stress was on the totality of one's vocation, not on *submission.* Peaceful asceticism was a concept alien to the desert warriors, and condemned by Muhammad as "monkery" (*rahbaniya*) typical of Christians. It is unlikely that Muhammad would have succeeded had he really meant "surrender" when he called his religion *Islam,* and it is just as unlikely that his early audience had not been aware of its broader, defiant meaning. This is confirmed by the fact that Muhammad did not use the words "Islam" and "Muslim" until he was firmly established in Medina following the battle of Badr. Until that time, his followers were simply called "believers" (*mu'minun*), the name used even after his death.

It was the rapid course of events in the first decades following the death of Muhammad—

> the hostile attitude taken by the previously islamized tribes, the restoration of order by Abu Bakr and his generals, the splendid feats of arms under Umar, which were followed by the islamization of large parts of the ancient world—that made clear to the Companions, and to the pious generation of their successors, that the term 'Islam' had obtained a temporal

---

[5] 2:191.
[6] 2:193.
[7] Mishkat II, p. 253.

meaning. It seemed as if the narrow path, originally the only way by which the city of Islam could be reached, had been enlarged and paved and become easy highway for the multitudes who came from all sides to embrace Islam.[8]

Under the "rightly guided caliphs," Muslims had evolved from soldiers willing to die for the faith into people submitting to it. That wars of conquest were not only divinely ordained but also materially profitable endeavors went without saying. Only after the Islamic Empire had been established the notion of an "inner" jihad—that of one's personal fight against his ego and sinful desires—also came into being, but it was predicated on the assumption that the external, real jihad was nearing its completion. The concept of spiritual struggle was never meant to replace, let alone abrogate, the original, warlike meaning.

Muhammad may not have performed any miracles in his lifetime, but his followers took the victorious spread of Islam by the invading Arab armies as a sure sign of divine favor. Following the first four caliphs, the conquered lands were turned into an Arab empire ruled by a small elite of Muslim warriors who lived entirely on the spoils of war, the poll and land taxes paid by the subjugated peoples. They did not engage in economically productive activity and lived in isolation from the local people, in fortified garrisons spread across North Africa and the Middle East.

In the early decades of the conquest, Islam was still identified with Arab culture to such an extent that conversion also meant association with one of the Arab tribes as a client. The converts, then and in subsequent centuries, had not only lost their names for Arab ones, but also a sense of their own past and culture. Their pre-Islamic ancestors could no longer be respected: did not the Prophet see his own father in hell? As V.S. Naipaul has noted,

There has probably been no imperialism like that of Islam and the Arabs. . . . Islam seeks as an article of faith to erase the past; the believers in the end honour Arabia alone; they have nothing to return to. Islam requires the convert to accept that his land is of

---

[8] Arent Wensinck, *Muslim Creed*, pp. 22–23.

no religious or historical importance; its relics were of no account; only the sands of Arabia are sacred.[9]

The vanquished were "culturally disemboweled," condemned to the enforced psychosis of renouncing their old and highly developed identities for a crude and violent desert blueprint that regulated the minutest details of their lives.

CALIPHATE

Muhammad's death was also the end of prophecy and the *umma* faced a challenge. He did provide for the institution of the *caliph* as Allah's viceroy on earth, but it was unclear who was to take that role. Muhammad's was a tough act to follow: he claimed universal authority, and the *haram* that he established had no natural limits.

The institution of the caliphate was an attempt to institutionalize the legacy of the prophet and to regulate politics on the basis of Allah's revealed will. The caliph alone is supposed to guarantee the legitimacy and legality of the state structure over which he presides, because he commands and demands authority on the basis of apostolic succession from the last of all apostles. Obedience to him is no less obligatory than that to the prophet. Accordingly, the caliphate was a concept of world government by the early converts that was not bound, in principle, by any geographical boundaries or regional loyalties.

There were three groups with a claim to succession. There were the early converts, who followed Muhammad on his flight from Mecca and whose members had established family links through marriage. The leading citizens of Medina argued that they were the ones who had made Muhammad's rise possible, that without their faith in him and their pledge to him there would have been no Islam. Finally, the more recent converts who belonged to the Quraysh tribe could not claim such credentials, but they nevertheless aspired to authority and influence in the community on the grounds on their traditional preeminent tribal status.

---

[9] V.S. Naipaul, *Beyond Belief: Islamic Excursions Among the Converted Peoples*, N.Y., Random House, 1998.

Close companionship with Muhammad from among the early converts—coupled with Quraysh blood, for which he had expressed preference—soon prevailed, and his first four successors during the "apostolic" period of Islam were Abu Bakr, Umar, Uthman, and Ali. They ruled as caliphs from Mohammad's death in 632 to 661, oversaw the major Muslim conquests, and laid the rules governing their relations with the vanquished Jews and Christians that retain their validity to the present day. The four caliphs are remembered as *the rightly guided ones* because of their close association with Muhammad.

Abu Bakr, the first caliph and father of Aisha, one of Muhammad's wives, faced the uphill task of legitimizing his position. He was not a successor by virtue of prior designation or prophetic gift, yet was expected to combine religious and secular authority at a time when their development into a codified blueprint had hardly started. In the beginning, Muhammad's alliances with different tribes threatened to dissolve. Most heartland Arabs were nominally converted to the new faith by the time of his death, of which they had but a limited understanding beyond the easily grasped basic tenets; Islam was yet to be made fully coherent and codified. The "Wars of Apostasy," conducted during Abu Bakr's brief caliphate, clearly indicated that, for at least some, the conversion to Islam was an act of expediency or survival, rather than choice.

Early probing raids into the borderlands of Byzantium and Persia under Umar, the second caliph (634–644) and Abu-Bakr's designated successor, showed how weakened both had been by their mutual struggle. Initial successes bred ever-greater boldness. By the time of Umar's death, in addition to the entire Arabia, the Western Sassanian lands and the Byzantine provinces of Syria and Egypt had fallen to the Arabs; the rest of Persia soon followed. Persia succumbing to Islam was especially significant as it was a mature culture, equal if not superior to that of contemporary Europe.

The Byzantines suffered a major defeat at the Battle of Yarmuk in A.D. 636, Jerusalem was taken in 638, the Persians were defeated at Nihavand in 641, and the conquest of northern Egypt was completed in 640–641. The conquerors' energy and fighting skills, put to good use by Umar's considerable organizational skills and leadership qualities, were also aided by the presence of former imperial mercenaries and military slaves who coached the Arabs in the science of battlefield tactics and military technology. The core of the invading army was imbued with a spirit of irresistible zeal bred by the many easy victories. As early as 766, a Christian clergyman writing in Syriac spoke of the "locust swarm" of unconverted barbarians—Sindhis, Alans, Khazars, and others—who served in the caliph's army, and by the ninth century slave armies appeared all over the Islamic empire.[10]

Umar's career was cut short when a vengeful slave from Iraq killed him, but the decade of his rule exceeded in sheer geographic scope all Islamic conquests of subsequent times. It imbued the Muslims with a sense of invincibility that was certainly beneficial to their fighting morale in the period of expansion, but it also bred a sense of complacency that proved dangerous to the Muslim cause once the tide of history did turn.

Under the third caliph, Uthman ibn Affan, Umar's phenomenal conquests were consolidated and expanded. The presence of numerous Arabs, immigrants from previous decades and centuries, along the Fertile Crescent facilitated the conquerors' intercourse with the local population and offered a substantial group of local inhabitants that could be expected to easily transfer its loyalties to the invaders on the grounds of language, tradition, and blood, if not religion. Under Uthman, discord appeared since he was the first convert of high social and economic standing and a son-in-law of Muhammad, and his reign was marked by nepotism. The old Quraysh Meccan establishment was back in charge, and he made many enemies among the Old Guard of the Companions. Many were aggravated by his standardization of the Kuran. His gruesome death at the hands of rebels in 656 marked the beginning of the first *fitnah* ("trial"), rebellion against divine law, within the Muslim community. Uthman's body was turned away from the Muslim cemetery. His wife, with some of his friends, buried him by night in a Jewish cemetery without the ritual washings, while listening to the curses of the rebels who threw stones at them. The subsequent chaos and bloodshed came to be known as *al-Bab al-Maftuh*, "the door opened [to civil warfare]."

Ali, Muhammad's cousin and son-in-law, was the last of the "four rightly guided" caliphs, but from his new capital, Damascus, he could never establish his full authority amidst the accusations that it was he who

---

[10] Bernard Lewis, *Race and Slavery in the Middle East,* Oxford University Press, 1994.

had instigated Uthman's murder. Two of the discontents' leaders, Talha and al-Zubair, with the support of the most influential of Muhammad's widows, Aysha, rebelled against Ali. The resulting "Battle of the Camel" saw 10,000 Muslims slaughtered. Ali and his troops won, but soon faced another contender, Mu'awiya, the powerful and scheming governor of Syria, who also accused him—as did Aysha—of complicity in the assassination of Uthman. Another indecisive battle followed, after which Mu'awiya and Ali agreed to appoint arbiters and to abide by their solution. This undermined the authority of Ali, however, and caused the collapse of support among his followers. Ali was eventually killed in 661 by one of his disillusioned former supporters.

Ali's elder son and Muhammad's grandson Hasan was seen by many as the rightful heir to caliphate. When Mu'awiya opposed his succession and began to prepare for war Hasan initially wanted to fight but, plagued by many defections, soon abandoned the caliphate to his opponent. For the rest of his life, he lived quietly in Medina.

Hasan's younger brother Husayn ibn-Ali reluctantly went along with the arrangement while Mu'awiya was alive, and even accepted an annuity from him. He refused to recognize the legitimacy of his son and successor Yazid in April 680, however, and raised the banner of resistance in the Iraqi city of Kufah as an anti-caliph of sorts. In subsequent months he tried to set up a polity that would be based on "true" Islam, as opposed to what he regarded as the corrupt regime of the Umayyads.

Yazid sent a detachment of 4,000 men against Husayn, whose much smaller force was defeated at the battle of Kerbela in October 680. Husayn and most of his family were killed, and his severed head sent to Yazid in Damascus. This sealed the split in Islam between the Sunni and Shi'ite sects. The latter still regard Ali and his sons as the only legitimate line of succession and commemorate Husayn's death in the first ten days of Muharram—the date of the battle according to the Islamic calendar—as a period of lament. Of twelve venerated Shia caliphs, beginning with Ali and ending with Mohammed ("Imam al-Mahdi"), Husayn the martyr has a special place to this day.

In the subsequent history of Islam, the victims of massacres by Muslim rulers have frequently been Muslims, including members of their own families or families claiming descent from Muhammad himself.[11] Nevertheless, most Muslims look upon the early period of the four caliphs as the ideal model of umma that has never been attained in subsequent centuries, but should be striven to.

Ali's rival, Muawiyah, established the Umayyad caliphate, which produced 14 caliphs between 661 and 749, ruling the Muslim world from Damascus. In 749, the last of them, Marwan, and all the members of the Ummayad family were murdered except abd-al-Rahman, who fled to Spain—conquered by Muslims some three decades earlier—and founded an independent Ummayad caliphate there. Already under the Umayyads, the fearsome rulers of the desert had mellowed into palace sensualists. Luxurious residences replaced tents, and it is said of the caliphs Yazid I and II that they were "passionate friends of sport, music, and lady singers." Sensuality was replacing stern piety at the top.

The Abbasid dynasty (750–945), the most widely observed caliphate associated with 38 caliphs, moved the capital from Damascus to Baghdad, initially a village that was turned through slave labor into a splendid city with palaces, government buildings, and mosques. The first Abbasid caliph, Abdul Abbas, was a descendant of Muhammad's influential uncle, but under the new dynasty the Quraish dominance soon ended. The move to Mesopotamia entailed inheriting the Persian tradition of court ceremony, as well as arts and thinking. After his death, Abdul-Abbas was succeeded by his brother, and he, in turn, by his sons al-Mahdi and al-Hadi, and thereafter by the famous Harun-al-Rashid (786). It was under these rulers that the Islamic world reached the zenith of its power, prosperity, and learning.

The Abbasids, who ruled for just over 500 years (750–1258), transformed Islam into a transnational religion. Non-Muslim communities had been able to preserve a degree of self-rule and survive relatively intact the preceding century of initial Muslim conquest. The evolution of Islam into universal faith and the final development of codified Islamic theology and ideology changed the equation to the non-Muslims' lasting detriment.

Under the early caliphs, the conquests did not have the purpose of spreading Islam as such, but rather the establishment of the rule by Muslim Arabs in the conquered lands. Muhammad was frank about the exalted

---

[11] C.f. Ibn Warraq, 1995, p. 346.

94

status of his race: "Love the Arabs for three things—I am an Arab, and the Kuran is in Arabic, and the talk of those in Paradise is in Arabic."[12] The early Islamic state was a polity based primarily on persons and communities, not on territory, over which it did *rule* but did not *occupy* the entire area all of the time. This arrangement allowed for the continued existence and a degree of self-rule by the Jewish, Christian, Zoroastrian, and other communities.

The subject peoples were not immediately aware of the momentous quality of what had come to pass. That part of Arabia adjacent to the Syrian borders was, from the third century on, regarded as the "mother of heresies." Before the rise and spread of Nestorianism and Monophysitism, the Arian heresy was the prevailing creed of the Christian Arabs. In the fifth, sixth, and seventh centuries, Arianism was supplanted by Nestorianism and Monophysitism, which had then become the official creeds of the two most representative Churches of Syria, Egypt, Abyssinia, Mesopotamia, and Persia.[13] Like the Arabian Jews, the Christian Arabs did not, as a rule, particularly in the times immediately before and after Mohammed, attach much importance to the practical observance of their religion. For many dissident Christian groups that had been repeatedly denounced as heretical from Constantinople, it seemed preferable at first to be ruled by largely absentee non-Christian overlords who cared only about taxes and did not feel strongly one way or another about the finer points of Christology.

Slaughters did occur in the initial wave of conquest: during the Muslim invasion of Syria in 634, thousands of Christians were massacred; in Mesopotamia between 635 and 642, monasteries were ransacked and the monks and villagers slain; in Egypt the towns of Behnesa, Fayum, Nikiu and Aboit were put to the sword. The inhabitants of Cilicia were taken into captivity. In Armenia, the entire population of Euchaita was wiped out. The Muslim invaders sacked and pillaged Cyprus and then established their rule by a "great massacre." In North Africa, Tripoli was pillaged in 643 by Amr, who forced the Jews and Christians to hand over their women and children as slaves to the Arab army. They were told that they could deduct the value of their enslaved family from the poll-tax, the jizya. Carthage was

---

[12] *Al Hadis*, Vol. 4, p. 594.
[13] *The Catholic Encyclopaedia*, "Arabia."

razed to the ground and most of its inhabitants killed. Nevertheless, since dead bodies paid no taxes while the captives were economic assets, once the conquerors' rule was firmly established a degree of normalcy was reestablished at the level of local communities.

At the time of Muhammad's birth, Christianity had covered, outside Europe, the ancient Roman province of Asia, extending across the Caucasus to the Caspian Sea, Syria with the Holy Land, and a wide belt of North Africa all the way to the Atlantic Ocean. Christians numbered over 30 million by A.D. 311, in spite of imperial persecution that often entailed martyrdom. Most of them lived not in Europe but in Asia Minor and Africa, the home of many famous Christian fathers and martyrs, such as St. Paul of Tarsus, Augustine of Hippo, Polycarp of Smyrna, Tertullian of Carthage, Clement of Alexandria, John Chrysostom of Antioch, and Cyprian of Carthage. The Seven Churches of Revelation were all in Asia Minor. (Smyrna was the last of these and kept her light burning until 1922, when the Turks destroyed it, along with its Christian population.)

For the millions of trapped eastern Christians, as well as the Jews, the Zoroastrians of Persia, and the Hindus and Buddhists of the Subcontinent, the heirs to the most advanced civilizations of the time, a long night was descending.

THE CRUSADES: CHRISTENDOM STRIKES BACK

Between Muhammad's death and the second siege of Vienna, just over a thousand years later, Islam expanded—at first rapidly, then intermittently—at the expense of everything and everyone in the way of its warriors. Unleashed as the militant faith of a nomadic war band, *Islam turned its boundary with the outside world into a perpetual war zone.*

For a long time, the outcome of the onslaught was in doubt. The early attack on Christendom almost captured Constantinople when that city was still far and away the important center of the Christian world. Instead, the Greeks stood their ground against Islam for another six centuries. But the Muslims also conquered Spain, and had they gone further, the Kuran—in Gibbon's memorable phrase—might have been "taught in the schools of Oxford" to a circumcised people. The Muslims crossed the Pyrenees, promising to stable their horses in St. Peter's at Rome but were at last defeated by Charles Martel at Tours, exactly a century after the Prophet's

96

death. This defeat arrested their western conquests and saved Europe. The last attempt in pre-postmodern times took the Sultan's janissaries more than halfway from Constantinople to Dover (1683), via the Balkans. On both occasions the tide was checked, but its subsequent rolling back took decades, even centuries.

The Crusades were but a temporary setback to Islamic expansion, and the source of endless arguments that sought to establish some moral equivalence between Muslims and Christians at first, and eventually to elevate the former to victimhood and condemn the latter as aggressors. Far from being wars of aggression, the Crusades were a belated military response of Christian Europe to over three centuries of Muslim aggression against Christian lands, the systemic mistreatment of the indigenous Christian population of those lands, and harassment of Christian pilgrims. The postmodern myth, promoted by Islamic propagandists and supported by some self-hating Westerners—notably in the academy—claims that the peaceful Muslims, native to the Holy Land, were forced to take up arms in defense against European-Christian aggression. This myth takes A.D. 1095 as its starting point, but it ignores the preceding centuries, starting with the early caliphs, when Muslim armies swept through the Byzantine Empire, conquering about two-thirds of the Christian world of that time.

In 1009, Hakem, the Fatimite Caliph of Egypt, ordered the destruction of the Holy Sepulchre and all the Christian establishments in Jerusalem. For years thereafter, Christians were persecuted even more cruelly than in the early period of Muslim rule. In 1065, thousands of Christian pilgrims who had crossed Europe under the leadership of Günther, Bishop of Bamberg, while on their way through Palestine had to seek shelter in a ruined fortress where they defended themselves against Muslim attackers, in violation of earlier pledges that they would enjoy safe access to the holy sites. The rise of the Seljuk Turks compromised even the tenuous safety of Christian pilgrims.

Byzantium had reconquered much of Syria and Palestine under Nicephorus II and John I, including Antioch in 969, but the Turkish onslaught from the north made that recovery short-lived. They conquered Armenia and the whole of Asia Minor, where their descendants still live. In 1070 they took Jerusalem, and in 1071 Diogenes, the Greek emperor, was defeated and made captive at Mantzikert. Syria was the next to become the prey of the Turks. Antioch succumbed in 1084, and by 1092 not one of the great metropolitan sees of Asia remained in the possession of the Christians.

In spite of the Great Schism of 1054, the Byzantine emperors deemed the renewed threat from the east serious enough to seek help from Rome. The battle of Manzikert was the indirect cause of the Crusades, heralding Byzantium's loss of control in Asia Minor. This loss of control lay behind the appeal to the West. In 1073, letters were exchanged between Emperor Michael VII and Pope Gregory VII, who planned to send an army of 50,000 men to repulse the Turks. Gregory's successor, Urban II, took up those plans and convened a council at Clermont-Ferrand. A great number of knights and men of all conditions came and encamped on the plain of Chantoin, outside the city. On November 27, 1095, the Pope himself addressed the assembled multitudes, exhorting them to go forth and rescue the Holy Sepulchre. Amid cries of *Deus hoc vult!*—God wills it!—all pledged themselves by vow to depart for the Holy Land and received the cross of red cloth to be worn on the shoulder.

There was more than just a whiff of Muhammad in the papal guarantee of plenary absolution—a direct pass to heaven to the Crusaders should they die, or great riches if they lived. The Pope sent letters to various courts, and the movement made rapid headway throughout Europe:

> Preachers of the crusade appeared everywhere, and on all sides sprang up disorganized, undisciplined, penniless hordes, almost destitute of equipment, who, surging eastward through the valley of the Danube, plundered as they went along and murdered the Jews in the German cities. One of these bands, headed by Folkmar, a German cleric, was slaughtered by the Hungarians. Peter the Hermit, however, and the German knight, Walter the Pennyless (Gautier Sans Avoir), finally reached Constantinople with their disorganized troops. To save the city from plunder, Alexius Comnenus ordered them to be conveyed across the Bosphorus (August 1096); in Asia Minor they turned to pillage and were nearly all slain by the Turks. Meanwhile, the regular crusade was being organized in the West and, according to a

well-conceived plan, the four principal armies were to meet at Constantinople.[14]

Peter the Hermit was the most effective of preachers, and the lines of battle were clearly drawn: it was us against them, Christendom against the "Evil Empire of Mahound." The driving impulse was not that of conquest and aggression, but of recovery and defense, and liberation of the Christians who still in many places constituted the majority of the population. The Crusades were not Christendom's answer to Umar, they were a reaction to what he and his successors had done.

By May 1097 the armies were assembled, but their presence helped to bring about irremediable misunderstandings between the Greeks and the Latin Christians. Emperor Alexius mistrusted his tentative Western allies, whose designs for the imperial lands to be reconquered were indeed ambiguous. After an early victory over the Turks at the battle of Dorylæum on July 1, 1097, the Crusaders advanced through Asia Minor, constantly harassed by a relentless enemy, suffering from heat, and sinking under the weight of their armor. They rested and recuperated among the Armenians of the Taurus region, made their way into Syria, and on October 20, 1097, laid siege to the fortified city of Antioch. On the night of June 2, 1098, they took the city by storm, but subsequent plague and famine decimated their ranks.

Rest, replenishment of men and supplies, and recuperation of worn-out survivors continued through the winter. It was not until April 1099 that the Crusader army marched on to Jerusalem, and on June 7 besieged the city. The attack began July 14, 1099—the date destined to live in anti-Christian infamy centuries later—and the next day the Crusaders entered Jerusalem from all sides and slew its inhabitants, regardless of age or sex. The soldiers of the Church Militant, as it turned out, could not only outfight but also out-massacre their Mohammedan foes. In 1112, with the aid of Norwegians and the support of Genoese, Pisan, and Venetian fleets, Crusaders began the conquest of the ports of Syria, which was completed in 1124 by the capture of Tyre. Ascalon alone kept an Egyptian Muslim garrison until its fall in 1153.

The Crusades were initially successful because Islam was by no means a monolithic body-politic. The caliphate's authority was purely notional:

---

[14] "Crusades," *The Catholic Encyclopaedia* (1908).

Egypt was under the rule of the Fatimids, a Shi'ite sect, while the Sunni Turks from central Asia were gaining the upper hand in Shi'ite Persia, as well as Iraq, Syria, and Palestine. By the beginning of the "Glorious Twelfth," the Christian states—the Kingdom of Jerusalem, the Countship of Tripoli, the Principality of Antioch, and the Countship of Edessa—controlled an unbroken but tenuously held belt of territory roughly corresponding to the Fertile Crescent between the Euphrates and the Sinai. It was long and thin: the preoccupation with the holy places and ports precluded any serious attempt to develop strategic depth, or to create a viable local economic and demographic base for the new Christian states.

The necessity of defending these fragile *Outremer* domains, coupled with the lack of reliable local recruits, resulted in the creation of the religious orders of knighthood: the Hospitallers and the Templars. They attracted the younger sons of feudal houses and acquired both in Palestine and in Europe considerable property. Their bravery and discipline—allegedly but unprovenly cemented by certain unspeakable practices within the Templar brotherhood—could not compensate for the Christian states' lack of cohesion and discipline, however. The help they received from the West was too scattered and intermittent. The Principality of Edessa was the first to succumb to the Muslim counteroffensive on Christmas Day 1144, and Damascus fell in 1154.

In 1169 an energetic and able prince of Kurdish blood and Sunni religious allegiance, Salah-ed-Dîn (Saladin), succeeded his uncle as the Grand Vizier of Egypt and in 1171 helped overthrow the Shi'ite Fatimid dynasty; the event seemed of intra-Muslim significance at first, but the tide was about to be turned against the Christian transplant. While the Muslim response to the initial success of the Crusaders was a call for jihad, until Saladin's rise their internal divisions precluded and delayed concerted action. Appealing to the religious fervor of Egyptian and Syrian Muslims in subsequent years, Saladin was able to take possession of Damascus and to conquer all of Mesopotamia except Mosul, threatening the Kingdom of Jerusalem from all sides. On July 4, 1187, Saladin's army defeated the Christians on the shores of Lake Tiberias, and he entered Jerusalem on September 17. The fortified ports of Tyre, Antioch, and Tripoli were the only remaining Christian strongholds. Saladin respected his foes as brave warriors and freed many Crusader prisoners who were too poor to pay ransom. He also provided secure access for Christian pilgrims to Jerusalem and other holy places.

The news of Jerusalem's fall caused consternation in Europe, and Emperor Frederick Barbarossa led the next Christian assault in 1189—the Third Crusade, the most brutal of all—at the head of an army of 100,000. He was drowned while trying to cross a river in Asia Minor on horseback, however, and many German princes returned home. Others, under the emperor's son, Frederick of Swabia, reached Antioch and proceeded to Acre, where finally all the crusading troops assembled. The siege of the city had already lasted two years when Philip August, King of France, and Richard the Lionheart, King of England, arrived on the scene, and Acre surrendered on July 13, 1191. Soon, however, the old quarrel between the French and English kings broke out again, and the former left Palestine. Richard was now leader of the Crusade, but he failed to take Jerusalem and "compensated himself for these reverses by brilliant but useless exploits which made his name legendary among the Mohammedans."[15]

After Saladin's death his possessions were divided among his lesser successors, who lost Jerusalem again to the Crusaders in 1229, but the latters' strength and unity was waning and by 1244 the city fell again to the Muslims, this time continuously until its conquest by the Israelis in 1967. The deathblow to the Crusaders was given by al-Malik al-Zahir Baybars, a Mamluke who previously had stopped the Mongols. He destroyed the venerated Church of Nativity in Nazareth. Caesarea capitulated under the condition that its 2,000 knights would be spared, but once inside the city, the Muslims murdered them all. When Antioch fell to the Muslims, 16,000 Christians were put to the sword, and 100,000 are recorded to have been sold as slaves.

While it all lasted the warriors on both sides nevertheless developed a degree of grudging respect for each other. They believed, and by the tenets of their religions they were justified in believing, that they were doing God's work. They fought each other, but there were long periods of truce when they traded, met, and talked. The Crusaders discarded their heavy armor and adopted the flowing robes better suited to the local clime, while Saladin's warriors grasped and willingly accepted something of the

---

[15] Ibid.

knightly code and mystique that had been quite alien to the early followers of the Prophet.

Saladin was a brave and capable soldier, a great builder, and a generous and merciful ruler. Richard the Lionheart was, if not exactly merciful, "the greatest knight and most heroic fighter of his age."[16] Saladin repeatedly expressed admiration for the piety of Christian pilgrims, and, a generation or so later, Joinville refers approvingly to Saladin's ecumenical observation that a bad Muslim could never make a good Christian.

Even in the days of Richard and Saladin the confusion had already set in, however. The lords of Outremer found it convenient to strike all kinds of unseemly bargains with their foes and allied themselves with Muslim rulers against both Constantinople and new groups of Crusaders who were threatening to upset the balance of power. Before too long, the Crusades turned into West European man's first colonial adventure, and in the Fourth Crusade, the soldiers who besieged and sacked first Zara, then the Orthodox Christian Constantinople, should have had some difficulty in maintaining the fiction of a religious enterprise.

One can be critical of the Crusades, primarily because of the great damage they have inflicted on the Christian East. What the Crusaders did to the Muslim inhabitants of Jerusalem in 1099 was as bad as what the Muslims had done to countless Christian cities before and after that time, but the carnage was less pardonable because, unlike the Muslims', it was not justifiable by Christian religious tenets. From the distance of almost a millennium, however, it is time to see the phenomenon as Christendom's reaction to Muslim aggression. It was a reconquest of something taken by force from its rightful owners, "no more offensive than was the American invasion of Normandy":

> Muslims in the Middle East—including Bin Laden and his creatures—know as little about the real Crusades as Americans do. Both view them in the context of the modern, rather than the medieval world.... They were a desperate and largely unsuccessful attempt to defend against a powerful enemy.[17]

---

[16] Thomae Fleming, "East is East, and West is Wuss," *Chronicles: A Magazine of American Culture*, February 1999.

[17] Thomas F. Madden, "Crusade Propaganda: Abuse of Christianity's Holy War," *National Review Online*.

By the end of the thirteenth century, the last Crusader remnants in Palestine and Syria were wiped out. That may have been the end of the "authentic" Crusades—those specifically aimed at liberating the Holy Land from Muslim yoke, as opposed to the campaigns against heretics and papal enemies—but it was by no means the end of jihad. Mamluk Egypt and the Ottoman Empire were to grow and expand at the expense of Christendom until the tide was checked for the ensuing three centuries at the gates of Vienna in 1683.

INTOLERANCE CODIFIED

On the eve of the First Crusade, the prominent Islamic scholar Abu Ala Al-Mawardi prepared the formal blueprint for the Islamic government, based on the Kuran, the Tradition, and the practice of the previous four centuries of conquest. It reiterated the division of the world into the House of Islam, where umma has been established, and the House of War inhabited by *harbis*, that is, the rest of the world. The House of Islam is in a state of permanent war with the lands that surround it; it can be interrupted by temporary truces, but peace will only come with the completion of global conquest. The progression was from *Dar al Sulh*—when the Muslims are a minority community, and need to adopt temporarily a peaceful attitude in order to deceive their neighbors (Mecca before Muhammad's move to Medina is the model for which the Muslim diaspora in the Western world provides contemporary example)—to *Dar al Harb*, when the territory of the infidel becomes a war zone by definition. This happens as soon as the Muslim side feels strong enough to dispense with pretense. The example was provided by Muhammad, who accepted a truce with Mecca when he was in an inferior position but broke it as soon as his recuperated strength allowed and offered his pagan compatriots the choice of conversion or death. In Europe today, the early signs of this forthcoming stage, amounting to a low-intensity civil war, are visible in ethnic disturbances in English and French cities, when young English-born Pakistanis or French-born North Africans venture out from their no-go areas.

The final objective all along is *Dar al Islam*, where Muslims dominate and infidels are at best tolerated and at worst expelled or massacred. This applies even to "the people of the book":

103

Declare war upon those to whom the Scriptures were revealed but believe neither in God nor the Last Day, and who do not forbid that which God and His Apostles have forbidden, and who refuse to acknowledge the true religion until they pay the poll-tax without reservation and are totally subjugated. The Jews claim that Ezra is a son of God, and the Christians say, "The Messiah is a son of God." Those are their claims that do indeed resemble the sayings of the infidels of old. May God do battle with them![18]

The Muslims are obliged to wage struggle against unbelievers and may contemplate tactical ceasefires, but never its complete abandonment short of the unbelievers' submission. This is the real meaning of jihad. Indeed, in certain contexts and in certain times it may also signify "inner striving" and "spiritual struggle," but to generations of Muslims before our time—and to an overwhelming majority of believers who are our contemporaries—the meaning of jihad as the obligatory and permanent war against non-Muslims has not changed since Al-Mawardi's time. At all times, according to Allah/Muhammad, "Those who believe fight in the cause of God."[19] For the fallen and victorious alike, the rewards are instant and plentiful: "for whoever fights on God's path, whether he is killed or triumphs, we will give him a handsome reward."[20]

The conquered peoples were "protected persons" only if they submitted to Islamic domination by a "Contract" *(Dhimma)* and paid poll tax *(jizya)* and land tax *(haraj)* to their masters. Any failure to do so was the breach of contract, enabling the Muslims to kill or enslave them and confiscate their property. The cross could not be displayed in public, and "the people of the book" had to wear special clothing or a belt. Their men were not allowed to marry Muslim women, their slaves had to be sold to a Muslim if they converted, and they were not allowed to carry weapons. They had to take in Muslim travelers, especially soldiers on a campaign, but they had no right to the spoils of war. Since the income from the poll tax was mostly used to finance jihad, Jews and Christians under Muslim rule were effectively forced to bankroll the subjugation of their co-religionists who were still free.

---

[18] 9:29–30.
[19] 4:76.
[20] 4:74.

A host of additional petty rules were either enacted or adopted that were meant to humiliate non-Muslims. Some of them were summarized in the "Pact of Umar," in which the conquered Christians of Syria were forced to solemnly declare:

> We shall not build in our cities or in their vicinity any new monasteries, churches, hermitages, or monks' cells. We shall not restore, by night or by day, any of them that have fallen into ruin or which are located in the Muslims' quarters. We shall keep our gates wide open for the passerby and travelers. We shall provide three days' food and lodging to any Muslims who pass our way. We shall not shelter any spy in our churches or in our homes, nor shall we hide him from the Muslims… We shall not hold public religious ceremonies. We shall not seek to proselytize anyone. We shall not prevent any of our kin from embracing Islam if they so desire. We shall show deference to the Muslims and shall rise from our seats when they wish to sit down. . . . We shall not ride on saddles. We shall not wear swords or bear weapons of any kind, or ever carry them with us. We shall not sell wines. We shall clip the forelocks of our head. We shall not display our crosses or our books anywhere in the Muslims' thoroughfares or in their marketplaces. We shall only beat our clappers in our churches very quietly. We shall not raise our voices when reciting the service in our churches, nor when in the presence of Muslims. Neither shall we raise our voices in our funeral processions. We shall not build our homes higher than theirs.[21]

This was not a "pact," implying a treaty between theoretically equal partners entering a voluntary agreement. Umar warned the conquered that disobedience meant death: "Anyone who violates such terms will be unprotected. And it will be permissible for the Muslims to treat them as rebels or dissenters; namely, it is permissible to kill them."

Al-Mawdudi adds that "Muslims have the right to confiscate places of worship in such towns as have been taken by storm," as has been done with

---

[21] From Al-Turtushi, Siraj al-Muluk, pp. 229–230, www.fordham.edu/halsall/source/pact-umar.html.

St. John's in Damascus, Hagia Sophia in Constantinople, and countless others. The precedent is valid to this day.

"Protection" was also abolished if the dhimmis resisted Islamic law, gave allegiance to a non-Muslim power, enticed a Muslim from his faith; harmed a Muslim or his property; or committed blasphemy. "Blasphemy" included denigration of the Prophet Muhammad, the Kuran, the Muslim faith, the *Shari'a*, by suggesting that it has a defect, and by refusing the decision of the *ijma*—the consensus of the Islamic community or umma.[22] The moment the "pact of protection" is abolished, the jihad resumes, which means that the lives of the dhimmis and their property are forfeited. (To this day, those Islamists in Egypt who kill and pillage Copts claim that these Christians have forfeited their "protection" because they do not pay the jizya.) This relationship, typical of a war-treaty between the conqueror and the vanquished, remains valid for Muslims because it is fixed in theological texts.

In his *Rights of Non-Muslims in Islamic State,* al-Mawdudi asserts that an Islamic state is by its very nature bound to distinguish between Muslims and non-Muslims, "and, in an honest and upright manner, not only publicly declares this state of affairs but also precisely states what rights will be conferred upon its non-Muslim citizens and which of them will not be enjoyed by them." Accordingly, non-Muslims cannot vote or be elected, and no Muslim can be sentenced to die for murdering a non-Muslim.

> Nothing in the law of Muhammad states that the blood of the disbeliever is equal to the blood of the Muslim, because faith is necessary for equality. The people of the Covenant (Jews or Christians) do not believe in Muhammad and Islam, thus their blood and the Muslim's blood cannot be equal. These are distinctive texts which indicate that a Muslim is not to be put to death for (murdering) one of the people of the covenant or an unbeliever, but a free Muslim must be killed for a free Muslim, regardless of the race."[23]

If a Muslim murders another Muslim, he will be sentenced to death unless the victim's relatives accept a blood ransom. However, if the

---

[22] 3:106.
[23] Ibn Timiyya Vol. 14, p. 85.

106

murdered is non-Muslim, his relatives have no choice but to accept the blood payment. A non-Muslim's testimony is not acceptable or even allowed in court against Muslims or even against other non-Muslims. On the other hand, if a non-Muslim merely curses a Muslim, he must either be sentenced to death or be converted to Islam. Furthermore, if one of the people of the Book murdered another, and then the murderer was converted to Islam, he would not be subject to punishment. Those who aver that "there is no god but Allah and Muhammad is his apostle" were thus promised escape from the sentence of death with virtual impunity.

Discrimination was universal, not only legal. Non-Muslims could not be employed in the upper echelons of the civil service and in educating or in any way exercising authority over Muslims. Umar, the second caliph, refused to allow a Christian to continue in his post of the tax accountant in Syria and attacked one of his aides with a whip for employing a Christian to oversee the accounts of Iraq. In the end, as Islamic scholars state, "Some who were less qualified than the Christians were appointed; that would be more useful to Muslims for their religion and earthly welfare. A little of what is lawful will be abundantly blessed, and abundance of what is unlawful will be wasted."[24] No one but "a mature, sane Muslim should assume the office of judge" and no non-Muslim should ever "hold a position in which he can have power over a Muslim."

The resulting inequality of rights in all domains between Muslims and dhimmis was geared to a steady erosion of the latter communities by attrition and conversion. The position of the Christians, preferable to that of the Jews in Muhammad's lifetime, eventually became more difficult than that of the Jews. The Greek Orthodox among them were suspected of loyalty to the Patriarch and the Emperor in Constantinople, which was the main symbol of the Christian enemy until its fall in 1453. All of them were regarded as natural would-be allies of Christendom, an assumption as natural in view of the captives' position under Islam as it was unjustified by their actual behavior. By the time of Timur's invasions at the end of the fourteenth century, the Christians became a minority in their own lands where, no other religion had been known until the Muslim conquest.

Millions of Christians from Spain, Egypt, Syria, Greece, and Armenia; Latins and Slavs from southern and central Europe; as well as Jews,

---

[24] Abd El Schafi, *Behind the Veil*, p. 139.

henceforth lived under Shari'a, forming what Bat Ye'or calls the civilization of *dhimmitude*.[25] They endured for centuries the lives of quiet desperation interrupted by the regular pangs of acute agony. In all these societies the dynamics of Islamization were at work, different in form perhaps, between Spain and Syria, but always following the same pattern determined by the ideology and laws of jihad and Shari'a. The objective in all cases, and the outcome in most, was also the same: to transform native Christian majorities into religious minorities. The initial choice of the vanquished was not "Islam or death" but "Islam or super-tax;" but over time Shari'a ensured the decline of Eastern Christianity, the sapping of the captives' vitality and capacity for renewal.

The same dynamic applied to that jewel of supposed Islamic tolerance, Muslim Spain. Abd-er-Rahman III became sultan in 912, and in 929 he assumed the title of caliph. He reunited Moorish Spain and carried war to the Christian "barbarians." In 920 he put the garrison of Muez to the sword, and in 923 he entered Pamplona and destroyed its cathedral. Elsewhere cities that offered armed resistance "were subjected to the full rigor of Islamic custom, summary execution of all adult males, and the enslavement of women and children," the fate of Cordova, Zaragoza, and Merida.[26] Whenever the rigor of the Muslim rule slackened, the traditionalists strove to put it right. The religious opposition to the less intolerant Islam of the Almoravids gave rise to the Almohads, who gained control over all of the Maghrib for the only time in its history. They also controlled Muslim Spain. Their rule was marked by merciless religious persecution: Jews and Christians were compelled to convert or leave, and no suspect Muslim was safe:

> My heart is in the east, and I in the uttermost west—
> How can I find savor in food? How shall it be sweet to me?
> How shall I render my vows and my bonds, while yet
> Zion lieth beneath the fetter of Edom, and I in Arab chains?
> A light thing would it seem to me to leave all the good things of
> Spain—

---

[25] Bath Ye'or, *The Decline of Eastern Christianity under Islam*, op.cit.
[26] R.Fletcher, *Moorish Spain,* Weidenfeld & Nicolson, 1992.

Seeing how precious in mine eyes to behold the dust of the desolate sanctuary.[27]

Moorish Spain was not a tolerant and enlightened society even in its most cultivated epoch. There was beauty, but little tolerance. The Jews of Granada were butchered in 1066, the Christians were deported to Morocco in 1126. Learning did exist, but it was restricted to a small elite that was constantly at risk from persecution. In Moorish Spain, oppression or anarchy were the rule, good order and civilized behavior a fondly remembered exception.[28]

CONQUEST OF INDIA

On the eastern front, China's T'ang dynasty saw off the Muslim armies as smartly as Charles Martel. But India fell. Muslim invaders began entering India in the early eighth century, on the orders of Hajjaj, the governor of Iraq. Starting in 712 the raiders, commanded by Muhammad Qasim, demolished temples, shattered sculptures, plundered palaces, killed vast numbers of men—it took them three days to slaughter the inhabitants of the port city of Debal—and carried off their women and children to slavery. After the initial wave of violence, however, Qasim tried to establish law and order in the newly conquered lands, and to that end he even allowed a degree of religious tolerance. Upon hearing of such practices, his superior, Hajjaj, wrote back:

> It appears from your letter that all the rules made by you for the comfort and convenience of your men are strictly in accordance with religious law. But the way of granting pardon prescribed by the law is different from the one adopted by you, for you go on giving pardon to everybody, high or low, without any discretion between a friend and a foe. The great God says in the Kuran [47.4]: "O True believers, when you encounter the unbelievers, strike off their heads." The above command of the Great God is a great command and must be respected and followed. You should not be so fond of showing mercy, as to nullify the virtue of the

---

[27] Yehuda Halevi, *1141* (translated from the Hebrew by Nina Salaman, 1924).
[28] R. Fletcher, *Moorish Spain,* Weidenfeld & Nicolson, 1992.

act. Henceforth, grant pardon to no one of the enemy and spare none of them, or else all will consider you a weak-minded man.[29]

In a subsequent communication, Hajjaj reiterated that all able-bodied men were to be killed, and that their underage sons and daughters were to be imprisoned and retained as hostages. Qasim obeyed, and, on his arrival at the town of Brahminabad, massacred between 6,000 and 16,000 men.

Until that time India was one of the world's great civilizations. Tenth century Hindustan matched its contemporaries in the East and the West in the realms of speculative philosophy, mathematics, and natural science. Medieval India, until the Islamic invasion, was a richly imaginative culture, one of the six or seven most advanced civilizations of all times. Its sculptures were vigorous and sensual, its architecture ornate and spellbinding.

Qasim's early exploits were continued in the early eleventh century, when Mahmud of Ghazni "passed through India like a whirlwind, destroying, pillaging, and massacring," zealously following the Kuranic injunctions to kill idolaters, whom he had vowed to chastise every year of his life:

In the course of seventeen invasions, in the words of Alberuni, the scholar brought by Mahmud to India, "Mahmud utterly ruined the prosperity of the country and performed there wonderful exploits, by which the Hindus became like atoms of dust scattered in all directions, and like a tale of old in the mouth of the people. Their scattered remains cherish, of course, the most inveterate aversion toward all Muslims." . . . Mathura, the holy city of Krishna, was the next victim. "In the middle of the city there was a temple larger and finer than the rest, which can neither be described nor painted." The Sultan [Mahmud] was of the opinion that 200 years would have been required to build it. The idols included "five of red gold, each five yards high," with eyes formed of priceless jewels. "The Sultan gave orders that all the temples should be burnt with naphtha and fire, and leveled with the ground."[30]

---

[29] Quoted by Ibn Warraq, 1995, pp. 220–221.
[30] Ibid, p. 211.

In the aftermath of the invasion, in the ancient cities of Varanasi, Mathura, Ujjain, Maheshwar, Jwalamukhi, and Dwarka, not one temple survived whole and intact. In his *The Story of Civilization,* Will Durant lamented the results of what he termed "probably the bloodiest story in history." He called it "a discouraging tale, for its evident moral is that civilization is a precious good, whose delicate complex order and freedom can at any moment be overthrown by barbarians invading from without and multiplying from within." The bitter lesson, Durant concluded, was that "eternal vigilance is the price of civilization. A nation must love peace, but keep its powder dry."

Islamic invaders "broke and burned everything beautiful they came across in Hindustan," displaying, as an Indian commentator put it, the resentment of the less developed warriors who felt intimidated in the encounter with "a more refined culture."[31] The Muslim sultans built mosques at the sites of torn down temples, and many Hindus were sold into slavery. As far as the invaders were concerned, Hindus are kafirs par excellence. They, and to a lesser extent the peaceful Buddhists, were not "of the book" but at the receiving end of Muhammad's injunction against pagans: "Kill those who join other gods with God wherever you may find them."[32]

The mountainous northwestern approaches to India are called Hindu Kush, "the Slaughter of the Hindu," a reminder of the days when Hindu slaves from Indian Subcontinent died in the harsh Afghan mountains while being transported to Muslim courts of Central Asia. The slaughter in Somnath, the site of a celebrated Hindu temple, where 50,000 Hindus were slain on Mahmud's orders, set the tone for centuries.

The Buddhists were the next to be subjected to mass slaughter in 1193, when Muhammad Khilji also burned their famous library. By the end of the twelfth century, following the Muslim conquest of their stronghold in Bihar, they were no longer a significant presence in India. The survivors retreated into Nepal and Tibet, or escaped to the south of the Subcontinent. The remnants of their culture lingered on even as far west as Turkestan. Left to the tender mercies of Muslim conquerors and their heirs, they were systematically destroyed, sometimes—as was the case with the four giant

---

[31] Rizwan Salim, "What the invaders really did," *Hindustan Times*, December 28, 1997.

[32] 9:5–6.

111

statues of Buddha destroyed by the Taliban in Afghanistan in March 2001—as late as the first year of the third millennium.

That cultivated disposition and developed sensibility can go hand in hand with bigotry and cruelty is evidenced by the example of Firuz Shah, who became the ruler of northern India in 1351. This educated yet tyrannical Muslim ruler once surprised a village where a Hindu religious festival was celebrated and ordered all present to be slain. He proudly related that, upon completing the slaughter, he destroyed the temples and in their place built mosques.

The Moghul emperor Akbar is remembered as tolerant, and only one major massacre was recorded during his long reign (1542–1605), when he ordered that about 30,000 captured Rajput Hindus be slain on February 24, 1568, after the battle for Chitod. But Akbar's acceptance of other religions and toleration of their public worship, his abolition of poll-tax on non-Muslims, and his interest in other faiths were not a reflection of his Islamic spirit of tolerance. Quite the contrary, they indicated his propensity for free-thinking experimentation in the realm of religion that finally led him to complete apostasy. Its high points were the formal declaration of his own infallibility in all matters of religious doctrine, his promulgation of a new creed, and his adoption of Hindu and Zoroastrian festivals and practices.

Things were back to normal under Shah Jahan (1593–1666), the fifth Mogul Emperor and a grandson of Akbar the Great. Most Westerners remember him as the builder of Taj Mahal and do not know that he was a cruel warmonger who initiated 48 military campaigns against non-Muslims in less than 30 years. Taking his cue from his Ottoman co-religionists, on coming to the throne in 1628 he killed all his male relations except one who escaped to Persia. Shah Jahan had 5,000 concubines in his harem, but nevertheless indulged in incestuous sex with his daughters Chamani and Jahanara. During his reign, in Benares alone 76 Hindu temples were destroyed, and Christian churches at Agra and Lahore were demolished. At the end of the three-month siege of Hugh, a Portuguese enclave near Calcutta, he had 10,000 inhabitants "blown up with powder, drowned in water, or burnt by fire." More than 4,000 were taken captive to Agra where they were offered Islam or death. Most refused and were killed, except for the younger women who went to harems.

The massacres perpetrated by Muslims in India are unparalleled in history, bigger in sheer numbers than the Holocaust, or the massacre of the

Armenians by the Turks; more extensive even than the slaughter of the South American native populations by the invading Spanish and Portuguese. They are insufficiently known in the outside world, however:

> The British, in pursuing their policy of divide-and-rule, colluded to whitewash the atrocious record of the Muslims so that they could set up the Muslims as a strategic counterbalance to the Hindus. During the freedom struggle, Gandhi and Nehru went around encrusting even thicker coats of whitewash so that they could pretend a facade of Hindu-Muslim unity against British colonial rule. After independence, Marxist Indian writers, blinkered by their distorting ideology, repeated the big lie about the Muslim record.[33]

Militant Islam sees India as "unfinished business," and it remains high on the agenda of oil-rich Muslim countries such as Saudi Arabia, which are spending millions every year trying to convert Hindus to Islam.

OTTOMAN NIGHTMARE

With the fall of Baghdad to the Tatars it seemed that the end of Islam was nigh, but a sturdy race of converted barbarians would save the day. Arab historian Ibn Khaldoun hailed the rise of the Ottomans, and the institution of slavery by which they came, as the manifestation of Allah's mercy "when the Abbasid state was drowned in decadence and luxury" and overthrown by the heathen Tatars "because the people of the faith had become deficient in energy and reluctant to rally in defense." At that moment Allah "rescued the faith by reviving its dying breath and restoring the unity of the Muslims in the Egyptian realms":

> He did this by sending to the Muslims, from among this Turkish nation and its great and numerous tribes, rulers to defend them and utterly loyal helpers, who were brought . . . to the House of Islam under the rule of slavery, which hides in itself a divine blessing. By means of slavery they learn glory and blessing and are exposed to divine providence; cured by slavery, they enter the

---

[33] Francois Gautier, *Rewriting Indian History*, New Delhi, Vikas Publishing, 1996.

Muslim religion with the firm resolve of true believers and yet with nomadic virtues unsullied by debased nature, unadulterated by the filth of pleasure, undefiled by ways of civilized living, and with their ardor unbroken by the profusion of luxury.

Thus the Ottoman Empire became the standard bearer of Islam: "one intake comes after another and generation follows generation, and Islam rejoices in the benefit which it gains through them, and the branches of the kingdom flourish with the freshness of youth." The bearers of the standard came to Anatolia at the turn of the second millennium as mercenary soldiers. Osman I, from whom the name *Osmanli* ("Ottoman") is derived, proclaimed the independence of his small principality in Sogut near Bursa, on the border of the declining Byzantine Empire, in the early thirteenth century, and attracted other tribal leaders to his banner. Within a century, the Osman Dynasty had extended its domains into an empire stretching from the Balkans to Mesopotamia. Its growth was briefly disrupted by the Tatar invasion and Sultan Bayezit's defeat at the Battle of Ankara (1402).

Under Mehmet I "the Restorer," the Turks were back in business and conquered a ruined and impoverished Constantinople under Mehmet II in 1453. For three days the conquerors indulged in murder, rape, and pillage. The survivors were enslaved, and the Ottoman Empire thus succeeded the Byzantine Empire. Some decades later it also succeeded the Arab Caliphate, the mantle of descent from Muhammad, after the conquest of Egypt (1517).

Islam may have rejoiced, but there was precious little cause for rejoicing in Asia Minor and in the Balkans as further Christian communities came under Muslim rule. At first, the expanding Ottoman Empire, like the expanding Arab Empire of earlier times, enhanced "the rule of slavery" by conquest and capture, and great numbers of Balkan Christians were enslaved in the early onslaught. The conquered populations were subsequently subjected to the practice of *devshirme*.

The annual "blood levy" of Christian boys in peacetime was a novelty even by the Arabian standards. In Arabia those families unable to pay the crushing jizya were obliged to hand over their children to be sold into slavery, and to deduct their value from their assessment. But Turkish "devshirme," introduced by Sultan Orkhan (1326–1359), consisted of the periodic taking of a fifth of all Christian boys in the conquered territories:

114

On a fixed date, all the fathers were ordered to appear with their children in the public square. The recruiting agents chose the most sturdy and handsome children in the presence of a Muslim judge. Any father who shirked his duty to provide children was severely punished. This system was open to all kinds of abuse. The recruiting agents often took more than the prescribed number of children and sold the "surplus" children back to their parents. Those unable to buy back their children had to accept their being sold into slavery. . . . The devshirme is an obvious infringement of the rights of the dhimmis—a reminder that their rights were far from secure, once and for all.[34]

One November morning in 1516, in a memorable literary account, one such boy, an Orthodox Serb of nine, was snatched from his mother from the village of Sokolovici, near the Bosnian town of Visegrad:

In time he became a young and brave officer at the Sultan's court, then the Great Admiral of the Fleet, then the Sultan's son-in-law, a general and statesman of world renown, Mehmed Pasha Sokollu, who waged wars that were for the most part victorious on three continents and extended the frontiers of the Ottoman Empire, making it safe abroad and by good administration consolidated it from within. For these sixty odd years he served three Sultans, experienced both good and evil as only rare and chosen persons may experience them, and raised himself to heights of power and authority unknown to us, which few men reach and fewer men keep. This new man that he had become in a foreign world where we could not follow even in our thoughts must have forgotten all that he had left behind in the country whence they had once brought him. He surely forgot too the crossing of the Drina at Visegrad, the bare banks on which travelers shivered with cold and uncertainty, the slow and worm-eaten ferry, the strange ferryman, and the hungry ravens above the troubled waters. But that feeling of anxious discomfort which had remained in him never completely disappeared.[35]

---

[34] Ibn Warraq, op. cit., 1995, p. 231.
[35] Ivo Andric, *The Bridge on the Drina*.

For about three centuries starting in 1350, military expeditions made forays into Christian villages to kidnap boys for training as janissaries. Contrary to previous Islamic law and practice, enslavement of the subject peoples was thus legitimized even if they did not rebel against their conquerors.

The "blood levy" was the most hated of all taxes by far, and it necessitated deliberate mutilation of many healthy Christian boys by their parents to render them safe from capture. The practice left a deep scar on the collective memory of the Balkan Christians, notably Serbs and Bulgarians, and contributed to their thorough loathing of all things Turkish that persists to this day. And yet contemporary Turkish propagandists present the tragedy of the kidnapped boys and their families as the Ottoman equivalent of a full scholarship to Harvard or Yale: "From the poor families' point of view, it was a great chance for their sons to be offered a high level of education, especially in the palace which would provide good future prospects."[36]

The materially and culturally rich Christian civilization of Byzantium and its dynamic and creative Slavic offspring in Serbia and Bulgaria were destroyed. The coarse descendants of Turkoman nomads thus enjoyed the fruits of the Western Christian infamy of 1204 (when Constantinople was sacked by the Franks and other Western "Christians"), which paved the way for May 29, 1453, when the city and remaining empire fell to the Muslims. Before that awful day, some Byzantines had pronounced, still feeling the Fourth Crusade's sting, that they "would rather see the Muslim turban in the midst of the city than the Latin miter." As despicable as the Great Betrayal of 1204 was, the Byzantine Greeks soon found out that evil was outdone by a greater evil.

Once the emperor and his badly outnumbered soldiers were slain on the walls of Constantinople, bands of Turks went on a rampage. Pillaging and killing went on for three days. Thousands of civilians were enslaved, soldiers fought over boys and young women. The blood ran in rivers down the steep streets from the heights of Petra toward the Golden Horn. All the treasures of the Imperial Palace were carried off. Books and icons were burnt once the jeweled covers and frames had been wrenched off. In the monastery of the Holy Savior, the invaders first destroyed the icon of the

---

[36] www.turkishodyssey.com/turkey/history/history3.htm.

Mother of God, the Hodigitria, the holiest icon in all Byzantium, painted—so men said—by Saint Luke himself. When the Turks burst into the Hagia Sophia,

> The worshippers were trapped. A few of the ancient and infirm were killed on the spot; but most of them were tied or chained together. Many of the lovelier maidens and youths and many of the richer-clad nobles were almost torn to death as their captors quarreled over them. The priests went on chanting at the altar till they too were taken. . . . The inhabitants were carried off along with their possessions. Anyone who collapsed from frailty was slaughtered, together with a number of infants who were held to be of no value. . . . [Byzantium] was now half in ruins, emptied and deserted and blackened as though by fire, and strangely silent. Wherever the soldiers had been there was desolation. Churches had been desecrated and stripped; houses were no longer habitable and shops and stores battered and bare. The Sultan himself as he rode through the streets had been moved to tears.[37]

The difference between the Crusaders' senseless debauchery and the Turks' calculated barbarism is visible in the treatment of both subjects by a great painter. While acknowledging the shame of the "Entry of the Crusaders into Constantinople," through his 1840 painting of the same name, it was Eugene Delacroix's depiction of a Turkish monstrosity that became the Guernica of the nineteenth century. "The Massacre at Chios: Greek families awaiting death or slavery" is a masterpiece of horror depicting the systematic extermination of the entire population of an Aegean island, graphically illustrated how being a Greek, Armenian, Serb, or indeed any other Christian in the Ottoman Empire meant living in daily fear of murder, rape, torture, kidnap of one's children, slavery, and genocide.

In the end, to an enslaved Eastern Christian the "Frank" was remembered as a treacherous cousin; the Turk was the irreconcilable enemy:

---

[37] Sir Steven Runciman, *The Fall of Constantinople, 1453*, Cambridge University Press, 1969.

They took the City, they took her: they took Thessalonica:
They took even Saint Sophia, they took the great monastery,
which had three hundred semantra and seventy-two bells:
Every bell had a priest, and every priest a deacon.
In the Great Church where the holy gifts were revealed, the King of all,
there came to them a voice from heaven, from the mouth of the angels:
"Leave off your psalter, put away the holy gifts.
Send word to the land of the Franks to come and take them:
Let them come and take the golden cross and the holy gospel,
and the holy table, lest it be profaned."
And when Our Lady heard this, the icons wept:
"Be still, dear Mistress, do not weep, do not cry:
Again with the years, with time, again this place will be yours."[38]

The Ottoman zenith was reached in the sixteenth century, when the Turks controlled Egypt, Syria, Mesopotamia, the Arabian Peninsula, held Persia at bay, and pushed into central Europe after defeating the Hungarians at Mohacs. The decline of the empire began late in that century. It was rapid, and visible in the corruption and degeneracy of the sultans and of their ruling class. Following the downfall of Grand Vizier Mehmed Sokolu, the influence of the favored women of the harem over Sultan Murad III was inordinate. When he died in 1595, his son Muhammad had his 19 brothers murdered to prevent them from usurping his throne, and seven of his father's pregnant concubines were sewn into sacks and thrown into the Marmara. He did not kill his many nephews but kept them under arrest in the *Kafes,* the "Cage" of the Seraglio, where they vegetated in constant dread of their lives and learned nothing of the art of governance.

In the next century, on the death of Murad IV, the throne came to Ibrahim, who had not stepped out of the "Cage" since the age of two. Depraved cruelty of the Ottoman Empire peaked with this monster who executed his grand vizier who dared mutter some remarks about his

---

[38] Quoted by Fr. Hugh Barbour, O. Praem. in his paper "A Latin's Lamentation Over Gennadios Scholarios" at The Lord Byron Foundation's conference "Overcoming the Schism," Chicago, May 9, 1998.

excesses, and in anger threw his baby son into a cistern. One morning after a debauch, feeling jaded with his harem, Ibrahim had all three hundred women put into sacks and thrown into the Bosphorus. Only one survived by being picked up by a ship bound for France. Even when he was finally strangled, the devshirme class was split into many political parties and fought for power, manipulated sultans, and used the government for their own benefit. Corruption, nepotism, inefficiency, and misrule spread.

The Ottoman Empire from time to time shrewdly applied limited toleration of select minorities. The act that resonates with modern Turkish propaganda was the invitation to the Jews of Spain to resettle in its lands after expulsion, some of them in Sarajevo. But the status of Jews and Christians, nominally regulated through the *Millet* system, deteriorated with the gradual decline and ultimate degeneration of the Ottoman Empire. In reality, even the Jews of Europe, discriminated against, harassed, and persecuted in the Roman Catholic lands, had not nearly experienced the type of nightmarish cruelty and carnage Ottoman Christians endured for five centuries. As for the Jews expelled from Spain, they were invited by the Sultan not because of any motivations involving tolerance, but to replace the vast swathes of Christians that had been eliminated, and thus to maintain the area's commerce and the Sultan's tax base. While the Ottoman Jews were also subjected to discrimination and periods of cruel persecution, the fact that they held a favored status within the Empire over the subhuman *giaours* (infidel Christian dogs) is as much a reason for celebration of the Ottomans' "tolerance" as the fact that the Nazis were "tolerant" of occupied Slavs in comparison to their treatment of the Jews.

As Turkey declined, its provincial governors and warlords—often, though not always, local converts to Islam with a suppressed guilty grudge against their former co-religionists—grew stronger, and increasingly asserted rebellious independence. Notably in the Balkans, it was demonstrated in far harsher treatment of their Christian subjects than was either mandated or normally practiced from the Bosphorus.

Early in the nineteenth century, Napoleon conquered Egypt and briefly controlled it. This proved to be a blessing in disguise, for it forced the moribund Ottomans to face reality while helping open up Egypt to contact with the West, especially through the introduction of printing and modern education to the Arab world. Sultan Selim III (reigned 1789–1807) attempted to reform the Ottoman system by destroying the Janissary corps and replacing it with the *Nizam-i Cedit* (new order) army modeled after the new military institutions being developed in the West. This attempt so angered the Janissaries and others with a vested interest in the old ways that they overthrew him and massacred most of the reform leaders.

Defeats at the hands of Russia and Austria, the success of national revolutions in Serbia and Greece, and the rise of the powerful independent Ottoman governor of Egypt Mohammed Ali so discredited the Janissaries, however, that Sultan Mahmut II was able to massacre and destroy them in 1826. He inaugurated reforms, which continued during the *Tanzimat* reform era (1839–1876) and the reign of Abdulhamit II (1876–1909). "Westernization" of state institutions was accompanied by an escalating oppression of the Christians.

The weakening of Turkey enabled ascendant European powers first to take an interest in the destiny of the remaining Christian communities under Muslim rule, and next to try and alleviate their condition. The effort was conducted through bilateral agreements between the Ottomans and the victorious European powers (Russia and Austria), or voluntary contacts with the friendly ones (Britain and France). Some improvement resulted in the granting of a Western-style constitution in 1839, which eventually led to the abolishment of the old Millet system and, at least, nominal equalization of rights between the three main religious communities. In part, these reforms were defensive in nature, as the Turkish government hoped to placate the Europeans and, by enacting desired legislation, remove the grounds for interference.

They did not have much effect on the ground, however. Indeed, the last century of Ottoman rule—from the defeat of Napoleon until the dissolution of the Ottoman Empire at the end of the First World War—witnessed a more thorough and tragic destruction of the Christian communities in the Middle East, Asia Minor, the Caucasus, and the Balkans, than at any prior period. Almost the entire Greek population of the island of Chios, tens of thousands of people, was massacred or enslaved in 1822 (as we have seen in reference to Delacroix). The following year, the number of victims of the slaughter at Missolongi is known precisely: 8,750. Thousands of Assyrians were murdered in the province of Mossul in 1850, and in 1860 some 12,000 Christians were put to the sword in Lebanon. The butchery of 14,700 Bulgarians in 1876 was almost routine by Turkish standards. At the town of Batal, 5,000 out of 7,000 inhabitants were

120

murdered, the fact that was unsuccessfully suppressed by the British government of Prime Minister Benjamin Disraeli, but nevertheless made public by journalists.[39]

In many cases, the massacres of Christians resulted from local Muslim revolts against any decree granting them greater rights than those that were regarded as divinely ordained by Caliph Umar. At the same time, the great Western powers—the heirs of those who had looted Constantinople in the Crusades and refused to help when the Turks were breaking through the walls with a cannon built by an Hungarian Catholic, who forced the last emperors to foreswear their Orthodox faith at the Council of Florence as the price of Western help that never came—those same Western powers, and Great Britain in particular, actually supported the Turkish subjugation of Christian Europeans on the grounds that the Mohammedan empire was a "stabilizing force" and a counterweight against Austria and Russia. The scandalous alliance with Turkey against Russia in the Crimean War reflected a pernicious frame of mind that has manifested itself more recently in the overt, covert, or *de facto* support of certain Western powers for the Muslim side in Bosnia, Kosovo, Macedonia, Chechnya, Cyprus, Sudan, East Timor, and Kashmir.

From the dozens of anti-Christian pogroms in the nineteenth century, the "Bulgarian Atrocities" are remembered because they provoked a cry of indignation from Gladstone (to the chagrin of Disraeli), who asserted, "No government ever has so sinned, none has proved itself so incorrigible in sin, or which is the same, so impotent in reformation." But Gladstone's opponents, the advocates of Turkophile policy at Westminster, went beyond *Realpolitik* in arguing for the lifeline to the Sick Man of the Bosphorus: they devised the theory that the Ottomans were in reality agreeable and tolerant, and only needed a friendly, supportive nudge to become just, or almost, like other civilized people:

> If, in the more remote past, Bourbon France had made common cause with the Sublime Porte (the scandalous *Union of the Lily and the Crescent*) against Habsburg Austria, the arrangement at least had the virtue of cynical self-interest: Catholic France was hardly expected to praise the sultan's benevolence as part of the

---

[39] William Stearns Davis, *A Short History of the Near East* (quoted in Horton, op. cit.).

bargain. But by the 1870s, Disraeli's obsession with thwarting Russian ambitions in the Balkans prompted the Tories' unprecedented depiction of Turkey as tolerant and humane, even in the face of the Bulgarian atrocities. Even so, Britain's Christian conscience, prodded by Gladstone's passionate words, was sufficient to bring down Lord Beaconsfield's government in 1880.[40]

(When it was all over, speaking of Disraeli, Gladstone wrote to the Duke of Argyle: "He is not such a Turk as I thought. What he hates is Christian liberty and reconstruction." 125 years later, the problem of Islamophilia in the West is not love of "the Turk" but hatred of the West.)

In a speech at Blackheath in 1876, Gladstone told the Ottomans: "You shall retain your titular sovereignty, your empire shall not be invaded, but never again, as the years roll in their course, so far as it is in our power to determine, never again shall the hand of violence be raised by you, never again shall the flood gates of lust be opened to you."

This was not to be. Regular slaughters of Armenians in Bayazid (1877), Alashgurd (1879), Sassun (1894), Constantinople (1896), Adana (1909) and Armenia itself (1895–1896) claimed a total of 200,000, but they were only rehearsals for the horrors of 1915. In the awful annals of the twentieth century, two instances of genocide stand out. One of them, the Jewish Holocaust of 1942–1945, has spawned an enormous amount of literature. The other, the Turkish massacre of Armenians in 1915, has been virtually ignored by everyone except the Armenians themselves. The irony is that their fate was almost a prototype of the mass murder of Jews in Europe. *"Who remembers the [extermination of the] Armenians?"* Hitler asked those members of his inner circle who feared that Germany's reputation would suffer because of its persecution of the Jews. Along the route to Adana and beyond, Turkish women were given the dagger *(hanjar)* to give the final stab to dying Armenians in order to gain credit in the eyes of Allah as having killed a Christian.[41] Survivors of the massacre ended up scattered throughout the Middle East and in other parts of the world.

---

[40] James Jatras, "Insurgent Islam and American Colaboration," *Chronicles: A Magazine of American Culture*, February 1999.

[41] Michael J. Arlen, *Passage to Ararat,* Ballantine Books, 1975.

Further south, the slaughter of Christians in Alexandria in 1881 was only a rehearsal for the artificial famine induced by the Turks in 1915–1916 that killed over 100,000 Maronite Christians in Lebanon and Syria. So imminent and ever-present was the peril, and so fresh the memory of these events in the minds of the non-Muslims, that illiterate Christian mothers dated events as so many years before or after "such and such a massacre."[42] Across the Middle East, the bloodshed of 1915–1922 finally destroyed ancient Christian communities and cultures that had survived since Roman times—groups like the Jacobites, Nestorians, and Chaldaeans. The carnage peaked after World War I ended.

DUSK OF LEVANTINE CHRISTIANITY

The tragedy of Christian communities under Turkish rule, as Gladstone saw it, was not "a question of Mohammedanism simply, but of Mohammedanism compounded with the peculiar character of a race":

They were, upon the whole, from the black day when they first entered Europe, the one great anti-human specimen of humanity. Wherever they went, a broad line of blood marked the track behind them, and, as far as their dominion reached, civilization disappeared from view. They represented everywhere government by force as opposed to government by law. Yet a government by force cannot be maintained without the aid of an intellectual element. Hence there grew up, what has been rare in the history of the world, a kind of tolerance in the midst of cruelty, tyranny, and rapine. Much of Christian life was contemptuously left alone, and a race of Greeks was attracted to Constantinople which has all along made up, in some degree, the deficiencies of Turkish Islam in the element of mind.[43]

"The attitude of the Muslims toward the Christians and the Jews is that of a master toward slaves," reported the British Vice Consul in Mosul, 1909, "whom he treats with a certain lordly tolerance so long as they keep

---

[42] George Horton, *The Blight of Asia,* Indianapolis, 1926.
[43] Quoted on Turkish Foreign Ministry web site: www.mfa.gov.tr/grupe/eg/eg06/09.htm.

their place. Any sign of pretension to equality is promptly repressed." It is ironic but unsurprising that the persecution of Christians culminated in their final expulsion from the newly founded Republic of Turkey in the early 1920s under Mustafa Kemal known as Ataturk, the same man who also abolished the caliphate and separated the mosque and state. The fact that this ethnic cleansing was carried out under the banner of resurgent Turkish nationalism, rather than Ottoman imperialism or Islamic intolerance, mattered but little to the victims. The end result was the same: churches demolished or converted into mosques, and communities that used to worship in them dispersed or dead.

The burning of Smyrna and the massacre and scattering of its 300,000 Christian inhabitants is one of the great crimes of all times. It marked the end of the Greek civilization in Asia Minor, which at its height had also given the world the immortal cities of Pergamus, Philadelphia, and Ephesus. On the eve of its destruction, Smyrna was a bustling port and commercial center. The seafront promenade, next to foreign consulates, boasted hotels modeled after Nice and elegant cafes. Yellowing postcards show its main business thoroughfare, the *Rue Franque,* with the great department and wholesale stores, crowded by the ladies in costumes of the latest fashion. The American consul-general remembered a busy social life that included teas, dances, musical afternoons, games of tennis and bridge, and soirées given in the salons of the rich Armenians and Greeks: "In no city in the world did East and West mingle physically in so spectacular a manner as at Smyrna, while spiritually they always maintained the characteristics of oil and water."[44]

Sporadic killings of Christians, mostly Armenians, started immediately after the Turks conquered it on September 9, 1922, and within days escalated to mass slaughter. It did not "get out of hand," however; the Turkish military authorities deliberately escalated it. Greek Orthodox Metropolitan Chrysostomos remained with his flock. "It is the tradition of the Greek Church and the duty of the priest to stay with his congregation," he replied to those begging him to flee. The Muslim mob fell upon him, uprooted his eyes and, as he was bleeding, dragged him by his beard through the streets of the Turkish quarter, beating and kicking him. Every now and then, when he had the strength to do so, he would raise his right

---

[44] Ibid.

hand and bless his persecutors, repeating, "Father, forgive them." A Turk got so furious at this gesture that he cut off the Metropolitan's hand with his sword. He fell to the ground and was hacked to pieces by the angry mob.

The carnage culminated in the burning of Smyrna, which started on September 13, when the Turks put the Armenian quarter to torch, and the conflagration engulfed the city. The remaining inhabitants were trapped at the seafront, from which there was no escaping the flames on one side, or Turkish bayonets on the other: "At the destruction of Smyrna there was one feature for which Carthage presents no parallel. There was no fleet of Christian battleships at Carthage looking on at a situation for which their governments were responsible."[45] English, American, Italian, and French ships were indeed anchored in Smyrna's harbor. Ordered to maintain neutrality, they would or could do nothing for the 200,000 desperate Christians on the quay:

> The pitiful throng—huddled together, sometimes screaming for help but mostly waiting in a silent panic beyond hope—didn't budge for days. Typhoid reduced their numbers, and there was no way to dispose of the dead. Occasionally, a person would swim from the dock to one of the anchored ships and tried to climb the ropes and chains, only to be driven off. On the American battleships, the musicians on board were ordered to play as loudly as they could to drown out the screams of the pleading swimmers. The English poured boiling water down on the unfortunates who reached their vessel. The harbor was so clogged with corpses that the officers of the foreign battleships were often late to their dinner appointments because bodies would get tangled in the propellers of their launches. . . . A cluster of women's heads bound together like coconuts by their long hair floated down a river toward the harbor.[46]

That was the end of Christianity in Asia Minor. Elsewhere in the Muslim world following the end of World War I, and notably in the newly independent or semi-dependent Arab states, European presence meant that

---

[45] Ibid.
[46] Nicholas Gage, *Greek Fire*, Alfred A. Knopf, 2000.

it was no longer possible to enforce more drastic forms of discriminatory practices against the surviving Christian population. But this was merely a temporary improvement, not a permanent solution of their position:

> But at the very time that Europe achieved its military and geopolitical advantage, the moral and religious decline that culminated in the autogenocides of 1914 and 1939 had become evident. Having found in their grasp places their Crusader predecessors had only dreamed of reclaiming: Jerusalem, Bethlehem, Antioch, Alexandria, Constantinople—effete and demoralized European governments made no effort to re-christianize them and, within a few decades, meekly abandoned them. The moral disarmament of contemporary post-Christian Europe is now nearly universal. After World War I, with the installation of nominally "pro-Western" governments in many Muslim countries fashioned from the wreckage of the Ottoman Empire, the West seems to have convinced itself of the existence of benign Islam.[47]

Even without being fully or permanently liberated, for the first time in more than a millennium, the representatives of Christian communities in Lebanon and Egypt were allowed to participate in the government, Christian churches were again freely built, and the notion of jizya disappeared from political discourse. One notable exception, even in the period of Western domination between two world wars, was Saudi Arabia, which remains to this day a fortress of stern Wahabbism, as determined to convert the Western world to Islam as it is to decapitate any one of its own subjects who violates the tenets of the Faith.

The pendulum has swung back in recent decades. The perceived slight of infidel presence and direct or indirect dominance in the Arab world has also resulted in the backlash in the form of Islamic religious revival. Notably in the aftermath of the Arab defeats by Israel of 1967 and 1973, Christians were subjected to new restrictions. In Egypt, the construction of new churches was obstructed, a quota system was instituted regarding university admissions, Christians were barred from high government

---

[47] Jatras, *Chronicles,* 1999, op. cit.

126

positions, and they were even accused of complicity with Zionism on the grounds of conciliatory statements from the Vatican about the Jews.

The process of Islamic resurgence reached a new peak in 1979 with the fall of the Shah and the Islamic revolution in Iran. It is notable that only religious communities predating the arrival of Islam in Persia are tolerated, while the later ones, such as Bahais, are regarded as apostates subject to death penalty. As late as 1955, Istanbul's Christians suffered what William Dalrymple called "the worst race riot in Europe since *Kristallnacht.*" Following the last pogrom, the Christians have retained only nominal presence in Turkey, completely contingent on the good will of the government in Ankara. Further east, in Asia Minor and the Lepanto, some Christian communities survived, but their numbers are a pale shadow of what they were only two centuries ago. Entire peoples have been obliterated since that time.

What has happened to the Christian majorities in the Middle East, North Africa, Bosnia, and Kosovo, has happened to the Hindus in the Subcontinent. In 1941, in what would become Pakistan, there were approximately 25 percent Hindus, and 30 percent in what would later become Bangladesh; in 1948, only 17 percent in Pakistan and 25 percent in Bangladesh; in 1991, a bare 1.5 percent remained in Pakistan and less than 10 percent in Bangladesh.

It is remarkable that in this age of rampant victimology, the persecution of Christians by Muslims has become a taboo subject in the Western academy. A complex web of myths, outright lies, and deliberately imposed silence dominates it. Thirteen centuries of religious discrimination, causing suffering and death of countless millions, have been covered by the myth of Islamic "tolerance" that is as hurtful to the few descendants of the victims as it is useless as a means of appeasing latter-day jihadists. The silence and lies, perpetrated by the Western academy and media class, facilitates the perpetuation of religious discrimination and persecution even today.

We are, nevertheless, often told by contemporary apologists for Islam that the usual *modus operandi* of the early Muslims—attacking other people's lands, pillaging, raping, robbing, and extorting—should be judged in its "context," that this was normal behavior at the time. The same understanding, however, is not extended towards those Europeans—often coarse and decidedly unpleasant characters that joined the Crusades—who

127

attempted to turn the tables and take the battle back into the enemy camp, and whose actions those same Western friends of Islam so sternly condemn.[48] The emerging sense from the language is that the militant expansion of the Muslims was appropriate and understandable, but defeats that were inflicted on them by their rivals were not, and the truth about the life of non-Muslims under Islam remains censored:

> Why do we never hear about such things? Do not expect them to form the subject of any future PBS documentary, with a title like "Empire of Blood" or "Forgotten Holocaust." Such programs are about as improbable as studies publicizing the millennium-long Muslim hegemony over the African slave trade. The story of the non-Muslims' experiences under Islamic rule is as politically incorrect to tell, and therefore as little known in today's America, as the remarkable life of Muhammad himself.[49]

We don't hear about them because the upholders of the myth of Islamic tolerance are secular Western freethinkers who hate persecution and discrimination—sexual, racial, religious, or any other—with one exception: when Christians are the victims. Recent attempts by some apologists for Islam in the West—notably a British journalist by the name of Noel Malcolm—to present the sordid *casino* of Ottoman overlordship in southeast Europe as "tolerant," or even enlightened, are as intellectually dishonest as they are factually insupportable. At no time was the arrangement concerning "the people of the book" meant to be a constitutional edifice based on mutual rights and obligations; at all times it was a device of jihad, a mechanism for their immediate exploitation and eventual destruction.

The myth of "tolerant Islam" did not die with the collapse of the Turkish Empire. Rather, it took another form: that of the National Arab Movement, which promoted an Arab society where Christians and Muslims would live in perfect harmony. In the same way as the myth of the Ottoman tolerance was created to block the independence of the Balkan nations, so the Arab multi-religious fraternity was an argument to destroy the national

---

[48] Notably e.g. *Muhammad: A Biography of the Prophet* by Karen Armstrong.
[49] Philip Jenkins, "Empires of Faith: Islam and the Academy," *Chronicles: A Magazine of American Culture*, September 2001.

liberation of non-Arab peoples of the Middle East: Kurds, Armenians, Assyrians, Maronites, and Jews:

> And although from the beginning of this century until the 1930s, a stream of Christian refugees were fleeing massacres and genocide on the roads of Turkey, Iraq, and Syria, the myth continued to flourish. After the Israelis had succeeded in liberating their land from the laws of jihad and dhimmitude, the myth reappeared in the form of a multi-cultural and multi-religious fraternal Palestine, which had to replace the State of Israel. Its pernicious effects led to the destruction of the Christians in Lebanon. One might have thought that the myth would end there. But suddenly the recent crisis in Yugoslavia offered a new chance for its reincarnation in a multi-religious Muslim Bosnian state. What a chance! A Muslim state again in the heartland of Europe. And we know the rest, the sufferings, the miseries, the trials of the war that this myth once again brought in its wake.[50]

Even after September 11, the myth lives on all over the Western world, perhaps even more strongly than before. It seems that Huntington's notion of "civilizational blocks," like it or not, has the virtue of expressing something real in Western attitudes. A British analyst has called it "Frankish blinkers." Huntington speaks of "the West," but if he had written "the Franks," the term would have supplied more historical depth:

> When the western Crusaders came into the Byzantine world eight centuries ago, they were all called "Franks"—French, German, or English. Just like their contemporary descendents, they had superb military technology, immense self-confidence, and a good nose for profit and plunder. They waved their swords in the name of God, but they acted as though there was something wrong and inferior about the Orthodox Christians. When they murdered Rhineland Jews in 1096, when they massacred Muslims in Jerusalem in 1099, this was all very new; when they sacked

---

[50] Bat Ye'or: *Myths and Politics: Origin or the Myth of a Tolerant Pluralistic Islamic Society,* Paper delivered at the annual conference of The Lord Byron Foundation, Chicago, August 1995.

Constantinople in 1204, it was a trend. By the time the kings of the Latin West calmly watched the Turks take Constantinople in 1453, it was engrained.[51]

We are dealing with a prejudice that is not easy to pin down. Is it the hostility toward Orthodoxy displayed by the "knowledge class" in the modern Western world? Is it the benign or not so benign neglect of Orthodox culture and nations by Western political and cultural elites? Is it the facile treatment of Orthodoxy by academia and pluralistic theologians according to their own standards and values—standards and values that bear no relation to the essence of Orthodoxy? Is it the opacity of Orthodoxy to Western Christianity, and the corresponding confused response of Roman Catholics or Protestants, partly approving and partly disapproving, according to their own theological principles? Is it even perhaps the mistaken understanding of many Orthodox themselves, whether laypeople or clergy, of the true nature and purpose of Orthodoxy? Is it an intellectual, a cultural, a political, a social problem, or a religious problem? Are mistaken notions about Orthodoxy, or hostile reactions to Orthodoxy, to be attributed to its *confusedly* perceived difference from "the West"—or is the antipathy toward Orthodoxy due to *clearly* perceived difference?

It is correct to say that all of these attitudes are involved at one level or another, but this does not really go to the heart of the matter. For the heart of the matter is a matter of the *heart*—more precisely, a matter of a schism in the soul of modern man, which has separated the mind from the heart.

The old contempt for Islam went way beyond humanity and courtesy in our time, to become a theological maneuver, expressing a distaste for Western tradition by promoting Islam into a parity of esteem and enabling the apologists of jihad to advance the claim that theirs is not an aggressive but a defensive concept. The exact meaning of its "defensive" character is provided by the Tradition: jihad "has its material and moral functions (e.g., self-preservation and the preservation of the moral order in the world). . . . The sword has not been used recklessly by the Muslims; it has been wielded purely with humane feelings in the wider interest of humanity."[52] Those "wider interests" are immutable as they have been defined by Allah:

---

[51] Michael Stenton, "Frankish Blinkers," Unpublished paper presented at The Lord Byron Foundation's conference "Bridging the Schism," Chicago, May 1998.

[52] Sahih Muslim III, pp. 938, 941.

130

"fight and slay the pagans wherever ye find them and seize them."[53] The famous Surra of the Sword leaves no room for ambiguity.[54] It abrogates the over-quoted "Let there be no compulsion in religion."[55]

Recent attempts by Islamic apologists, to assure the West that only the "spiritual" definition of jihad really applies, amount to distorting history and brushing up centuries of very physical "striving" by generations of Muslim warriors. It is true that "Muslims are called by the Qur'an and the example of the Prophet of Islam to strive for Peace through all available means," but the "Peace" that is called upon believers to implement is impossible unless it is established under Islamic rule.[56] The author quite correctly admits that "in Qur'anic terms, peace does not only mean absence of war, it is also a positive state of security in which one is free from anxiety or fear." He does not specify, however, that this state of security is only available in Dar el-Islam, once Islam defeats its enemies and conquers their lands.

This is exactly the same definition of "peace" that was used by the Soviet empire in the period of its external expansion (1944–1979): it is the objective, but it is fully attainable only after the defeat of "imperialism as the final stage of capitalism" and the triumph of the vanguard of the proletariat in the whole world.

What matters to non-Muslims today, and to non-Communists 60 years ago, is not the metaphysical meaning of "Peace" within the community of the believers, but the consequences of their dialectic for the rest of us. Those who invented jihad in the seventh century intended it for particular purposes and are the authors of the concept and, as such, they should be respected intellectually. "If some of their heirs wish to change the meaning of what was normal then, they should say so, and act upon it. In the Christian world, modern Christians outlawed crusading; they did not rewrite history to legitimize themselves. Those who believe that the jihad-holy war is a sin today must have the courage to delegitimize it and outlaw it as well."[57]

---

[53] 9:5

[54] 9:29

[55] 2:256

[56] "A Christian Perception of Islam: the Struggle for Dialogues and Peace," *Palestine Times*, 8/1997.

[57] Dr. Walid Phares: "Jihad is Jihad," *Palestine Times*, 11/1997.

Islam is and always has been a religion of intolerance, a jihad without an end. Despite the way the apologists would like to depict it, Islam was spread by the sword and has been maintained by the sword throughout its history. William Muir, one of the greatest orientalists of all times (1819–1905), summed it up at the end of a long and distinguished career when he declared his conviction "that the sword of Muhammad and the Qur'an are the most fatal enemies of civilization, liberty, and truth which the world has yet known." They have combined to create the Arab empire, once described as "an unmitigated cultural disaster parading as God's will," but parading, in its modern metamorphosis, as the creed of equality:

> This fiction has been presented as a fact with an unparalleled skill. In fact, the Prophet Muhammad divided humanity into two sections, the Arabs and the non-Arabs. According to this categorization, the Arabs are the rulers, and the non-Arabs are to be ruled through the yoke of Arab cultural imperialism: Islam is the means to realize this dream, because its fundamentals raise superiority of Arabia sky-high, inflicting a corresponding inferiority on the national dignity of its non-Arab followers. From the Arabian point of view, this scheme looks marvelous, magnificent and mystifying . . . yet under its psychological impact, the non-Arab Muslims rejoice in self-debasement, hoping to be rewarded by the Prophet with the luxuries of paradise. The Islamic love of mankind is a myth of even greater proportions. Hatred of non-Muslims is the pivot of Islamic existence. It not only declares all dissidents as the denizens of hell, but also seeks to ignite a permanent fire of tension between Muslims and non-Muslims; it is far more lethal than Karl Marx's idea of social conflict which he hatched to keep his theory alive.[58]

The Tradition is surprisingly modern when it describes wars of global conquests, slaughter and enslavement of countless millions as an activity with a "moral function," undertaken "in the interest of the humanity." Never are people killed more easily, and in greater numbers, than when it is done for their own good. The jihadi campaigns fought by the Muslims in

---

[58] Anwar Shaikh, *Islam: The Arab National Movement.* U.K.: The Principality Publishers, 1995.

Spain, France, India, Iran, throughout the Balkans, or at the very gates of Vienna, were as defensive as Stalin's winter war with Finland, or the "counterattack" against Poland by Hitler.

The only distinction between Islamic terror through the centuries— against Medinan Jews, Arabian pagans, Greeks, Serbs, Persians, Hindus, Armenians, African blacks, and countless others—and its twentieth century totalitarian counterparts, as practiced in the workhouses of the Final Solution and the Gulag, concerned methods. Unlike Arabs, Turks, and their local collaborators through the centuries, the mass murderers in European totalitarian powers adopted the "style" of a developed industrial state. Their terror relied on complex equipment and intricate administrative network, while Islamic terror was "primitive" and "traditional." Nazis and Stalinists relied on coordinated plans, orders, reports, invoices, lists, cost-benefit calculations and statistics. On the other hand, from Muhammad and Usman to Abdul Hamid, Mustafa Kemal, and the modern Sudanese Army, the orders have been mostly oral, the apparatus of terror arbitrary, the selection of targets and methods of killing sometimes random.

Nazi and Stalinist terror was for the most part *depersonalized* and *bureaucratic*, it was *cold, abstract, objective*; the warriors for Islam were *direct, personal* and *warm*. Their terror was and is often directed against their first neighbors; it was and is *passionate* and *subjective*. The terror of the *Reichkommissars* and *Politkommissars*, with its somberness, discipline, and bureaucratic pedantry, was "puritanical," while the Muslims in all ages and locations indulge literally in orgies of violence. The Malaysian Islamist leader Anwar Ibrahim was unintentionally frank when he declared "We are not socialist, we are not capitalist, we are Islamic." The differentiation is *vis-à-vis* rival political systems and ideologies, not religions:

> While fundamentalist Islam differs in its details from other utopian ideologies, it closely resembles them in scope and ambition. Like Communism and Fascism, it offers a vanguard ideology; a complete program to improve man and create a new society; complete control over that society; and cadres ready, even eager, to spill blood.[59]

---

[59] Daniel Pipes, "There Are No Moderates: Dealing with Fundamentalist Islam," *National Interest, Fall 1995.*

The similarity between the contemporary revolutionary-utopian Islamist project and the Marxist-Fascist propagandistic discourse of six or seven decades ago is truly remarkable:

> The state is held responsible for securing the safety of each individual and making medical care and education available to everyone. It would not only match what the industrialized countries provide to their citizens, instead, it would excel them; it would respect every individual and value him; it would also preserve and safeguard his religion, his property and his honour. The state would aim at satisfying the needs of every individual realistically. . . . Employees' wages should be increased to make them refrain from thinking about taking bribes or stealing. . . . The state should abolish all fiscal fees and rates, water and sewage rates, school fees, import and export licenses and fees, council rates, ground rent, road tax, and fiscal stamps. One of its main functions is to secure the essential needs of all its subjects and to enable each individual to acquire his luxuries, according to his ability.[60]

The overall totalitarian character of the Islamic state is frankly admitted by this author, who devotes pages upon pages to the need for an effective Islamic security apparatus of external intelligence and domestic vigilance. The *Fuehrerprinzip* that had become inseparable from Muhammad's legacy in Medina is taken for granted: "the state in Islam is one single institution, which is the Khalifa," the Leader responsible for and in control of all government departments. All the existing institutions will be abolished:

> The Khalifa would take charge of serving the Ummah and he alone would have the mandatory power to establish the pyramidical framework of the state according to Islam. The present ruling system should be abolished, whether it were royal or republican. Ministries, parliament and local authorities should also be abolished. All syndicates, trade unions, charity organizations and political parties based on other than Islam

---

[60] www.almuhajiroun.com/lnews/special-%2024%20hrs%20afta%20k. php.

should be abolished. The former political ruling system should be uprooted.

Marxist-Fascist and Islamist projects have in common the lust for other people's lives and property, and the desire to exercise complete control over their subjects' lives. All three have been justified by a self-referential system of thought and belief that perverts meanings of words, stunts the sense of moral distinctions, and destroys souls.

BLUEPRINT FOR CONQUEST

As global threats, Nazism and Communism are dead, and while vigilance is called for against future resurgence, ghosts do not threaten anyone. Islam, by contrast, is still with us, and has global consequences, however obscure and coarse its origins. But "radical Islam" is not a twentieth century phenomenon that has somehow veered away from the original model based on a different set of religious, legal, and political assumptions. It is almost three centuries since Muhammad ibn Abd al-Wahhab was born, and he is alive today more than ever.

Wahhab was a zealous Muslim revivalist (b. 1703) who lived in the period of the Ottoman Empire's early decline. He nevertheless sensed it, and considered that Islam in general, and Arabia in particular, needed to be spiritually and literally re-purified and returned to the true tenets of the faith. Like Muhammad, he married a wealthy woman older than himself, whose inheritance, once she died, enabled him to engage in theological and political pursuits. His strictly orthodox legal training, combined with a brief encounter with Sufism—which he rejected—produced a powerful and appealing mix. From the Sufis he took the concept of a fraternal religious order, but rejected initiation rituals and music in any form. He also condemned the decorations of mosques, however nonrepresentational, and sinful frivolities such as smoking tobacco. His Kuranic literalism also sought to diminish the grip of establishment scholars steeped in analogical reasoning. In particular, he rejected veneration of saints, and sites and objects connected with them, and gave rise to a movement that sees itself as the guardian of "true" Islamic values. His ideas were espoused in the *Book of Unity,* which gave rise to the name of the movement, *al-Muwahhidun,* or Unitarians.

135

By the middle of the eighteenth century, Wahhab—like Muhammad before him—found a politically powerful backer for his religious cause. In 1744 he struck a partnership with Muhammad ibn-Saud, the leader of a powerful clan in central Arabia, and moved to his "capital," the settlement of ad-Dir'yah (Riyadh). Since that time the fortunes of the Wahhabis and the Ibn Saud family have been intertwined. Under Ibn-Saud's successor, Abdul-Aziz, the Wahhabis struck out of their desert base at Najd with fury unseen in a millennium. In what looked for a while like the repetition of Muhammad's and the Four Caliphs' phenomenal success a thousand years earlier, they temporarily captured Mecca and Medina and marched into Mesopotamia, forcing the Ottoman governor to negotiate humiliating terms, and invaded Syria.

This was an unacceptable challenge to the sultan, the heir to the caliphate and "protector of the holy places." In 1811 he obtained the agreement of Ali Pasha, the *de facto* autonomous ruler of Egypt following Napoleon's withdrawal, to launch a campaign against the Wahhabis. After seven years, they were routed. In 1818 the Turks broke the first Wahhabi state. Later the sect revived under Faysal to provide the focus of Arab resistance to the Ottoman Empire, which they considered degenerate and corrupt, but the fortunes of the Ibn-Saud family declined due to a dispute with another northern Arabian clan. They had to seek refuge in the neighboring province of Mosul, in today's Kuwait.

In 1902 a daring and bellicose prince of the Ibn-Saud family, named after Abdul-Aziz the warrior, returned with 40 horsemen and took control of Riyadh. That was the beginning of his campaign to recover control over Arabia. In 1912 the Wahhabi revival prompted the founding of a religious settlement at Artawiyah, 300 miles north of Riyadh, under the auspices of the *Ikhwan*, the Brotherhood. This was a stern Arabian variety of Puritan Plymouth, in which people were dragged from their homes and whipped for failing to attend Friday prayers.

As the First World War engulfed not only Europe but also the Middle East—once Turkey threw in her lot with the Central Powers—an old foe of the house of Ibn-Saud, the governor of Mecca by the name of Hussein, switched sides and supported the British in the hope that they would support him as the ruler of an independent Arabian state once the conflict was over. In the end, his perfidious protectors, in the best tradition of the shortsighted Albion, betrayed him. Not even the illustrious Colonel

Lawrence ("of Arabia") could change the outcome: in a preview of the subsequent self-defeating Balkan game concerning Josip Broz Tito and General Mihailovich, the policy-makers in London tried to be too clever by half, stabbed their friends in the back, helped their foes, and undermined the British long-term interest in the process. A depiction of the state of affairs on the other shore of the ocean, more than half-century later, conveys the spirit:

> It is hardly a surprise that business executives who would sell their grandmothers to Abdul Abulbul Amir for oil drilling rights would see the world as a reflection of their balance sheets, nor is it a surprise that secular, socially progressive opinion is viscerally anti-Christian. What is not expected is that so many Western Christians, Americans in particular, are willing to believe the worst about their Eastern Christian cousins, who, only lately freed from Islamic (and later, in most cases, communist) servitude, are desperately attempting to avoid a repeat of the experience. Today, when all of the Russian north Caucasus is subject to plunder and hostage-taking raids staged from Shari'a-ruled Chechnya, when not just Nagorno-Karabakh but Armenia proper is in danger of a repeat of 1915, when Cyprus and Greece receive unvarnished threats to their territorial integrity on a weekly basis for the offence of purchasing defensive weapons, and when the borders of Serbia are rapidly approaching those of the *pashaluk* of Belgrade in order to appease America's new friends in Bosnia and Kosovo, organized Roman Catholic and Protestant sentiment in America overwhelmingly sides with non- and anti-Christian elite opinion in its pro-Muslim, anti-Orthodox tendency.[61]

In the chaotic years after the demise of the Ottoman Empire, the Ikhwan proved to be an able and fanatical fighting force, securing victory for Ibn Saud, their leader and the founder of the present royal dynasty. In 1924, 3,000 of them looted and burned the town of Taif, killing 300 people for no apparent reason—an example to be repeated on countless occasions in our own time, from Algeria to the Spice Islands. In 1925 they carried out

---

[61] James Jatras, "Insurgent Islam," *Chronicles*, February 1999.

Ibn Saud's order that all revered burial sites in Mecca and Medina be destroyed. His men completely demolished a cemetery known as the "heavenly orchard" in Medina, where relatives and many early companions of the Prophet were buried. In 1926 they proclaimed Abdul-Aziz the king of Hejaz, and within a decade he had united the rest of Arabia and imposed on them—*imitatio Muhammadi*—the Wahhabist view of the world, man, law, and Allah.

It is incorrect to say that the Wahhabi movement is to Islam what Puritanism is to Christianity, however. While Puritans could be regarded as Christianity's Islamicists *sui generis* with their desire to turn Christianity into a scriptural, literalist theocracy that it had never intended to become, Wahhabism is unmistakably "mainstream" in its demand for the return to the original glory of the early Islamic *Ummah*. Their iconoclastic zeal notwithstanding, the Wahhabis were no more extreme or violent than the models for Islam in all ages, the Prophet and his companions.

The descendants of Abdul Wahhab are still heading the Saudi religious establishment. They resisted the introduction of "heathen" contraptions such as radio, cars, and television, relenting only when the king promised to use those new media to promote the faith. They stopped the importation of all alcohol, until then sold to foreigners (1952), and banned women driving motor vehicles (1957). At the outset of the new millennium, the State Department report on human rights in the Kingdom of Saudi Arabia in 2000 offers an accurate glimpse of what is in store for the rest of humanity if and when Islam is globally triumphant:

> Freedom of religion does not exist. Islam is the official religion, and all citizens must be Muslims. Neither the government nor society in general accepts the concepts of separation of religion and state, and such separation does not exist. Under Shari'a, conversion by a Muslim to another religion is considered apostasy. Public apostasy is a crime punishable by death if the accused does not recant. Islamic religious education is mandatory in public schools at all levels. All children receive religious instruction. . . . Citizens do not have the right to change their government. The Council of Senior Islamic Scholars . . . reviews the government's public policies for compliance with Shari'a. The government [views] Islamic law as the only necessary guide

138

to protect human rights. There is legal and systemic discrimination based on sex and religion.[62]

The Saudi religious police, known as the Committee to Promote Virtue and Prevent Vice, routinely intimidate, abuse, and detain citizens and foreigners. The authorities abuse detainees, using beatings, sleep deprivation, and torture. "Punishments include flogging, amputation, and execution by beheading, stoning, or firing squad. The authorities acknowledged 120 executions during [2000], an increase from 100 in 1999." The men were executed by beheading, and the women were executed by firing squad. There were 27 amputations in 2000, including 7 multiple amputations (right hand, left leg). Persons convicted of less serious offenses, such as alcohol-related offenses, or being alone in the company of an unrelated person of the opposite sex, are flogged with a cane.

An eye for an eye works literally as well as figuratively in Islam: a Saudi court ordered that the eye of an Egyptian man be removed as punishment for an attack six years previously in which he was convicted of throwing acid on another Egyptian man. The victim, who lost his eye in the attack and suffered other disfigurement, had urged the court to implement Al-Qisas, the Shari'a provision stipulating that the punishment be commensurate with the crime. The convicted man at least had the consolation of having his eye removed at a hospital and under anesthesia.

Political detainees "commonly are held incommunicado in special prisons during the initial phase of an investigation, which may last weeks or months" without access to lawyers, but that doesn't matter anyway, since "defendants usually appear without an attorney before a judge, who determines guilt or innocence in accordance with Shari'a standards." Most trials are closed, and crimes against Muslims receive harsher penalties than those against non-Muslims. In the case of wrongful death, the amount of indemnity or "blood money" awarded to relatives varies with the nationality, religion, age, and sex of the victim. A sentence may be changed at any stage of review, except for punishments stipulated by the Kuran.

---

[62] U.S. Department of State, Saudi Arabia: Country Reports on Human Rights Practices - 2000. Released by the Bureau of Democracy, Human Rights, and Labor, February 23, 2001.

The king of the Saudis remains their imam. He and the Wahhabi religious establishment see it as their inviolable and sacred duty and purpose to evangelize the world, and the Saudi money—American and Western petrodollar windfall, actually—has paid for the construction of over 1,000 mosques in the United States, and several thousand in other parts of the world. All along, needless to say, no churches (let alone synagogues) can be built in Saudi Arabia. The destroyers of the holy places in Medina and Mecca in the 1920s are the spiritual, and in some cases perhaps literal, ancestors of the terrorist slaughter of September 11.

* * *

Fourteen centuries after Muhammad, the real question for the free world—and the term is more apt now than it had been at any time during the Cold War—the real question is not "Why does a Muslim wage jihad?" In a sane world, such a question would concern nobody but social anthropologists. It is "What makes a jihad-minded Muslim hate the West so much that he is prepared to kill any number of Westerners, and himself for good measure, to make that point?" It is certainly not rock and roll music that he hates, as Orianna Fallaci has noted, not the usual stereotypes like chewing-gum, hamburgers, Broadway, or Hollywood. The "tangible" objects of that resentful hate are the skyscrapers, the science, the technology, the jumbo jets. Accustomed as the Westerners are to the double-cross, blinded as they are by myopia, they'd better understand that a war of religion is in progress:

> A war that they call *Jihad*. Holy War. A war that might not seek to conquer our territory, but that certainly seeks to conquer our souls. That seeks the disappearance of our freedom and our civilization. That seeks to annihilate our way of living and dying, our way of praying or not praying, our way of eating and drinking and dressing and entertaining and informing ourselves. You don't understand or don't want to understand that if we don't oppose them, if we don't defend ourselves, if we don't fight, the Jihad will win. And it will destroy the world that, for better or worse, we've managed to build, to change, to improve, to render a little more intelligent, that is to say, less bigoted—or even not bigoted

140

at all. And with that it will destroy our culture, our art, our science, our morals, our values, our pleasures.[63]

Islam, a religion born of the desert, has created jihad and remains defined by jihad, its most important concept for the rest of the world. Through jihad, Islam has emerged as a quasi-religious ideology of cultural and political imperialism that knows no natural limits to itself. Unlike the "just war" theory originated in Christian thinking, which has evolved into a secular concept instituted in international laws and codes, including the Geneva Conventions, jihad is inherently religious as well as political: Islamic normative thinking does not separate the two. It has emerged from the desert, and it perpetually creates new mental, psychic, spiritual, and literal deserts of whatever it touches.

---

[63] "Anger and Pride" by Oriana Fallaci, *Corriere della Sera* on September 29, 2001 (translated from the Italian by Chris and Paola Newman).

CHAPTER FOUR

The Fruits

Shirk is the most appropriate word for translating the word "freedom" in Article 18 of the Universal Declaration for Human Rights, which is posed as an ideal to be attained: "Everyone has the right to freedom of thought, conscience, and religion; this includes freedom to change his religion."[1]

As this Muslim author readily concedes, *shirk*, the ultimate, unpardonable sin of blasphemy and the exact opposite of Islam, stands for freedom of thought, conscience, and religion. A Muslim is not free to believe or do what he wishes. He is under *Islamic* law, which is the only legal, legitimate, moral, and rational code. That is the most important "fruit" of Islam, from which a variety of others have sprouted.

The basis of the social and legal order and obligation in Islam is the Kuran, the final and perfect revelation of Allah's will that is to be obeyed by all creation.[2] There is no sovereign but Allah in Islam: "Therefore exalted be Allah, the King, the Reality: there is no god but He, the Lord of the Throne of Honor!"[3] Allah's divine sovereignty is irreconcilable with popular sovereignty, which is the essence of democracy.

The original Arab word for "kingdom" is *mulk,* from the Semitic root *m-l-k* that is common to both Arabic and Hebrew; in Islamic terminology, it has come to signify the realm in which only Allah is its King, even in the earthly domain. (To denote a kingdom in secular and political sense, the Arabic language commonly uses another derived form, that is *mamlakah.*) Islam therefore sees Muslims as worshippers and slaves of Allah (*ibaad Allah*). The Islamic law, the *Shari'a,* is therefore not a supplement to the "secular" legal code, it *is* the only such code and the only basis of obligation, because a Muslim's only true allegiance is to Allah, and to Muhammad: "He who obeys the Messenger, obeys Allah."[4]

---

[1] Fatima Mernissi, *Islam and Democracy,* London, 1993, p. 87.
[2] 4:105.
[3] 23:116.
[4] 4:8.

143

No mere human entity has the authority to enact laws: Allah's earthly plenipotentiary—*khalif*—merely enforces the law in this world, in accordance with Muhammad's revelation, as the divine "vicegerent on earth."[5] He cannot do or enact anything contrary to the Kuran or Sunnah, down to such details as making room for newcomers in a crowded mosque: "O, ye who believe! When it is said make room in assemblies, then make room."[6] The definition of what is just depends solely on Allah's will, to which none of the usual moral criteria found among humans is applicable. "Just" and "unjust" are not regarded in Islam as intrinsic characteristics of human actions; they are entirely changeable by divine decree.

The law is interpreted by muftis, who have the legal authority to give opinions (*fatwa*) in answer to an inquiry by a judge (*qadi*) or a private individual. The judgment requires extensive knowledge of the Kuran and the Hadith, as well as of legal precedents, but it does not allow for judicial activism or creativity: the body of sources is finite, and only *qiya*, or analogical reasoning, can be applied. During the Ottoman empire, the mufti of Istanbul was Islam's chief legal authority, presiding over the whole judicial and theological hierarchy. After its fall, the Grand Mufti of Jerusalem is regarded as *primus inter pares*. The actual decision is rendered by the qadi. Caliph Umar was the first to appoint a qadi to eliminate the impossible task of personally judging every dispute that arose in the community.

Islam is a revealed religion, strongly focused on its grounding in history, in the historical person of Muhammad, his revelation and his example. Events *as they happened*, starting with the Night of Power and with all subsequent recorded or alleged words and deeds of the Prophet, are the foundation of the faith, law, and social convention. Even his apparently trivial actions and utterances were passed on as rules and mode of conduct, in accordance with the Kuranic statement that Muhammad is "a beautiful pattern (of conduct)."[7] His sayings and acts guide the lives of all true Muslims to this day. Whereas *imitatio Christi* is a voluntary spiritual endeavor for a pious Christian, all *bona fide* Muslims are not only morally and spiritually but also legally obliged to imitate Muhammad.

---

[5] 2:30.
[6] 58:11.
[7] 33:21.

144

The Hadith offer the essential guide in this endeavor, because the Kuran provides but scant instruction regarding important daily aspects of faith and life. To give one example, the Tradition offers detailed instruction on the rituals of the faith, as performed by Muhammad, that is not elaborated in the Kuran. It has been said that what the Kuran teaches in black and white, the Hadith teaches in color. The hadithic literature contains literally thousands of similar binding precedents, and tens of thousands of nonobligatory ones that are regarded as "weak" in their provenance. The approved ones supply the precedents for legal requirements and religious duties (*ahkam*) and define what is allowed (*halal*) or forbidden (*haram*):

> Without the information we obtain from the Traditions, it would be impossible to construct a detailed system of worship, procedure of pilgrimage, list of unlawful food, or laws of inheritance. Many of the religious penalties, such as the punishment of the drunkard, the punishment of the married adulterer, are not mentioned in the Qur'an but uttered by Muhammad.[8]

In the Hadith where we find that Muhammed offers the eternal model of behavior for every little detail of everyday life: when to blow the nose, how to wear shoes, how to urinate, and how to conduct sexual union in marriage. Allah is so distant, inscrutable, and abstract that Muhammad as his prophet perhaps inevitably acquired quasi-divine status: no mere mortal, even the one with the gift of prophecy, is revered to the point of regulating whether one's hair is to be cut from left to right or vice versa. Bukhari attests that Muhammad did not resist the trend: "I have been sent in the best of the generations of the children of Adam, one generation after another generation, until I am born in the generation in which I am born."[9] He frankly saw himself as the pinnacle of all men: "Allah sent me to complete the excellent virtues and to perfect the good actions."[10] On the Day of Judgment, Muhammad says, "I shall be the leader of the Prophets and their spokesman and one who will intercede for them without boast."[11]

---

[8] Cf. El Schafi in *Behind the Veil.*
[9] *Al Hadis,* Vol 4, p. 316.
[10] *Al Hadis,* Vol 4, p. 328.
[11] *Al Hadis,* Vol. 4, p. 326.

The Muslims maintain that Islam is not "Mohammedanism," the religion of Muhammad, corresponding to Christianity, the religion of Christ: they do not worship Muhammad but Allah, and the former is only the messenger. Theoretically, this is so; yet *imitatio Muhammadi* as the source of daily moral and legal guidance elevates the prophet of Islam to quasi-divine status. The difference between Allah and Muhammad becomes blurred once a mortal and sinful man is recognized as the absolute authority on the will of the creator and sustainer of the universe.

That Muhammad himself wanted it that way there can be no doubt: "Whoso obeyeth the messenger obeyeth Allah, and whoso turneth away: We have not sent thee as a warder over them."[12] Islam is indeed "Mohammedanism," and *de facto* bi-theism. No theological sleight-of-hand can dispose of the problem.

SHARI'A

Contrary to the Christian concept of governmental legitimacy (Romans 13:1), Islam condemns as rebellion against Allah's supremacy the submission to any other form of law.[13] Muslims believe that Shari'a should be used as a standard test of validity of all positive laws, "a standard of values to which all law must be compiled with.[14] Christ recognized the realm of human government as legitimate when he said, "Render therefore to Caesar the things that are Caesar's, and to God the things that are God's" (Matthew 22:21). In Islam there is no such distinction between church and state.

Shari'a is not at all a "moral law" that guides one's personal map of moral distinctions, but a blend of political theory and penal law, requiring the punishment of violators through the sword of the state. It presupposes and demands the existence of an Islamic state as an executor to enforce the law. To be legitimate, all political power therefore must rest with those who enjoy Allah's authority on the basis of his revealed will sent down through his prophet.[15] Islam assumes a basic pattern of movement in the

---

[12] 4:80.

[13] 5:50.

[14] Ajijola, Alhaji, *What is Shariah?* Adam Publishers & Distributors, Delhi, India, 1998, pp. 303.

[15] 5:59.

universe, within which "politics is in fact no different from religion: truth comes from on high and on the way down is met by responsibility moving up. Society is regulated by law and in the Islamic state the source of law is divine."[16] Politics is not "part of Islam," as this would imply that in origin it is a distinctly separate sphere of existence which is then eventually amalgamated with Islam; politics is the inherent core of the Islamic imperative of Allah's sovereignty. Shari'a is therefore, strictly speaking, infallible.

Shari'a applies to all humankind just as Kuran applies to all creation, jinn and animal kingdom included. Any law that is inconsistent or in conflict with it should be null and void, not only to the Muslims, but to all humanity.[17] Jews, Christians, and pagans are subject to Shari'a, too, and from Muhammad's standpoint they are being hypocritical when they invoke the judgments and moral principles of prior revelations, because their real wish "is to resort together for judgment to the Evil One, though they were ordered to reject him."[18] Muhammad thereby abrogates all prophets prior to himself; resort to any other source of authority is not only unjustified, it is satanic.

Muhammad's pronouncements on law and morals were also subject to progression and abrogation of previous verses. In Mecca, when he was unable to enforce any rules, Muhammad did not try to impose on his converts a new code of behavior or laws to regulate their social, political, and economic life, let alone an entirely new moral standard. His demands initially were purely spiritual: understanding and public acceptance that there was no god but Allah, and that he, Muhammad, was his messenger. Otherwise the old customs and traditions were followed, including the drinking of wine, which the Kuran approved: "And of the fruits of the palms and the vines, you take from there an intoxicant and a provision fair."[19] A few years later, in Medina, wine and gambling were deemed more bad than good: "In both is heinous sin, and uses for men, but the sin in them is more heinous than the usefulness." The next step was to ban wine before prayer: "O believers, draw not near to prayer when you are drunken

---

[16] Yaqub Zaki. "The Qur'an and Revelation," in Dan Cohn-Sherbok (ed.), *Islam in a World of Diverse Faiths,* New York, St. Martin's Press, 1991.

[17] Alhaji, *What is Shariah?*, p. 303.

[18] 4:60.

[19] 16:67.

until you know what you are saying."[20] And finally, "O believers, wine and arrow-shuffling, idols and divining-arrows are an abomination, some of Satan's work."[21]

Other prohibitions, for instance that of usury, also went through stages. In Mecca it was not prohibited: "And what you give in usury that it may increase upon the people's wealth, increases not with God; but what you give in alms, desiring God's Face, those—they receive recompense manifold."[22] In Medina the tone changed, along with Muhammad's relations with the Jews, who were now worthy of God's wrath and curse because they had been forbidden to practice usury but did it anyway.[23] This implicit prohibition still did not apply to the Muslims. The next step was Muhammad's ban on "exorbitant usury," on "doubling and redoubling" one's investment.[24] Finally usury was prohibited categorically: "Give up the usury that is outstanding, if you are believers. But if you do not, then take notice that God shall war with you, and His Messenger; yet if you repent you shall have your principal, unwronging, unwronged."[25]

The non-Muslims are to be judged by the laws of the people of Islam in everything, "whether they like it or not, whether they come to us or not." The *Verse of the Sword* (9:5) abrogates any previous Kuranic injunction concerning Muslim treatment of the infidels. Contemporary Azhar scholars readily admit that the verse

> does not leave any room in the mind to conjecture about what is called defensive war. This verse asserts that Holy War, which is demanded in Islamic law, is not defensive war (as the Western students of Islam would like to tell us) because it could legitimately be an offensive war. That is the apex and most honorable of all Holy wars.[26]

It is unlawful to refer the conquered to the law of their faith. The Kuran says, "Pass your judgment on them according to what God revealed

---

[20] 4:43.
[21] 5:90.
[22] 30:39.
[23] 4:160.
[24] 4:160.
[25] 2:278–279.
[26] Buti, op. cit., pp. 323–324.

to you." Shari'a becomes the law of the land in all conquered domains, and all persons are subject to it. When the second caliph, Umar ibn Al-Khattab, presented the rules to the inhabitants of Syria, he told them plainly: "If any Christian violates any of these terms, it will be permissible to kill him." (Muslims still refer to Umar as "The Just Caliph.") One of the rules was that a Christian who curses a Muslim would be killed, even if the evidence comes only from the aggrieved party. It is easy to imagine "all the situations in which a Christian who is humiliated in his own land might get angry, react impulsively, and curse a Muslim. However, if he does, there is nothing left for him but to accept Islam or to be killed."[27]

The same fate was ordained for Muslims who presume to have second thoughts about their religion. The doubter is guilty of an unforgivable sin, because he takes himself away from Allah, his owner—which is theft—and weakens the *Ummah*, which is insurrection. The late King Hassan II of Morocco, who while not exactly "Islamic" in his personal life was nevertheless the imam of his domain, explained the situation back in 1990:

> If a Muslim says, "I have embraced another religion instead of Islam," he—before he is called to repentance—will be brought before a group of medical specialists, so that they can examine him to see if he is still in his right mind. After he has then been called to repentance, but decides to hold fast to the testimony of another religion not coming from Allah—that is, not Islam—he will be judged.

The notion that reluctance to embrace Islam is insanity is not new, and corresponds to the Soviet notion of treating political dissidents as psychiatric cases. An apostate, communist or Muslim, can be only mad, or bad—perhaps both. All mainstream Muslim scholars through the ages have agreed that apostasy is to be punished by death. Muhammad ordered it, and all the caliphs followed suit. Contemporary scholars also declare that the Muslim's freedom to change his faith is nonexistent.

The Bill of Legal Punishments published by the Azhar University in Cairo—the "Light of Islam" accepted as the highest scholarly authority on Shari'a—has been widely circulated in English among the Muslim diaspora in the Western world. It deals with the penalties imposed by Islamic law,

---

[27] *Behind the Veil*, p. 144.

such as amputation of the thief's hand and the scourging of the wine drinker. On page 12 it states that

> A person guilty of apostasy (man or woman) shall be put to death if repentance is not made within the period allowed which shall not exceed sixty days. Repentance of a person who commits apostasy more than twice shall not be accepted. An apostate is that Muslim who has renounced the faith of Islam irrespective of his adoption of another creed. The crime of apostasy is committed in the following ways: (1) making an explicit statement or committing an act definitely indicating renunciation of Islam; (2) denial of essential tenets of the faith; and (3) bringing into ridicule through word or action the Gracious Kuran.

On page 30, we find an explanatory note: "The ordained penalty for apostasy is based on the *Sunnahh*. The prophet, peace be on him, said, 'One who changes his faith is to be killed' (Al-Bukhari). It is also narrated by Al Dar Qutni that when a woman called Umm-Marwan had renounced Islam, the Prophet ordered that if she failed to repent she should be put to death."

All recognized sources agree that the verdict for the female apostate is the same as for the male. She must be called on to return to Islam for three days, prior to her death, "for an evildoer may have confused her understanding;" thus the possibility exists for her being released from her confusion. According to an approved hadith, Muhammad has said, "It is good if she repents. If she does not, she is to be killed, since by apostasy she should be treated like a woman who has fought against Muslims, being taken captive in a holy war; thus it is lawful to kill her with the sword. Moreover, her guilt is far more abominable than women who are taken captive in a holy war, since she has become a Muslim."

Islamic legal tradition is attentive of every detail: thus the killing of an apostate nursing woman must be postponed until her infant no longer needs her, if either no wet nurse can be found or if the babe cannot accept another woman in place of its mother. A divorced woman is to be killed without hesitation, unless she is menstruating (even if she should menstruate only every five years). If she has no period, owing to a weakness or questionable menopause, she is to be left in peace for three months, in case she is thought to be pregnant. If she is not thought to be pregnant, she is to be executed immediately after being called to repent. If unmarried, she is not to be acquitted.

The rightly guided caliphs continued this practice. It is known that Abu-Bakr ("the Truthful") fought against those who had deserted from the religion of Islam and killed many. The "Gracious Companions" were of the same view, and a consensus emerged on this issue. The Islamic League in Saudi Arabia broadened the definition to include persons "who alleged that the Qur'an is contradictory and includes some myths, who described the apostle Muhammad to imply that he was inflicted with vices. . . . The verdict of Islam is to sentence to death anyone who commits such things."

The death sentence for apostasy is strictly applied in Saudi Arabia. In September 1992, the Saudi government beheaded Sadek Abdel-Kerim Malallah after he was convicted of slandering Allah and the Prophet. His was "a sacrilegious crime punishable by death, irrespective of repentance," declared the Saudi interior ministry. This position has been accepted by the state authorities even in some Islamic countries normally not regarded as "fundamentalist." The semi-official Egyptian daily *Al Ahram* informed its readers in 1977 that the state assembly had approved a bill to enact the penalty for apostasy:

> The apostate who intentionally relinquishes Islam by explicit declaration or decisive deed must be put to death. Apostasy is established by one confirmation or by the testimony of two men. The apostate is forbidden to administer his properties. He will be given 30 days to repent before the execution of the sentence of death. But if one converted to Christianity was 10–14 years old, he will only be scourged fifty times.[28]

This law has not been implemented in Egypt so far, but it remains on the statute books. It is notable that the testimony of two men—by definition, two Muslim men—is sufficient to establish the crime. If they claim that a Copt had declared that there is no god but Allah and that Muhammad is his apostle, but subsequently changed his mind, the accused has the choice between embracing Islam or suffering martyrdom.[29]

---

[28] *Al-Ahram*, August 6, 1977.
[29] Cf. *Behind the Veil*, p. 14.

Incidentally, even a Muslim who neglects prayers is regarded as an apostate and must be killed if he does not repent.

Penalties for theft are not based on the Tradition but on the Kuran, which is clear on this point: "As for the thief, both male and female, cut off their hands. It is the reward of their own deeds, an exemplary punishment from Allah." The Tradition explains that a hand is cut off for stealing anything that costs one-fourth of a dinar and over; admittedly, currency conversion presents some difficulties. In those days a quarter-dinar did not buy much: "May God curse the thief. If he steals an egg, his hand must be cut off, or if he steals a rope, his hand must be cut off."[30]

Early legal doctrines and practices were codified by the Hanbalite school of law, the predominant school of Islamic jurisprudence, named after the theologian Ahmad ibn Hanbal (780–855). Today, 12 centuries later, Azhar scholars do not veer from the straight and narrow in their Statute of Legal Penalties: a person found guilty of theft will have the right hand amputated for the first offense, the left foot for the second offense, and remain imprisoned "till the time of evident repentance for subsequent offenses." It was Muhammad's habit to cut off the thief's hand and to hang it around his neck to make an example of him and to humiliate him. The same punishment was applied to a woman who was accustomed to borrowing things and failing to return them, in spite of the intercession of her companions.[31] (Inexplicably, however, those who loot public property and embezzle the state's treasury are exempt from this punishment.)

Between them the Kuran and sunna stand above reason, conscience, or nature. A thing is right—including acts and laws abhorrent to the superceded biblical or "irrelevant" natural morality—because Allah says so, speaking through his prophet, or because Muhammad has thus spoken or acted. The lack of any pretense to moral basis of Shari'a is explicit: there is no "spirit of the law" in Islam, no discernment of the consequences of deeds. The revelation and tradition must not be questioned or any other standard of judgment—least of all any notion of "natural" justice inherent to men as such—can be invoked, let alone applied.[32] It cannot be penetrated by reason, its apparent inconsistencies notwithstanding, and the attempt must not be made. Every Muslim who is capable and qualified to give a

---

[30] Sahih of Al-Bukhari, part 8, pp. 199–201.

[31] Bukhari, part 8, page 199.

[32] 5:45.

sound opinion on matters of Shari'a, is entitled to interpret the law of Allah when such interpretation becomes necessary, but where an explicit command of Allah or his Prophet already exists, no Muslim leader or legislature, or any religious scholar can form an independent judgment. Since Muhammad is the Seal of the Prophets, there can be no further development in any judicial matters where the Kuran and sunnah provide guidance.

STUPID, FAITHLESS WOMEN

The testimony of one man equals that of two women. . . . Female parties to court proceedings such as divorce and family law cases generally must deputize male relatives to speak on their behalf.... Women play no formal role in government and politics and are actively discouraged from doing so. . . . The government does not keep statistics on spousal abuse or other forms of violence against women, [which] appear to be common problems. Hospital workers report that many women are admitted for treatment of injuries that apparently result from spousal violence. . . . Women are not admitted to a hospital for medical treatment without the consent of a male relative. By law and custom, women may not undertake domestic or foreign travel alone. . . . In public a woman is expected to wear an *abaya* (a black garment that covers the entire body) and to cover her head and face. . . . Some government officials and ministries still bar accredited female diplomats in the country from official meetings. . . . Daughters receive half the inheritance awarded to their brothers. . . . Islamic law enjoins a man to treat each wife equally. In practice, such equality is left to the discretion of the husband. Some women participate in *Al-Mesyar* (or "short daytime visit") marriages, in which the women relinquish their legal rights to financial support and nighttime cohabitation. Additionally, the husband is not required to inform his other wives of the marriage, and any children resulting from such a marriage have no inheritance rights. Women must demonstrate legally specified grounds for divorce, but men may divorce without giving cause. In doing so,

153

men are required to pay immediately an amount of money agreed upon at the time of the marriage, which serves as a one-time alimony payment. If divorced or widowed, a woman normally may keep her children until the age of 7 for boys, 9 for girls.

The above is not a quote from a history book describing conditions in medieval Arabia; it comes from the U.S. Department of State's *Country Report on Human Rights Practices in the Kingdom of Saudi Arabia* for A.D. 2000. It also tells us that women must not drive cars, and must not be driven, except by an employee, or husband, or a close relative—and even then must not occupy the front seat. In addition, the Report says, divorced foreign women are prevented from visiting their children, once they are awarded to the deceased husband's family. The authorities monitor any gathering of persons, especially women, and disperse women found in public places, such as restaurants. Women may study abroad—but only at the undergraduate level—if accompanied by a spouse or an immediate male relative. Women own 4 percent of the businesses, but they must deputize a male relative to represent the business. Women may not accept jobs if there are no adult male relatives present with whom they may reside and who agree to take responsibility for them. Contact with male supervisors or clients is generally allowed only by telephone or fax machine.

With the exception of the reference to cars, phones, and faxes, all stipulations are legally, and therefore morally, quite impeccable from the Islamic point of view. In the Kingdom of Saudi Arabia, the Kuran and Sunna are formally accepted as the country's constitution and the source of its legal code.

The status of women in Islam is comparable to that of the human rights in Cuba: theoretically exalted if you subscribe to the theory, utterly deplorable in practice, and impolite to discuss frankly in the enlightened Western circles. Second-hand apologetics and propaganda notwithstanding, the original sources for "true" Islam—the Kuran and Hadith—speak for themselves. They provide ample and detailed evidence on Islamic ideology, theory, and subsequent Shari'a practice regarding the role and rights of women. This practice is in force through much of the Islamic world today. According to the *New York Times* (May 17, 2002), a judge in Pakistan sentenced a young woman to death for "adultery" by stoning. She had been raped by her husband's brother. The judge defended his action by saying

154

that he had merely followed the Kuran-based law that mandated this punishment. The fact the woman, Zafran Bibi, was raped was of no consequence. The woman had accused her brother-in-law of raping her and this was a confession to her crime of "having intercourse outside of marriage." The *Times* noted that this case fit "a familiar pattern."

The Kuran is unambiguous: "Men are in charge of women because Allah has made the one of them excel the other."[33] It also acknowledges the theoretical equality of *the works* of the sexes before Allah, and the oneness of origin of men and women: "I will not suffer the work of him among you that worketh, whether of male or female, to be lost. The one of you is the issue of the other."[34]

The "works" of men and women may be held in equal regard, but they do not have equal worth as people. The men are superior, and it is for the women to act as their husbands act by them, but the men are a step above them.[35] In relation to each other, according to Allah's message to men, "Your wives are as a soil to be cultivated unto you; so approach your tilth when or how ye will."[36] Men are the protectors and maintainers of women, because Allah has given the one more strength than the other, and because they support them from their means—"therefore the righteous women are devoutly obedient." Those that are not—the majority—inhabit the nether regions of hell. Muhammad has stated that most of those who enter hell are women, not men. Contemporary Azhar scholars of Egypt agree: "Oh assembly of women, give charity, even from your jewelry, for you (comprise) the majority of the inhabitants of hell in the day of resurrection." According to al-Bukhari, the prophet saw Hell, and the majority of its dwellers were women, because "they are not thankful to their husbands."[37]

The disobedient wives are to be admonished at first, refused sexual favors next, and finally beaten, albeit "lightly."[38] The verse was revealed in connection with a woman who complained to Mohammad that her husband hit her on the face, which was still marked by the slap. At first he told her

---

[33] 4:34.
[34] 3:195.
[35] 2:228.
[36] 2:223.
[37] Sahih of Al-Bukhari, Vol. 7, p. 96.
[38] 4:34.

to get even with him, but then added: "Wait until I think about it." The revelation followed, after which the Prophet said: "We wanted one thing but Allah wanted another, and what Allah wanted is best." The slap that leaves a visible mark counts as "light beating," that does not cause lasting injury. Azhar University scholars concur:

> If admonishing and sexual desertion fail to bring forth results and the woman is of a cold and stubborn type, the Qur'an bestows on man the right to straighten her out by way of punishment and beating, provided he does not break her bones nor shed blood. Many a wife belongs to this querulous type and requires this sort of punishment to bring her to her senses!

A professor at the College of Law at the University of Qatar makes the same point in his "Family Problems' Solution":

> If a woman is afraid that her husband may turn away from her or detest her, she will hasten to bring understanding and reconciliation. But if the husband is afraid that his wife may rebel against him, he hastens to bring mutual understanding by means of exhortation, then by abandonment of the bed, then by the scourging which deters.[39]

Physical violence against one's wife, far from being a crime punishable by law, remains divinely ordained and practically advised in modern Islam. After all, in Muhammad's rendering of the story of the righteous Job, Allah ordered him to beat his wife. We read: "Take in thine hand a branch and smite therewith and break not thine oath."[40] If a wife sought consolation outside wedlock, Allah mandates extreme punishment: "If any of your women are guilty of lewdness, take the evidence of four (reliable) witnesses from amongst you against them; and if they testify, confine them to houses until death do claim them, or Allah ordain for them some (other) way."[41]

Muslim propagators in the West "explain" that the Islamic teaching and practice on admonishing and beating wives and withdrawing sexual favors from them is in line with the latest achievements of clinical

---

[39] Ahmad Ahmad, *The Individual Guarantee in the Islamic Law*, p. 63.
[40] 38:44.
[41] 4:15.

156

psychology. It is apparently not only correct, but positively beneficial to them because "women's rebelliousness (*nushuz*) is a medical condition" based either on her masochistic delight in being beaten and tortured, or sadistic desire to hurt and dominate her husband. Either way,

> such a woman has no remedy except removing her spikes and destroying her weapon by which she dominates. This weapon of the woman is her femininity. But the other woman who delights in submission and being beaten, then beating is her remedy. So the Qur'anic command: 'banish them to their couches, and beat them' agrees with the latest psychological findings in understanding the rebellious woman. This is one of the scientific miracles of the Qur'an, because it sums up volumes of the science of psychology about rebellious women.[42]

There is no fundamental distinction in status between the Muslim and the non-Muslim woman: men are, on principle, in charge of them, and they are less valuable than men. She is not to be trusted to marry a non-Muslim, whereas a man can do so, and expect, nay insist, that the wife converts. While condemning the pagan Arab practice of burying unwanted newborn girls alive, the Kuran also acknowledges the lesser worth of daughters:

> And when any of them is given the good tidings of a girl, his face is darkened and he chokes inwardly, as he hides him from the people because of the evil of the good tidings that have been given unto him, whether he shall preserve it in humiliation, or trample it into the dust.[43]

Adjusted people would value all children equally, regardless of gender, and Allah's preference for sons cannot portend anything good. The boys' special status and codified superiority indicate that their purpose is in the fulfillment of the needs of the father, which explicitly denies an attitude of nurturing towards the child.

The Law of Inheritance accordingly dictates that a son gets double the inheritance of a daughter; and in Islamic courts a man's witness is worth

---

[42] *The Australian Minaret,* Australian Federation of the Islamic Councils, November 1980, p.10.
[43] 16:48, 59.

twice that of a woman's.[44] Al-Ghazali, still revered as one of the greatest Muslim scholars of all time, states that Allah has punished women in eighteen ways, including physical functions (menstruation, pregnancy, childbirth) and divinely ordained handicaps: lesser share in inheritances, liability for divorce but inability to initiate divorce, seclusion, exclusion from many religious rituals and ceremonies, and disqualification for positions as rulers and judges. (European judges did not include women until a century ago, but the equivalents of Empress Theodora, Elizabeth I, and Catherine the Great, Maria Theresa, and Victoria do not exist in the Muslim world.)

Islamic marriage does not envisage any consent from the bride if she is still under paternal control: Abu Bakr, who was Muhammad's friend, thus wed him to his daughter, Aisha, when she was six, though the actual consummation of that "marriage" took place when she was nine, and Muhammad 54. It does not produce any community of property between husband and wife, and the wife is permanently dependent on the support of her husband. That support may be withdrawn in case of disobedience.

To the outright divine command of every wife's obedience to her husband, Muhammad has added a few comments of his own. When asked who among women is the best, he replied: "She who gives pleasure to him (husband) when he looks, obeys him when he bids, and who does not oppose him regarding herself and her riches fearing his displeasure."[45] As for the "rights" of women, even in basic necessities the needs of the husband take precedence: "You shall give her food when you have taken your food, you shall clothe her when you have clothed yourself, you shall not slap her on the face, nor revile (her), nor leave (her) alone, except within the house."[46]

The husband's sexual needs have to be satisfied immediately and unquestioningly: "When a man calls his wife to his bed, and she does not respond, the One Who is in the heaven is displeased with her until he is pleased with her. . . . When a man invites his wife to his bed and she does not come, and he (the husband) spends the night being angry with her, the angels curse her until morning."[47] This is consistent with the consensus of

---

[44] 2:282.

[45] Mishkat I, p. 216.

[46] Mishkat I, p. 212.

[47] Sahih Muslim II, p. 723.

Islamic scholars that "sexual intercourse is an action, and the woman does not act," and that her pleasure in the sexual act is to give pleasure to her husband.

According to an undisputable hadith, Muhammad once said to a group of women: "I have not seen anyone more deficient in intelligence and religion than you. A cautious, sensible man could be led astray by some of you." The women asked what was deficient in their intelligence and religion, and he replied:

> "Is not the evidence of two women equal to the witness of one man?" They replied in the affirmative. He said: "This is the deficiency of your intelligence. . . . Isn't it true that a woman can neither pray nor fast during her menstrual period?" The women replied in the affirmative. He said: "This is the deficiency in your religion."[48]

Interestingly, Muhammad does not command women to fast or to pray during their menstrual period, and then takes that as conclusive evidence of their lack of faith. The fact that in Shari'a the testimony of a woman is equal to one half of a man's testimony[49] and that she inherits only a half of her male siblings' portion[50] is also presumably justified by the woman's lack of faith and intelligence so often remarked upon by the prophet.

In our own time, General Zia ul-Haq, the military dictator of Pakistan for many years, had reintroduced discriminatory legislation reducing women's rights to one-half those of men when they sign business contracts. Some women's groups protested that the new law "insulted women and debased their dignity." Dr. Aly Farrukha, Director of Islamic Studies in Chicago, replied: "The issue of a woman's testimony in court is a divine order which necessitates that a woman who is a witness should be accompanied by another woman in order to remind her if she forgets (some details) and to correct her if she makes an error. This verdict does not intend to insult women, but rather to help them."[51]

In addition to all other deficiencies, the woman has no fewer than ten 'awrat, shameful orifices including, or resembling, her external genitals:

---

[48] Sahih of Al-Bukhari, vol. 1, Hadith No. 301. See also vol. 3, Hadith No. 826.
[49] 282.
[50] 4:11.
[51] *The League of the Islamic World*, February/March, 1985, p. 17.

"Ali reported to the Prophet, saying: 'Women have ten 'awrat. When she gets married, the husband covers one, and when she dies the grave covers the ten.'"[52] Furthermore, according to a "faultless" hadith, not only does the woman have ten 'awrat, she is seen as one herself: "The woman is 'awrat. When she goes outside (the house), the devil welcomes her."[53] Covering all orifices with a veil is not meant to preserve the chastity of women, but that of men prone to be scandalized by the spectacle. Muhammad accordingly forbade women to talk except by leave of their husbands, to go out except in emergency (and on Bairam), to use the middle of the road, to be greeted, or to greet. The fire-worshipper, the Jew, and the pig are listed alongside the woman as things that corrupt prayer.

The volumes of the Hadith mention violent scenes between Ali and Fatima, Muhammad's daughter. At times he forgot himself to the point of ill-treating this ailing woman, forcing her to take refuge in her father's house. When faced with these delicate situations, whether Ali or Uthman, Fatima or Ruqayya were concerned, he ordered his daughters "to comply with their husbands' moods." He declared, "If I were to order anybody to make a prostration to anybody, I would have ordered a woman to prostrate before her husband."[54]

This adage goes beyond a slave acknowledging her master; it resembles that of creator and creature, and borders on heresy on the Kuran's own terms, since worship belongs to God alone. Nevertheless, a mortal man is elevated to an almost divine plane when the destiny of his wife is at stake: her disobedience to him is unlawful, while her obedience is the key to eternal bliss: "Whosoever female dies while her husband is pleased with her will enter Paradise."[55] Muhammad also warned women: "Watch how you treat your husband, for he is your Paradise and your Hell."

Small wonder then that, in Muhammad's view, it is a noble sacrifice for men to share his life with women, creatures utterly deficient in mind, religion, and gratitude, and unable to repay the favor. Muhammad's example was followed by the early caliphs, the "well-instructed" ones. The second caliph, Umar, ordered Muslims to prevent the women from learning

---

[52] Kanz-el-'Ummal, Vol. 22, Hadith No. 858.

[53] *Ihy'a 'Uloum ed-Din* by Ghazali, Beirut, Vol II, Kitab Adab al-Nikah, p. 65.

[54] Mishkat I, p. 210.

[55] Mishkat I, "Duties of husband and wife," Hadith No. ii, 60.

to write and to resist "their capricious ways." Ali, Muhammad's devoted son-in-law and the fourth caliph, said that women are evil, and, worse still, a necessary evil: "Men, never ever obey your women. Never let them advise you on any matter concerning your daily life." According to Ali, they have three qualities worthy of an unbeliever: they complain of being oppressed when in fact it is they who oppress; they take solemn oaths and at the same time lie; they make a show of refusing the advances of men when, in fact, they long for them ardently.

In short, the woman is not a worthy and equal companion of man. Her deficiency in intelligence and religion render her unable to engage in discussion of lofty ideas, even if her husband were foolish enough to approve of any such attempt. One of Muhammad's widows, his favorite, A'isha, complained to the caliphs and companions: "You have put us on the same level with a donkey and a dog." Her words were prompted by Muhammad's verdict that if a man's prayer was disrupted by the passing of a donkey, a dog, or a woman in front of him, his prayer was not acceptable, and he had to perform ablution again and repeat his prayer.

Caliph Umar was once interrupted by his wife while talking to another man and told her off by saying, "You are a toy; if you are needed, we will call you."[56] Ever faithful to his father-in-law's example, he only reflected the Prophet's adage that "the woman is a toy; whoever takes her, let him care for her." This metaphor is further elaborated by Ghazali: "In the company of women, looking at them, and playing with them, the soul is refreshed, the heart is rested, and the man is strengthened to the worship of God." Ghazali concludes that this was the meaning of Allah's words "That he might rest in her."[57]

In Islam, divorce is undesirable but lawful and easy to obtain. The husband can divorce his wife by simply saying so three times, but a woman cannot divorce her husband unless she has his permission to do so. She can get a judicial dissolution of marriage for neglect, ill-treatment, or positive cruelty.[58] A man may divorce his wife without any misbehavior on her part, or without assigning any cause, and it is valid even if a man is acting under compulsion, if his words are uttered in sport or jest, or by a mere slip of the

---

[56] Al-Musanaf, Vol. 1, Part 2, p. 263.

[57] 7:189.

[58] A. Guillaume, *Islam,* p. 174.

161

tongue.[59] The husband may even say to himself, without announcing his intent to the wife: "If this thing does not happen, my wife is divorced by three"—and if "the thing" comes to pass, the wife finds herself divorced for reasons entirely unknown to her.

In our own time Arab press is full of family tragedies caused by the frivolous treatment of divorce in Islam, and the courts are overloaded with thousands of divorce suits that mean the eviction of children and wives who are helpless and dependent on their former husbands. By contrast, they may not seek divorce but only judicial annulment, on the grounds of the husband's physical sexual deficiency, mutilation, or malfunction prior to marriage; of evident madness and leprosy; impotence, for which a year of probation can be granted by the judge; or a husband's "vow" not to have intercourse with his wife for four months.

No marriage is valid without the payment of a dowry. The significance of its payment—sometimes in the form of a mere token—for the sexual use of the woman is rooted in the Kuran.[60] This is confirmed by Muhammad's ruling that a man who wanted to divorce his new bride, who turned out not to be a virgin but pregnant from previous adultery, still owed her the dowry: "He separated the two, commanded that the woman be flogged, and said to the man, 'The baby will be your slave.'"[61] Since the implications of the sexual rights secured by the payment of dowry extend to children of a previous marriage, the husband has the right to prevent his wife from looking after children, including infants, from her former husband. In any event, man is the privileged party in all cases of custody of the children. Their mother may be awarded temporary custody until the age of seven (for boys) or nine (for girls), provided she is of good character and does not leave the abode of the husband, does not remarry, and preserves sound morals.

"The wife," of course, designates any one of up to four of them (a limitation to which the Prophet himself was not subjected), as the Kuran sanctions polygamy: "If ye fear that ye shall not be able to deal justly with the orphans, marry women of your choice, two, or three, or four. But if ye fear that ye shall not be able to deal justly [with them], then only one, or [a captive] that your right hands possess, that will be more suitable, to prevent

---

[59] T.P. Hughes, *Dictionary of Islam.*

[60] 4:24.

[61] *Encyclopaedia of Islam*, "Nikah."

you from doing unjustly."[62] Ghazali's justification for polygamy is simple: "Some men have such a compelling sexual desire that one woman is not sufficient to protect them [from adultery]. Such men therefore preferably marry more than one woman and may have up to four wives."

If they want to get rid of them, the Kuran does not present a problem: "If you wish to exchange one wife for another and you have given unto one of them a sum of money, take nothing from it." The rule was practiced by Muhammad's successors and companions. Muhammad's second successor, Umar, married seven women in the course of his life, in addition to having two maid-slaves, Fakhiyya and Lahiyya, as concubines. Uthman was wed to eight women. Once he was widowed, Ali ibn Abi Talib—to whom Muhammad denied permission to marry a second wife beside his own daughter Fatima—married 10 wives and permanently maintained 19 concubines and maid-slaves for a total of 29 women. Muhammad's grandson Hasan ibn Ali, of whom Muhammad said that he is the master of the youth of paradise, during the course of his life married up to 70 women and had at least 31 children. Sometimes he used to divorce two women in a day. Even his father urged the residents of Iraq not to marry their daughters to him because he was a man who constantly divorced his wives, but the Kufa's people continued to marry their daughters to him, hoping that they would bear children descended from the Prophet. "It is no sin for you if you divorce women," the Kuran says, provided the dowry is repaid and suitable parting gifts presented.[63] Tedium of matrimony or simple carnal desire for another woman necessitated divorcing one to marry the other if the family budget could not accommodate both. The revered companions and the rightly guided caliphs provided the example.

If multi-matrimonial bliss provides insufficient diversity, Muslim men are free to have sex with their slave girls to their heart's content. According to Bukhari, Muhammad sometimes had sex with all his wives in one night, and at that time he had nine wives, and he once said of himself that he had been given the power of forty men.[64] Nevertheless, he enjoyed the obligatory services of his Coptic slave Mary better than the charms and favors of all his wives.

---

[62] 4:3.

[63] 2:236.

[64] Sahih of Al-Bukhari, vol. 7, Hadith No. 142. Also vol. 1, Hadith No.268.

Modern Islamic scholars argue for the practice of polygamy on scriptural grounds as well as for practical reasons. Sheikh Taysir Al-Tamimi, acting head of the Palestinian Authority's Shari'a Judicial System, had this to say, "To those who demand equality and whine about women's rights: By permitting polygamy, Islam protects the woman's humanity and emotions, secures her right to marry, and gain honor and esteem, instead of becoming a professional paramour lacking in rights, whose children are thrown onto the garbage heap."[65] Qatari Sheikh Walid bin Hadi set out the different rationales for polygamy—barrenness, demographic inequality, preventing adultery, and increasing the birth rate—but, as he explained, in the final analysis every man has his own reasons: "The Prophet said: Do not ask a husband why he beats his wife. . . . According to the same principle, Do not ask a husband why he takes a second wife.[66] Dr. Muhammad Al-Masir, a cleric from Egypt's Al-Azhar University, defends polygamy in the name of women's rights: "In the days of the Prophet, not even one woman remained without a husband—not a spinster, nor a widow, nor a divorcee. . . . I ask our women and daughters not to be egotistical." (This remark seems to presume the needs of a society engaged in eternal jihad, both in terms of caring for widows and for keeping as many women as possible in the production of future fighting men.)

"The wife" could also be a concubine, or legally paid prostitute under another name. The institution of temporary, contractual marriage—degrading to women no less than to the institution of "marriage"—was proclaimed lawful by Muhammad "for three nights" or more. It could be contracted for some money, or a dress, then the "husband" could desert the "wife," leaving her without any rights or obligations *vis-à-vis* any possible offspring. The soldiers of Islam in the field welcomed the revelation:

> We used to participate in holy battles led by Allah's Apostle and we had no wives with us. At that time, he allowed us to marry women with a temporary contract and recited to us this verse, 'Oh you who believe, make not unlawful the good things which Allah has made lawful for you."[67]

---

[65] *Al-Quds*, March 8, 2001.
[66] *Al-Rai* (Qatar), January 5, 2002, quoted by www.memri.com.
[67] 5:87.

By approving polygamy or temporary "marriage," Islam denies the value of true marriage, based on exclusive, devoted love and rooted in the natural (and scriptural) notion of family. Monogamy alone gives recognition, status, and value to a woman, as well as to the husband and their offspring. In a polygamist society there is no centralized family nucleus. There are many children, and every group of children rotates not around the father but around the mother. When a Muslim man takes another woman, she does not live with the former wife and her husband but in another house or tent, and there she raises her children. The husband may visit her once a week or once a month. If she is out of favor, her children will seldom meet, let alone play with, their father. In the polygamist society, the father is perceived as an absence. Instead of the father figure essential to normal development, there is a void, from Ishmael to Muhammad to Bin Laden, one of fifteen children by one of ten wives.

Islamic dogma, tradition, and practice are the foundation of a coherent and consistent outlook that has generated its own reality, visible in each and every traditionally Muslim country and in the transplanted centers of the Islamic diaspora in the West. Khaled Fouad Allam of the University of Trieste calls that "schizophrenia of the contemporary Muslim society, with signs of modernization in externals, with women doctors and lawyers, and, at the same time, deep-rooted structures that seek to apply Islamic law to civil rights in Muslim countries." The latter are self-congratulatory about Islam's treatment of women, even in their pitch to the West, claiming that "the Islamic system has achieved the right mixture of freedom and security that women seek and that is in the interest of the society as a whole":

> The regulations for the protection of women which were revealed in the seventh century can be easily verified by anyone in the twentieth century . . . [and] contain certain fundamental truths which will benefit whoever applies them. The present time of widespread rethinking of the role and rights of women is perhaps the appropriate time to look with fresh eyes at the Islamic point of view, which has contributed to the formation of stable societies in both sophisticated and underdeveloped peoples in vast areas of the world over the past fourteen centuries, which has retained the

continuity of its principles, and from which the Western world may have something to learn.[68]

For one-half of all Muslims living in those "stable societies," a tenth of the humanity, by the time of early puberty Purdah falls and "the rest of her life was going to be spent in that void where time was without meaning."[69] For those unwilling to submit, the punishment may be death, even if they are of royal blood: this was the fate of a Saudi princess and her boyfriend. Both were executed for adultery when they returned to their native land from Britain, where they had a romantic liaison as students. (When ATV in Britain and PBS in the United States were about to air a documentary based on this tragedy, "Death of a Princess," unprecedented pressure came from the British Foreign Office, from the U.S. State Department, the Saudi royal family, and the oil interests to cancel the show.[70])

The relegation of women to such an inferior position deprives Islamic societies of the talents and energies of half its people. As Bernard Lewis has warned, it also entrusts the other half's crucial early years of upbringing to undereducated and downtrodden mothers. The idea of "love" is removed from those men's understanding of sexuality, which is too often reduced to hurting others by violence. Gross mutilation of little girls, known as clitorectomy and rampant in Muslim Africa, and to a lesser extent in Arabia, is the direct result of a culture that deems female orgasm as indecent and threatening, because it implies mutuality. It reflects a gigantic rupture that Islam develops between men and women, where no harmony, affection, or equality is allowed to exist:

> In relationships between men, meanwhile, affection, solidarity, and empathy are left out of the picture. They threaten the hyper-masculine order. It is excruciating to imagine the sexual confusion, humiliation, and repression that evolve in the mindsets of males in this culture. But it is no surprise that many of these males find their only avenue for gratification in the act of humiliating the foreign "enemy," whose masculinity must be

---

[68] www.jamaat.org/islam/WomanIslam.html.

[69] V.S. Naipaul, *Beyond Belief: Islamic Excursions Among the Converted Peoples*, N.Y., Random House, 1998.

[70] www.pbs.org/wgbh/pages/frontline/us.

violated at all costs as theirs once was. Violating the masculinity of the enemy necessitates the dishing out of severe violence against him. In the recent terrorist strikes, therefore, violence against Americans served as a much-needed release of the terrorists' bottled-up sexual rage. Moreover, it served as a desperate and pathological testament of the re-masculinization of their emasculated selves.[71]

Mass murderers are frequently found to have histories of sexual abuse as children, and Islamic terrorists are no exception. Unlike their lone Western counterparts, however, the abuse of which they are the victims is systemic, and inherent to their societies. They are victimized by virtue of growing up and living in a dysfunctional culture of sexual repression and misogyny, where "love" is reduced to violent domination and its rejection reflects a deep-seated fear of individuality.

The treatment of women might be expected to disqualify Islam from the liberal establishment's point of view, but this has not happened. There is a reason for this. It is the failure of Islam to recognize, let alone support, the wife as her husband's closest and inseparable lover and partner, his life-long companion. Islam challenges Christian marriage in principle and in practice, and Muslim teaching on marriage and the family, though conservative about "patriarchy," undermines the traditional Western concept of matrimony. Paradoxically, Islam thus comes close to the contemporary, post-Christian ideology that relativizes "marriage" and "family."

HOMOSEXUALITY: "TRANSGRESSION BEYOND BOUNDS"

This sin, the impact of which makes one's skin crawl, which words cannot describe, is evidence of perverted instincts, total collapse of shame and honor, and extreme filthiness of character and soul. . . . The heavens, the Earth, and the mountains tremble from the impact of this sin. The angels shudder as they anticipate

---

[71] Jamie Glazov, "The Sexual Rage Behind Islamic Terror," www.frontpagemag.com/columnists/glazov/glazov10-04-01.htm.

the punishment of Allah to descend upon the people who commit this indescribable sin.[72]

There are many sins in Islam that may fit this description, from idolatry, atheism, and apostasy, to drunkenness, adultery, and questioning the divine origin of the Kuran. In this particular instance it refers to homosexuality, for which a death sentence remains on the statute books in several Islamic countries.

In Saudi Arabia, on April 16, 2001, five homosexuals were sentenced to 2,600 lashes and 6 years in prison, and four others to 2,400 lashes and 5 years' imprisonment for "deviant sexual behavior." Amnesty International subsequently reported that six men were executed on charges of deviant sexual behavior, some of which were related to their sexual orientation, but it was uncertain whether the six men who were executed were among the nine who were sentenced to flogging and imprisonment in April.[73]

It is difficult to establish precisely the number of homosexuals who have been executed in Iran since the Islamic revolution in 1979, since not all sentences are widely publicized, but estimates range from several hundred to 4,000.[74] According to Amnesty International, at least three homosexual men and two lesbians were publicly beheaded in January 1990. The Islamic Penal Law Against Homosexuals, approved in July 1991 and ratified in November of that year, is simple. Article 110: "Punishment for sodomy is killing; the Shari'a judge decides on how to carry out the killing." Article 129: "Punishment for lesbianism is 100 lashes for each party." Article 131: "If the act of lesbianism is repeated three times and punishment is enforced each time, the death sentence will be issued the fourth time."

While the Taliban ruled Afghanistan, it regularly executed homosexuals. Islamic jurists in Kabul and Kandahar only differed on the method of killing. One group of scholars believed the condemned should be taken to the top of the highest building in the city and hurled to death, while others advocated placing them in a pit next to a wall, which would then be toppled on them, so that they are buried alive. Both methods were

---

[72] Dr. Abdul Aziz Al-Fawzan, *The Evil Sin of Homosexuality,* www.islamweb.net/english/family/sociaffair/socaff-84.html.

[73] Associated Press, April 16, 2001.

[74] www.iranian.com/Letters/1999/September/gay.html.

solidly grounded in the Tradition, and both were applied. At least five men convicted of sodomy by Afghanistan's Shari'a courts had been "placed next to walls by Taliban officials and then buried under the rubble as the walls were toppled upon them." In one such incident, three homosexuals were punished in this way while Taliban leader Mullah Mohammad Omar watched, along with thousands of spectators. After the 30-minute waiting period, the three men were still alive, but two died the next day. What became of the third is unknown.[75] The punishment by stoning is derived from the Kuranic account of Sodom's destruction by a "rain of stones," which was itself the product of Muhammad's misunderstanding of the Hebrew story of "fire and brimstone" (i.e., sulfur):

> We also (sent) Lut: he said to his people: 'Do ye commit lewdness such as no people in creation (ever) committed before you? For ye practice your lusts on men in preference to women: ye are indeed a people transgressing beyond bounds.' And his people gave no answer but this: they said, 'drive them out of your city: these are indeed men who want to be clean and pure!' But We saved him and his family, except his wife: she was of those who lagged behind. And We rained down on them a shower (of brimstone): then see what was the end of those who indulged in sin and crime![76]

Kuranic claim that homosexuality had been unknown before it first appeared in Sodom is a uniquely Islamic concept; so is the notion that the reason for its destruction was exclusively due to the homosexual practices of its inhabitants, a clear departure from the Hebrew Scriptures. In addition to the Kuran many hadiths mention *liwat* (homosexual intercourse): "When a man mounts another man, the throne of God shakes," and "Kill the one that is doing it and also kill the one that it is being done to."[77] Muhammad's first successor, Abu Bakr, reportedly had a homosexual burned at the stake. The fourth caliph, Muhammad's son-in-law Ali, ordered a sodomite thrown from the minaret of a mosque. Others he ordered to be stoned. One of the earliest and most authoritative commentators on the Kuran, Ibn 'Abbas (died 687) blended both approaches into a two-step execution in which "the

---

[75] Amnesty International report, May 1998.

[76] 7:80–84.

[77] Further examples are listed at www.religioustolerance.org/hom_isla.htm.

sodomite should be thrown from the highest building in the town and then stoned." Later it was decided that if no building were tall enough, he could be shoved off a cliff. Regardless of the exact method, "Muslim jurists agree that, if proven of guilt, both of them should be killed. However, jurists differ on the methodology of capital punishment."[78] There are seven countries in the world that carry the death penalty for homosexual acts, and all of them justify this punishment with the Shari'a.

In practice, however, suppression and unavailability of liaison between males and females outside the prearranged wedlock has produced latent sexual tension in Islamic societies that has sought and found release in homosexual intercourse through the centuries. Those denied access to licit sexuality have sought and obtained outlets that produced chronic contradictions between normative morality and social realities. Male and female prostitution and same-sex practices—including abuse of young boys by their older male relatives—have been rampant in Islamic societies from the medieval to the modern period.[79]

It should be emphasized that those societies stress a distinction between the sexual act itself, which was deemed acceptable, and emotional attachment, which was unpardonable: "Sexual relations in Middle Eastern societies have historically articulated social hierarchies, that is, dominant and subordinate social positions: adult men on top; women, boys and slaves below."[80] A Muslim who is "active" in sexual relations with other men is not considered a "homosexual" (the word has no pre-modern Arabic equivalent); quite the contrary, his sexual domination of another man may even confer a status of hyper-masculinity. He may use other men as substitutes for women, and at the same time have great contempt for them.

In all cases it is the presence of love, affection, or equality among sexual partners that is intolerable. Equality in sexual relations is unimaginable in Islam, whether heterosexual or homosexual. Sex in Islamic societies has never been about mutuality between partners, but about the adult male's achievement of pleasure through domination.

---

[78] www.jamaat.org/qa/homo.html.

[79] Thomas L. Friedman, quoting the Iranian paper, *Entekhab*, writes, "'There are now 84,000 prostitutes operating on the streets of Tehran and 250 brothels, including some linked to high officials." "Iran by the Numbers," *The New York Times*, June 23, 2002.

[80] Bruce Dunne, "Power and Sexuality in the Middle East," *Middle East Report*, Spring 1998.

SLAVERY AND RACISM

While both the Old and New Testaments recognized slavery, the Gospels do not treat the institution as divinely ordained. The slaves are human, and all men are equal in the eyes of God regardless of their status in this life: "there is neither Jew nor Greek, there is neither bond nor free, there is neither male nor female; for ye are all one in Christ Jesus." Slavery was to early Christians a fact of life, and a thing of men.

The Kuran, by contrast, not only assumes the existence of slavery as a permanent fact of life, but regulates its practice in considerable detail and therefore endows it with divine sanction. Muhammad and his companions owned slaves, or acquired them in war. Muhammad's scripture recognizes the basic inequality between master and slave, and the rights of the former over the latter.[81] It also urges, without actually commanding, kindness to the slave.[82] As Bernard Lewis has noted, an important change from pagan—though not from Jewish or Christian—practices is that in the strictly religious sense, the believing slave is now the brother of the freeman in Islam and before God, and the superior of the free pagan.[83] This point is emphasized and elaborated in innumerable traditions, in which the Prophet is quoted as urging considerate and sometimes even equal treatment for slaves, denouncing cruelty, harshness, or even discourtesy, recommending the liberation of slaves and reminding the Muslims that his apostolate was to free and slave alike.

The Kuran assures the Muslim the right to own slaves (to "possess their necks") either by purchasing them or as bounty of war.[84] Muhammad had dozens of them, both male and female, and he regularly sold, purchased, hired, rented, and exchanged slaves when he became independently wealthy in Medina after Badr and the confiscation of Jewish property. Some of their names are recorded to posterity; as for the women, "whenever Muhammad took a woman as a captive, if he imposed the veil on her, Muslims would say he took her as a wife, but if he left her unveiled they would say, 'He owned her as a slave;' that is, she became a property of his right hand." The bounties have become lawful to the nation of

---

[81] 16:71; 30:28.
[82] 6:36; 9:60.
[83] 2:221.
[84] 58:3.

Muhammad. Ibn Timiyya wrote, "Slavery is justified because of the war itself; however, it is not permissible to enslave a free Muslim. It is lawful to kill the infidel or to enslave him, and it also makes it lawful to take his offspring into captivity."[85] In line with the racist views of Muhammad, the Arabs as "the noblest of all races" were exempt from enslavement.[86]

The "well-guided" four caliphs who came after Muhammad discouraged the enslavement of free Muslims, and it was eventually prohibited. The assumption of freedom as the normal condition of men did not extend to non-Muslims, however. Disobedient or rebellious dhimmis were reduced to slavery—that is, if their lives were spared—and prisoners captured in jihad were also enslaved if they could not be exchanged or ransomed. In 781, 7,000 Greek prisoners of war were enslaved after a battle at Ephesus. At the capture of Thessalonica in 903, 22,000 Christians were sold into Muslim slavery. The same happened in 1064 in Georgia and Armenia. In Africa, Arab rulers regularly raided black tribes to the south and captured slaves claiming their raids to be jihad; many Hindus were enslaved on the same pretext.

Divine sanction of slavery means that disobedience carries everlasting punishment. Obeying the master is the slave's key to paradise: "There are three (persons) whose prayer will not be accepted, nor their virtues be taken above: the runaway slave until he returns back to his master, the woman with whom her husband is dissatisfied, and the drunk until he becomes sober."[87] While maltreatment was deplored, there was no fixed Shari'a penalty. The slave had no legal powers or rights whatsoever. A Muslim slave-owner was entitled by law to the sexual enjoyment of his slave women. The Kuran mandated that a freeman should be killed only for another freeman, a slave for a slave, and a female for a female.[88] The Tradition says that "a Muslim should not be killed for a non-Muslim, nor a freeman for a slave."[89]

The slave trade inside the Islamic empire and along its edges was vast. It began to flourish at the time of the Muslim expansion into Africa, in the middle of the seventh century, and it still survives today in Mauritania and

---

[85] Ibn Timiyya, Vol. 32, p. 89.
[86] Ibn Timiyya, Vol. 31, p. 380.
[87] Mishkat al-Masabih, Book I, Hadith No. ii, 74.
[88] 2:178.
[89] *The Commentary of al-Baydawi*, p. 36.

Sudan. The Spanish and Portuguese originally purchased black African slaves for their American colonies from Arab dealers. Every year, for about 600 years, the Nubian kingdom was forced to send a tribute of slaves to the Muslim rulers in Cairo. Nubians and Ethiopians, with their slender features and thin noses, were preferred to the equatorial Bantus, for whom hard toil and lowly menial tasks were generally reserved.

Black slaves were brought into the Islamic world by a number of routes—from West Africa across the Sahara to Morocco and Tunisia, from Chad across the desert to Libya, from East Africa down the Nile to Egypt, and across the Red Sea and Indian Ocean to Arabia and the Persian Gulf. There are notable differences between the slave trade in the Islamic world and the trans-Atlantic variety. The former has been going on for thirteen centuries and it is an integral feature of the Islamic civilization, while the influx of slaves into the New World lasted a quarter as long and effectively ended by the middle of the nineteenth century. Over 10 million Africans were taken to the Americas during that period, while the number of captives taken to the heartlands of Islam—while impossible to establish with precision—is many times greater. Nevertheless there are tens of millions of descendants of slaves in the Americas, and practically none in the Muslim world outside Africa. For all its horrors, the Atlantic slave trade regarded its victims as valuable assets whose lives and progeny should be preserved, not for altruistic but for economic reasons; in the Muslim world, slaves were considerably cheaper, far more widely available, and regarded as a dispensable commodity.

Most slaves imported into the Americas were males, while in the Muslim world they were predominantly female. In the early caliphate, in Mesopotamia, considerable numbers of black slaves were used as labor on large estates, but the practice effectively ceased after a mass rebellion in the ninth century that at one moment even threatened Baghdad. Since that time the Muslim heartland has been apprehensive of using large contingents of male African slaves working in one location. They were used primarily as domestic servants, or, in the case of women, as sex objects—some harems had hundreds of concubines—and, in North Africa, as soldiers blindly obedient to their masters.

Many African slaves were eunuchs, and the method of their mutilation, before they could fetch the best price in the Islamic world, defies imagination:

Castration was admittedly against the Islamic law, but its letter—
the "spirit" being nonexistent—often offered a pragmatic way out
for the imaginative believer. Regarding African captives, a handy
contrivance was to buy already castrated slaves whose mutilation
occurred prior to the wretch's importation into the lands of the
Faithful. The dealers thus had a clear incentive to perform the
operation themselves along the route. For African captives,
nothing short of "castration level with the abdomen" would do;
no mere removal of the *cojones*, like with the Slavic and Greek
captives, by the mere removal of testicles. Only such radically
castrated eunuchs were deemed fit to be guardians of the harem:
that way there was no risk of their damaging any of the property
in the harem. The proceedings were too gruesome to describe in a
book of this kind. The mortality rates were enormous.[90]

As the Ottoman ruling class "descended further into sensual
degeneracy and even idiocy," the clever slaves—mostly kidnapped
Christian boys from the Balkans and the Caucasus—came to play an
increasingly important role as counselors, advisors, tutors, and, eventually,
even managers of the holy places of Mecca and Medina, where they were
treated with great respect.[91] In the period of its decline, the Ottoman harems
and landed estates were filled by Christian slaves captured in the Caucasus,
until the Russian liberation of the area in the early years of the nineteenth
century. The Tatars raided surrounding Christian lands from their
stronghold in the Crimea and sold captured Eastern Europeans in the slave
markets of Istanbul and other Turkish cities. This practice only ended with
the Russian annexation of the peninsula in 1783. The Muslims' view on
their two main sources of slaves, sub-Saharan Africa and Slavic Eastern
Europe, developed into the tradition epitomized by a tenth-century Islamic
writer:

> The people of Iraq have sound minds, commendable passions,
> balanced natures, and high proficiency in every art, together with
> well-proportioned limbs, well-compounded humors, and a pale

---

[90] *Islam's black slaves:* an interview with Ronald Segal by Suzy Hansen, www.salon.
com/books/int/2001/04/05/segal/index.html.

[91] Cf. Ronald Segal, *Islam's Black Slaves: The Other Black Diaspora,* Farrar, Straus,
& Giroux, 2001.

brown color, which is the most apt and proper color. They are the ones who are done to a turn in the womb. They do not come out with something between blond, blanched and leprous coloring, such as the infants dropped from the wombs of the women of the Slavs and others of similar light complexion; nor are they overdone in the womb until they are burned, so that the child comes out black, murky, malodorous, stinking, and crinkly-haired, with uneven limbs, deficient minds, and depraved passions, such as the Ethiopians and other blacks who resemble them. The Iraqis are neither half-baked dough nor burned crust, but between the two.[92]

Another important source of European slaves was piracy, with its autonomous power base in the Barbary Coast of Algiers. In 1516, Khair ed-Din, a Turkish privateer, laid siege to the Spanish fortress on the island of Penon and conquered it. For three subsequent centuries, the Muslim pirates were secure in Algiers. The captives of the Barbary corsairs could be freed by ransom or conversion. The rest were sold at auctions, and many died from fever, starvation, or the lash. Women were taken into harems as concubines of their captors.

The abolitionist sentiment in Europe and America was inseparable from Christian faith and world outlook. William Wilberforce and the Clapham Sect, inspired by the Wesleyan Revival, lobbied for abolition and finally succeeded in having the legislation adopted at Westminster that abolished slavery in the British Empire and turned Britain into a determined foe of slave traders everywhere. The evangelical revival movement provided momentum to the abolitionist movement in the United States.

Islam provides no analogous abolitionist imperative. Just as Britain and France were finally working to shut down the Atlantic slave trade, it was picking up in East Africa, and most of the slaves were being sold to kingdoms in Arabia and the Persian Gulf. The Arabian Peninsula in 1962 became the world's penultimate region to officially abolish slavery (Mauritania formally followed suit in 1982), yet years later Saudi Arabia alone was estimated to contain a quarter of a million slaves.

---

[92] Dinesh D'Souza, "Is Racism a Western Idea?" in *Christian Ethics Today*, March 1996.

Hoping to curtail the trade, in 1842 the British Consul General in Morocco made representations to the Sultan asking him what measures, if any, he had taken to abolish slave trade. The sultan replied, in a letter expressing bewilderment, that "the traffic in slaves is a matter on which all sects and nations have agreed from the time of the sons of Adam" until that day:

> The sultan continued that he was "not aware of its being prohibited by the laws of any sect, and no one need ask this question, the same being manifest to both high and low and requires no more demonstration than the light of day." The sultan was only slightly out of date concerning the enactment of laws to abolish or limit the slave trade, and he was right in his general historic perspective. The institution of slavery had indeed been practiced from time immemorial.[93]

A network of trade routes and markets extending all over the Islamic world and far beyond its frontiers lasted until well into the twentieth century. In some places the practice is still flourishing, notably in sub-Saharan Africa. To find truly endemic, raw anti-black racism and slavery today, one needs to go to the two Islamic Republics in Africa, Mauritania and Sudan. In both countries, those phenomena have their origin in the early period of Islamic expansion. As black kings and princes embraced Islam, they cooperated with the Arabians in the exportation of human cargo. Interestingly for a faith supposedly free from racial prejudice, Islamic judges declared that "the master does not have the right to force the female slave to wed to an ugly black slave if she is beautiful and agile, unless in case of utmost necessity."[94]

Black people had been enslaved on such a scale that the term *black* became synonymous with *slave*. The mixed-race, predominantly black but self-avowedly "Arab" denizens of the transitional sub-Saharan zone were indoctrinated into treating their completely black southern neighbors with racist disdain. (To this day it can be dangerous to one's life to ask a dark-looking but Arabic-speaking Sudanese or Mauritanian Muslim if he was "black.") The collaborators eventually surpassed their Arabic mentors in

---

[93] Bernard Lewis, *Race and Slavery in the Middle East,* Oxford University Press, 1994.

[94] Ibn Hazm, Vol. 6, Part 9, p. 469.

raiding tropical regions to capture slaves, mutilating the males by radical castration, raping females, and depopulating entire regions in the process.

For the black populations in Sudan and Mauritania, independence marked the end of a slavery-free respite under colonial rule. In both countries the forceful imposition of the wearing of the traditional Muslim dress, the *jalabia*, was followed by the compulsory circumcision and the giving of Arabic names to children as a precondition for entry into state schools. Slavery was "abolished" several times in Mauritania since independence, last on July 5, 1980. Yet the Anti-Slavery Society's findings (1982) and those of Africa Watch (1990) point to the existence of at least 100,000 "full-time" slaves and additional 300,000 half-slaves, all of them black, still being held by Arab-Mauritanians. Even the head of state from 1960 to 1978, Mokhtar Ould Daddah, kept slaves behind the presidential palace.[95] The Mauritanian government has not tried to eradicate slavery and failed; it has not tried at all.[96] Even the old Arab practice of forming slave armies is being revived in Mauritania, where thousands of *Haratines* were forcibly recruited, armed, and sent to take over black African villages in the south, where they massacred the inhabitants:

> The Haratines who have been settled on the lands of expelled blacks have been armed by the authorities and asked to organize their own defense. AI has been informed that some authorities are profiting from the subordination ties between masters and Haratines to enroll the latter in this militia. In general, this militia does not simply defend itself when attacked, but undertakes punitive expeditions against unarmed civilians living in the villages. In some cases, Haratines who object to this gratuitous violence are threatened with reprisals by the security forces who escort them on these expeditions.[97]

In 1983, the Arab-controlled government of Sudan instituted strict Islamic law in the entire country and subjected black Christians and other non-Muslims of the south in its decree. Then in 1992 a religious decree (fatwa) was ordered that gave justification to the military onslaught against

---

[95] John Mercer, Anti-Slavery Society Report of 1982.

[96] "Mauritania Slavery Alive and Well, 10 Years after the Last Abolition," *Africa Watch*, 1990.

[97] Amnesty International report on Mauritania, October 1990.

non-Muslims. Since that time, the United Nations and human rights groups have documented countless cases of slavery. People are taken as war booty to perform unpaid household labor and other tasks, or to be used for sexual gratification. The State Department had sent an assistant Secretary of State for African Affairs, Dr. Susan Rice, to investigate the problem. Her report was a horrific account of rampant slavery, with interviews with former slaves. However, it was quietly shelved by the Clinton Administration and denied media attention that it richly deserved by the standards of prevalent victimology.

Sudan shows that genocide need not be perpetrated by huge massacres. There are more insidious but equally effective ways of killing large numbers of people. The government in Khartoum is doing so by attrition: it is slowly and methodically grinding down the society and economy of the Nuba and starving the entire population. Meanwhile, in the garrison towns and Orwellian-sounding "peace camps," the government is remolding the political and social identity of the Nuba by force: the aim is to transform them into a deracinated underclass, the loyal servants of an extremist Islamic state. In each army attack, soldiers first arbitrarily gun down anyone they find. The government does not pay them salaries: their pay is the booty from the raids on Southern villages. The elderly and sick are usually killed on the spot and their food granaries set ablaze. The main objective of "combing" is to capture live, fit civilians:

> Thousands of men, women, and children are captured when their villages are surrounded, or are snatched while tending their crops, herding their animals, or collecting water. Many people run to hide in caves to escape government attacks, but they are driven even from these refuges by hunger and thirst, or by attacks using tear gas. Captives are taken to garrisons, forced to carry their own looted possessions, or drive their own stolen animals in front of them. These captives—or "returnees," as the government calls them—usually never see their families or villages again. Men are either killed or forcibly conscripted into a militia known as the *People's Defense Force*. Many are tortured. Women are raped and forced to work, often in special labor camps. All but the youngest children are separated for "schooling" (i.e., conversion

178

to Islam and training for a role in the new, extremist Islamic Sudan).[98]

The government also uses food as a means for luring Southern Sudanese Christians into its "peace camps" located in the desert. Food distribution in them is carried out exclusively by Islamic organizations, which use the promise of food as a means of converting Christians to Islam. The technique is very simple: If one does not bear an Islamic name, one is denied food. Without any means of alternative support the choice is, as ever, Islam or death.[99]

That it cannot be otherwise is explained by contemporary Islamic scholars, who are quite frank in admitting that Islam does not prohibit slavery but retains it and makes it lawful in two instances: for prisoners of war, "provided that the war is not between Muslims against each other—it is not acceptable to enslave the violators, or the offenders, if they are Muslims," and for "the sexual propagation of slaves which would generate more slaves for their owner."[100] Thousands of miles away from Africa, in Pakistan's Northwest Frontier Province, girls as young as five are auctioned off to the highest bidders.[101]

> Afghan girls between the ages of 5 and 17 sell for $80 to $100. The price depends on the color of their eyes and skin; if they are virgins, the price is higher. Mr. Arbab, an older man with a white shovel beard and a green turban, absently fingers his prayer beads as he calls out prices for the children. The girls are generally sold into prostitution or, if they are lucky, they may join harems in the Middle East.[102]

---

[98] *Facing Genocide: The Nuba of Sudan,* published by African Rights on 21 July 1995.

[99] Sabit A. Alley's paper delivered at the nineteenth Annual Holocaust and Genocide Program, Institute for Holocaust and Genocide Studies, New Jersey on March 17, 2001, www.iabolish.com /today/features/sudan/overview3.htm

[100] Dr. 'Abdul-Latif Mushtahari, *You Ask and Islam Answers*, pp. 51–52. The author is general supervisor at the Azhar University in Cairo.

[101] Andrew Bushel, "Sale of children thrives in Pakistan," *The Washington Times*, January 21, 2002.

[102] Ibid.

It is richly ironic that the founders of the Nation of Islam have urged African Americans to renounce Christianity as a tool of the oppressors, and that Elijah Muhammad's son upon dissolving the American Muslim Mission urged its members to become orthodox Muslims and thus "come home," spiritually at least, to their African roots. There is a double irony here since African Christianity pre-dates Islam by many centuries.

ISLAMIC ANTI-SEMITISM

"Islamic anti-Semitism" may sound illogical at first, as both Jews and Arabs are supposedly of the same or racially similar Semitic stock—and Islam is overwhelmingly an Arab religion, ideology, and way of life. The semantic confusion is due to the invention of the term "anti-Semitism" by a late nineteenth century German to give the anti-Jewish sentiment a "scientific" veneer. It was never meant to brand all Semitic peoples in the same category. Ever since it has denoted, and was meant to denote, different types and degrees of animosity to the Jews. It has found a perfect fit in Islam, when the drastic deterioration in the relations with the Jews occurred in the twentieth century resulting from the conflicting claims over Palestine. Inherent religious animosity is now fully coupled with anti-Jewish attitudes on ethnic and geopolitical grounds. Religious and political aspects of that struggle were as inseparable in the early seventh century as they are today.

Jews have lived in what are now Arab lands since the destruction of the first Temple in 586 B.C. The advent of Islam, and especially the tragic history of the Jewish tribes in Medina, made their continued survival look tenuous. Having been rejected by them, Muhammad set the tone reiterated in 1937 by the late King Ibn Saud to a British guest: "Verily, the word of God teaches us, and we implicitly believe it, that for a Muslim to kill a Jew, or for him to be killed by a Jew, ensures him immediate entry into Heaven and into the august presence of God Almighty."[103]

Muhammad's anti-Semitism is reflected in his suitably grim revelations in the Kuran. Time after time "the Children of Israel rebelled and disobeyed the Command of Allah, and became extremely arrogant."

---

[103] Quoted in "Oh Ye Who Are Jews . . . Long for Death" by Louis Rene Beres, Purdue University, www.gamla.org.il/english/article/ 2000/nov/ber2. Htm.

They have drawn on themselves wrath upon wrath, and their just reward in the form of "disgracing torment" yet awaits them.[104] Every time they make a covenant, some party among them throws it aside.[105] "And you will not cease to discover deceit in them."[106] So Allah brought them down and cast terror into their hearts, had some killed and others made captives, "And He caused you [Muslims] to inherit their lands, and their houses, and their riches, and a land which you had not trodden before."[107] The Muslims are able to do so because the Jews are cowards: "If they fight against you, they will show you their backs, and they will not be helped."[108] Until the Day of Resurrection they will be afflicted with humiliating agony.[109] They are accursed for their obstinate rebellion and disbelief, so "we have put enmity and hatred amongst them till the Day of Resurrection. Every time they kindled the fire of war, Allah extinguished it; and they (ever) strive to make mischief on earth."[110] Even when they seem united "their hearts are divided," and therefore "they fight not against you even together, except in fortified townships, or from behind walls. Their enmity among themselves is very great."[111] But even the stone behind which a Jew hides will say, "O Muslim! There is a Jew hiding behind me, so kill him." They have incurred the curse and wrath of Allah, who transformed them into monkeys and swine.[112] "Indignity is put over them wherever they may be;" "they have drawn on themselves the Wrath of Allah, and destruction is put over them" because they disobeyed Allah and used to transgress beyond bounds.[113] They cling greedily to this life even if it is a humiliating and villainous life, "and verily, you will find them the greediest of mankind for life."[114]

There could be no "golden age" for any community thus depicted by the deity of their rulers, and accordingly there was no "golden age" for the Jews in the Muslim world, either under Arabs or under Turks. There have

---

[104] 2:88–90.
[105] 2:100.
[106] 5:13.
[107] 33:26–27.
[108] 3:111.
[109] 7:167.
[110] 5:64.
[111] 59:14.
[112] 5:60.
[113] 3:112.
[114] 2:96.

been periods when they were able to live in relative peace, but their position was never secure. They were generally viewed with contempt by their Muslim neighbors, and their survival was always predicated on their abject subordination and degradation.

Mass murders of Jewish "protected people" started in Morocco as early as the eighth century, where Idris I wiped out whole communities. A century later, Baghdad's Caliph al-Mutawakkil designated a yellow badge for Jews, setting a precedent that would be followed centuries later in Nazi Germany, and synagogues were destroyed throughout Mesopotamia in 854–859. In Libya, then known as Tripolitania, Jews were considered as property of their Arab masters, who would bequeath the Jews to their heirs upon death. In the twelfth century, Egyptian Jews were the object of anti-dhimmi riots so successful that one observer noted the Jewish population had "greatly declined" in their wake.[115] On the other side of the Muslim empire, on December 30, 1066, Joseph HaNagid, the Jewish vizier of Granada, was crucified by an Arab mob that proceeded to raze the Jewish quarter of the city and slaughter its 5,000 inhabitants. Muslim preachers, who had angrily objected to what they saw as inordinate Jewish political power, incited the riot. And those were the most civilized Muslims in history, in Baghdad at the peak of one Islamic "golden age" and in Spain at the peak of another.

Nevertheless, the outpouring of Islamophile literature from the Western academy continues unabated. Its utopian character is sometimes almost openly admitted by those who construct the myth of an Islamic golden age of tolerance, whose goal is,

> to recover for postmodernity that lost medieval Judeo-Islamic trading, social and cultural world, its high point pre-1492 Moorish Spain, which permitted and relished a plurality, a convivencia, of religions and cultures, Christian, Jewish, and Muslim; which prized an historic internationality of space along with the valuing of particular cities; which was inclusive and cosmopolitan, cosmopolitan here meaning an ease with different

---

[115] *Middle East Digest*, September 1999.

cultures: still so rare and threatened a value in the new millennium as in centuries past.[116]

Elsewhere, the story was even grimmer. In 1465, Arab mobs in Fez slaughtered thousands of Jews, leaving only 11 alive, after a Jewish deputy vizier allegedly treated a Muslim woman in "an offensive manner." The killings touched off a wave of similar massacres throughout Morocco.[117] A new bout occurred in North Africa in the twelfth century, where the Almohads either forcibly converted or decimated their Jewish subjects; in Libya in 1785, where Ali Burzi Pasha murdered hundreds of Jews; in Algiers, where Jews were massacred in 1805, 1815, and 1830; and in Marrakesh, where more than 300 Jews were murdered between 1864 and 1880. Decrees ordering the destruction of synagogues were enacted in Egypt and Syria (1014, 1293–1294, 1301–1302) and Yemen (1676). Despite the Kuran's prohibition, Jews were forced to convert to Islam or face death in Yemen (1165 and 1678), Morocco (1275, 1465, and 1790–1792), and Baghdad (1333 and 1344).[118]

> It would not be difficult to put together the names of a very sizeable number of Jewish subjects or citizens of the Islamic area who have attained to high rank, to power, to great financial influence, to significant and recognized intellectual attainment; and the same could be done for Christians. But it would again not be difficult to compile a lengthy list of persecutions, arbitrary confiscations, attempted forced conversions, or pogroms.[119]

The situation of Jews in Arab lands reached a low point in the nineteenth century. Throughout North Africa they were forced to live in ghettos. In Morocco, which contained the largest Jewish community in the Islamic Diaspora, Jews were made to walk barefoot or wear shoes of straw when outside the ghetto. In 1884, the Sultan of Morocco said Jews had to work on Shabbat, could only "clean foul places and latrines," had to part

---

[116] John Docker: "Arabesques of the Cosmopolitan and International" (paper was delivered at the symposium: *Visions of a Republic*, The Powerhouse Museum, Sydney, 6 April 2001).

[117] Maurice Roumani, *The Case of the Jews from Arab Countries: A Neglected Issue*, Tel Aviv, World Organization of Jews from Arab Countries, 1977, pp. 26–27.

[118] Bat Ye'or, *The Dhimmi*, Fairleigh Dickinson University Press, 1985.

[119] G.E. Von Grunebaum, "Eastern Jewry Under Islam," *Viator*, 1971, p. 369.

with merchandise at half-price and accept counterfeit coinage, to name a few of the provisions.[120] Muslim children freely humiliated them by throwing stones. Writing in nineteenth century Syria, one Jew lamented, "When a Jew walked among them [the Muslims] in the market, one would throw a stone at him in order to kill him, another would pull his beard, yet another spit on his face. He became the symbol of abuse."

As the nineteenth century neared its end, the frequency of anti-Jewish violence increased, and many were executed on charges of apostasy. Ritual murder accusations against the Jews became commonplace in the final decades of the Ottoman Empire. The danger for Jews became even greater at the time of the partition of Palestine in 1947. In Iraq, the cleansing commenced in 1941, during the festival of Shavuot, when 180 Jews were murdered in a *farhoud* [pogrom] in Baghdad. The Syrian delegate at the United Nations, Faris el-Khouri, warned: "Unless the Palestine problem is settled, we shall have difficulty in protecting and safeguarding the Jews in the Arab world."[121] This was a self-fulfilling prophecy: Over 1,000 Jews were killed in the ensuing anti-Jewish rioting in Iraq, Libya, Egypt, Syria, and Yemen, triggering the mass exodus of Jews from Arab countries.[122] In the early 1940s, there were close to 1 million Jews throughout the Arab world. There are only a few thousand left today, mainly elderly. Some 600,000 went to Israel; those from North Africa to France or Canada, and others to the United States, Australia, and South America. The number of Jewish refugees from the Arab world exceeds the number of Palestinian refugees from the time of Israel's founding.

If the life of Jews under Islam was on the whole not as harsh as those of Christians, this was because they were not perceived as a threat: they did not have a potential source of loyalty or support in the outside world. The difference was one of degree, not of kind. Admittedly 'Umar ended the ban preventing Jews to live in Jerusalem, and Saladin, after conquering the city from the Crusaders, told the Jews that they could come back; but at all times theirs was a position of natural inequality. Even at the time of supposed "Jewish-Islamic symbiosis," the Jews were forced to live in ghettos as second class citizens.

---

[120] *Middle East Digest*, September 1999.
[121] *The New York Times*, February 19, 1947.
[122] Maurice Roumani, op.cit., pp. 30–31.

With the emergence of Zionism in the early twentieth century, the Muslims faced a "Jewish problem" for the first time since Mohammad. This time they faced it from a position of weakness, with the Jews for the first time since the destruction of the Temple poised to reestablish a polity that would be territorial as well as spiritual and cultural. The result was a massive outpouring of raw hatred, as atavistic and vitriolic as anything seen in Hitler's Germany, with the important difference that Nazism could not claim any scriptural grounding or divine mandate, even if it had wished for one.

It was a rude awakening for the Muslim world, after the phenomenal success of the earlier centuries, to find itself by the early twentieth century on what looked like the losing side of history. It was even more difficult to explain the decline, bearing in mind the Kuranic promise that the Umma consisted of the best of all people. The many weaknesses produced the sense that something had gone terribly wrong, but it did not result in creative self-examination. The question never was "What have we done?" but always "What have they done to us?" The Mongols, Turks, and Western imperialists have all had their share of blame apportioned, but, inevitably, in the 1930s the Jews were included among the "them" who were to blame.

Hitler's Germany sensed this and made a concerted, and remarkably successful, effort to plant "modern" anti-Semitism in the Arab world. As Bernard Lewis points out, "The struggle for Palestine greatly facilitated the acceptance of the anti-Semitic interpretation of history, and led some to attribute all evil in the Middle East—and, indeed, in the world—to secret Jewish plots." Even before Israel was created, that struggle turned into an existential battle of identity, with the complete denial of the legitimacy of Jewish existence as a central component of this campaign. When the Mufti of Jerusalem declared at the Dome on the Rock in 2001 that the negation of Jewish existence is an existential need of Islam, he was reflecting a majority, mainstream Muslim position, and continuing a well-established tradition.

In 1945, one name was missing from the Allies' list of war criminals, that of Haj Mohammed Amin al-Husseini, the Mufti of Jerusalem and the former President of the Supreme Muslim Council of Palestine. In May 1941, the Mufti declared jihad against Britain, "the greatest foe of Islam," and made his way to Berlin. When he met Hitler, on November 21, 1941, he declared that the Arabs are Germany's natural friends, ready to cooperate with the Reich with all their hearts by the formation of an Arab Legion. Hitler promised that as soon as the German armies pushed into the southern Caucasus, the Arabs would be liberated from the British yoke.

The Mufti's part of the deal was to raise support for Germany among the Muslims in the Soviet Union, the Balkans, and the Middle East. He conducted radio propaganda through the network of six stations and set up anti-British espionage and fifth-column networks in the Middle East. Partly thanks to his recruiting efforts, the Muslims in Bosnia and Kosovo volunteered for SS units famous for their savagery in the Balkans. His recruitment efforts among Soviet POWs from Islamic regions were proportionately somewhat less successful.

In the annual protest against the Balfour Declaration held in 1943 at the Luftwaffe hall in Berlin, the Mufti praised the Germans because they "know how to get rid of the Jews, and that brings us close to the Germans and sets us in their camp."[123] Echoing Muhammad after Badr, on March 1, 1944, the Mufti called in a broadcast from Berlin: "Arabs! Rise as one and fight for your sacred rights. Kill the Jews wherever you find them. This pleases God, history, and religion. This saves your honor." Already in 1941 he pledged "to solve the question of the Jewish elements in Palestine and in other Arab countries as required by national interests, and *in the same way as the Jewish question in the Axis lands is being solved*" [emphasis added]. Bernard Lewis says that, in addition to the old goal of Arabia being free of the presence of Jews, "he aimed at much vaster purposes, conceived not so much in pan-Arab as in pan-Islamic terms, for a Holy War of Islam in alliance with Germany against World Jewry, to accomplish the Final Solution of the Jewish problem everywhere." According to German officials who knew him,

> The Mufti had repeatedly suggested to the various authorities with whom he was maintaining contact, above all to Hitler, Ribbentrop, and Himmler, the extermination of European Jewry. He considered this as a comfortable solution of the Palestinian problem.

---

[123] B. Schechtman, *The Mufti and the Führer: The Rise and Fall of Haj Amin el-Husseini.* New York, 1965.

Perhaps the "Nazis needed no persuasion or instigation," as he was later to claim, but the foremost Arab spiritual leader of his time did all he could to ensure that the Germans did not waver in their resolve. He went out of his way to prevent any Jews to be allowed to leave Hungary, Romania, and Bulgaria, which were initially willing to let them go: "The Mufti was making protests everywhere—in the Office of the (Foreign) Minister, in the antechamber of the Secretary of State, and in other departments, such as Home Office, Press, Radio, and in the SS headquarters." In the end, Eichmann said, "We have promised him that no European Jew would enter Palestine any more." In 1943, he wrote to the Hungarian foreign minister:

> If there are reasons which make their removal necessary, it would be indispensable and infinitively preferable to send them to other countries where they would find themselves under active control, for example, in Poland, in order to protect oneself from their menace and avoid the consequent damage.

The choice of Poland as the Mufti's favored location for the deportation of Europe's Jews was chillingly uncoincidental.

After the war, with the Mufti re-established as the leader of the Palestinian Arabs, the Muslim line was that he had "killed nobody" and had only done his duty against Zionism. The "sense of duty" is evident in his letter of June 5, 1944, addressed to the Reichsfuehrer SS and Minister of the Interior Heinrich Himmler, in which the Mufti referred back to their conversation in which he asked Himmler to take all the measures to prevent the Jews from leaving Nazi-controlled Europe. On July 27, 1944, he wrote to Himmler again: "I ask you, Reichsfuehrer, to do everything necessary to prevent the Jews from emigrating."

In return, it was with the architect of the holocaust, Heinrich Himmler, that Islam had found its most ardent admirer and promoter in the pre-multicultural Europe. Himmler's hatred of "soft" Christianity was matched by his liking for Islam, which he saw as a masculine, martial religion based on the SS qualities of blind obedience and readiness for self-sacrifice, untainted by compassion for one's enemies. While Hitler did not think much of Himmler's neo-pagan mysticism, he was happy to let Islam become the "SS religion." By creating an SS division composed of Bosnian Muslims, Himmler was only taking the first step in the planned grand alliance between Nazi Germany and the Islamic world. One of his closest aides, *Obergruppenführer* Gottlob Berger, boasted that "a link is created between Islam and National-Socialism on an open, honest basis. It will be directed in terms of blood and race from the North, and in the ideological-spiritual sphere from the East."

The most potent heirs to the Nazi worldview in our own time as regards the Jews are not skinheads and Aryan Nation survivalists. They are schools, religious leaders, and mainstream intellectuals in the Muslim, meaning primarily Arab, world. Quite apart from the ups and downs of the misnamed "peace process" in the Middle East, quite apart from the more or less bellicose posture of the government of Israel, the crude way they actively demonize all Jews *as such* is startling.

The most prominent and influential daily newspaper in the Arab world is *Al-Ahram,* a semi-official organ of the Egyptian government, itself the second-largest recipient of American foreign aid. In June 2001 it carried an op-ed article, "What exactly do the Jews want?"—and the answer was worthy of the *Voelkische Beobachter* six decades earlier:

> The Jews share boundless hatred of the gentiles, they kill women and children and sow destruction. . . . Israel is today populated by people who are not descendants of the Children of Israel, but rather a mixture of slaves, Aryans, and the remnants of the Khazars, and they are not Semites. In other words, people without an identity, whose only purpose is blackmail, theft, and control over property and land, with the assistance of the Western countries.[124]

The second most influential Egyptian daily is *Al-Akhbar*, which went a step further on April 18, 2001: "Our thanks go to the late Hitler, who wrought, in advance, the vengeance of the Palestinians upon the most despicable villains on the face of the earth. However, we rebuke Hitler for the fact that the vengeance was insufficient."

It is hard to imagine hatred more vitriolic than that which reproaches the Nazis for not completing the Final Solution more thoroughly. What is remarkable is not that such sentiments exist, but that they are freely circulated in the mainstream media and internalized by the opinion-making

---

[124] Dr. Mustafa Mahmud in *Al-Ahram,* 23 June 2001.

elite throughout the Muslim world. In the same league we find the claim that the Holocaust in fact never happened and that the Jews and Israelis are the real Nazis. The Jewish-Nazi theme is a favorite of Arab caricaturists, some of whom use the swastika interchangeably with the Star of David, or juxtapose them. Graphic depiction of the Jews appear to have been lifted directly from the pages of *Der Stuermer*.

Syria is in the forefront. Mustafa Tlass, Syria's foreign minister, published a booklet, *The Matza of Zion*, about the infamous Damascus Trial of 1840, and concluded that Jews use non-Jewish blood for ritual purposes. The "Jewish Section" of the Makhabarat, the Syrian secret police, exercised strict control over the lives of the remaining members of the community. Just like Soviet citizens before 1989, Jews could travel abroad only if other family members remained behind in order to ensure the return of the traveler. Within the country there were tight restrictions on Jewish mobility and Jews had to seek permission to travel more than several kilometers from their homes. The documents of Jews were marked with a special designation indicating that the bearer was a Jew. Jews were not permitted to serve in the Syrian government, army, police or nationalized industry.

Even in countries not directly engaged against Israel, such as Morocco, demonization of the Jews is widespread. In October 1996 an op-ed article appeared in the Moroccan weekly *al-Usbu'* that provides an apt illustration of the genre. It claimed that "the Jews are a special kind of human being" by virtue of being spiteful and criminal, and congenitally dishonest:

> They are not content with the usurpation of the lands but they aim at the annihilation of mankind entirely in order to fulfill their devilish dreams. They cannot be satisfied without seeing the shedding of Moslem blood. The only arm which will enable us to confront this Jewish racist octopus is to know the Jews, and we cannot know them unless we read the Holy Kuran. You, the Moslem rulers, read the Kuran and forget about the politicians' accounts. The Jews are the enemy number one of the Moslems.

Among the recurring themes in the press of Islamic countries is that Judaism is a sinister religion and that Jews are a grotesque life form. Jews are also often represented as part of a diabolical cabal that strives at world domination; *The Protocols of the Elders of Zion* are often cited in this context by *bona fide* academic experts as credible evidence of Israel's intentions. Political and economic expert Dr. Amira Al-Sinwani thus summarized *The Protocols* for the Egyptian government-controlled daily *Al-Akhbar*:

> *The Protocols of the Elders of Zion*, published at the First Zionist Congress in the city of Basel, Switzerland in 1897, rose from the depths of darkness. They were later printed in French, in 1905. In 1921, the publication of these protocols was completely banned, except for the Arabic version. We all understand why Israel conceals these protocols when we look at the calls for destruction and the immorality—among them the call to destroy the world and set up "a world Jewish government that will rule this land— that is, rule the world."

To support the claim Dr. Al-Sanwani referred to a book published in 1935 in Nazi Germany, *A Handbook on the Jewish Question*.[125] While in the Arab world the Protocols are widely distributed but mostly by private editors, after 1979 in Iran an English and a French translation were printed and distributed by a publishing house sponsored by the government. From 1984 these booklets, including a map with a representation of the "Zionist serpent," were distributed by Iranian embassies and consulates in Europe. It is widely available in the entire Islamic world and is often cited by papers in other Arab countries.

In the aftermath of September 11, the most widely spread view all over the Muslim world—even at top governmental levels—is that "the Jews" carried out the attacks. Syrian foreign minister Mustafa Tlass, who has revived the "blood libel," claimed during a meeting in Damascus with a delegation from the British Royal College of Defense Studies that the Mossad planned the operation as part of a Jewish conspiracy.[126] Former Egyptian ambassador to Afghanistan Ahmad Al-'Amrawi stated that the Zionist movement and American intelligence organizations planned the

---

[125] www.memri.com, quoting original source. Charles Krauthammer also referred to this article, in his March 6, 1998, column in *The Washington Post* entitled "Arafat's Children."

[126] *The Jerusalem Post*, October 19, 2001.

attacks. Lebanese Druse leader Walid Jumblatt told *Al-Ayyam* daily that he thought the Mossad and American intelligence did it.

Columnist after columnist, in one leading paper after another, in Iran, Egypt, Jordan, Syria, and elsewhere expressed the opinion that "what happened is the work of Jewish-Israeli-American Zionism, and the act of the large Zionist Jewish mind controlling the world economically, politically, and through the media," and that "they, more than anyone, are capable of hiding a crime they carry out, and they can be certain that no one will ask them what they have done."[127]

Syrian ambassador to Tehran even declared that Syria has documented proof of the Zionist regime's involvement in the September 11 terror attacks on the U.S., and that "4,000 Jews employed at the World Trade Center did not show up for work before the attack clearly attests to Zionist involvement in these attacks."[128] He added that Israeli Prime Minister Ariel Sharon's unexpected postponement of his visit to the U.S. was "additional proof linking the Zionists with this tragedy." Even the most respected daily in the Arab world, pro-government *Al-Ahram,* joined the fray: "At the WTC, thousands of Jews worked in finance and the stock market, but none of them were there on the day of the incident. Out of 6,000 killed, of 65 nationalities from 60 countries, not one was a Jew!"[129]

While the United Nations has declared anti-Semitism a form of racism that must be condemned, Arab intellectuals are preaching it as gospel.[130] As Fouad Ajami of the Johns Hopkins University has observed in *The Dream Palace of the Arabs*, "the custodians of political power" in the Arab world determined some time ago that diplomatic accommodation would be the order of the day, but the intellectual class was given a green light to ensure that no peace with "the other" was possible. When faced with concerns about anti-Semitism in the Arab media, officials claim that is the price of a "free" press—even in countries that have none.

A gruesome, tangible testimony to Islamic anti-Semitism came with the ritualistic murder of the kidnapped *Wall Street Journal* reporter Daniel Pearl in Pakistan in February 2002. A videotape delivered to Pakistani

---

[127] Cf. comprehensive analysis of Arabic media reports on www.memri.com.

[128] IRNA (Iran), October 24, 2001.

[129] *Al-Ahram*, October 7, 2001.

[130] David A. Harris, "Peace and Poison in the Middle East," *The Washington Post*, May 2, 2000.

officials, just under four minutes long, showed the execution. Pearl was made to "confess" his Jewishness: "My name is Daniel Pearl. I'm a Jewish-American." He stated his address and repeated his sole defining characteristic as far as his captors were concerned: "My father is Jewish. My mother is Jewish. I am a Jew." Later on, looking at the camera, he said, "We've made numerous family visits to Israel." He added that there is a Heim Pearl Street there, named after his great-grandfather, who was one of the founders of a town. At that point the tape was interrupted and edited, after which Pearl spoke with some difficulty, making sympathetic reference to the prisoners held in Guantanamo Bay and comparing their predicament to his own. After another edit, he looks at the camera and says, "We as Americans cannot continue to bear the consequences of our government's actions, such as the unconditional support of the State of Israel." He is not reading a text but is speaking from memory, visibly struggling to remember what he is supposed to say. After this portion of the tape, which runs about a minute and a half, comes the final, gruesome segment of just under a minute, in which Daniel Pearl is butchered in the tradition of Muhammad's final solution for the Jews of Medina. Almost 14 centuries later, the Prophet's heirs are keeping the tradition alive.

The glaringly anti-Semitic character of Pearl's slaying has received surprisingly little attention from the media in the Western world. They were embarrassed, rather than outraged, by the connotations and preferred to present the story in terms of a "human tragedy," of "mindless violence," and to stress the noble sacrifice of a reporter ready to give his all in pursuit of a good story. It was even hinted that he was really pushing his luck anyway, and that his death was due to a normal occupational hazard. By minimizing the fact that his death, its fact, and its method, were primarily due to his *Jewishness*—and to his murderers' Islamicism—they paved the way for similar incidents in the future.

One need not speculate how the media would have reacted had a similar atrocity been committed by the neo-Nazis, or some weird sect other than Islam. An example was provided by the slaying of Matthew Shepherd. Within days of falling victim to a homophobic hate crime, he was promoted to the pantheon of politically correct victimhood, and continues to be perpetually memorialized in TV quasi-documentaries, books, conference papers, even street names. Gruesome, state-sanctioned executions of

192

homosexuals in the Muslim world meanwhile remain little known and seldom warrant official Western reaction.

The situational morality of the Western opinion creators prompts them not to judge events as such. They don't treat "morality" as a function of objective behavior but in accordance with the place of the actor within the ideological system. In those terms, anti-Semitism—including hard-core Holocaust denial—is utterly unforgivable, except when practiced by a "protected" group sanctified by its anti-Western "otherness," e.g., Muslims.

MYTH OF A "GOLDEN AGE"

With a few exceptions, the contemporary Islamic world is an overwhelmingly unpleasant place. There have been times, however, when some Muslim lands were fit for a cultivated man to live in. Baghdad under Harun ar-Rashid (his well-documented Christian-slaying and Jew-hating proclivities notwithstanding), or Cordova very briefly under Abd ar-Rahman in the tenth century, come to mind. We all know about all that, if for no other reason than because those isolated episodes are endlessly invoked by Islam's Western apologists and admirers as the auxiliary proof of the key tenet: that Christendom was the root of all evil in the world. It is therefore necessary to examine the validity of the claim that the "golden age" of Islam provides a viable counter-model to the barbarity of today's Wahhabism or Shi'ite radicalism.

The period in question largely coincides with the second dynasty of the caliphate, that of the Abbasids, named after Muhammad's uncle Abbas, who succeeded the Umayyads and ascended to the caliphate in A.D. 750. They moved the capital city to Baghdad, absorbed much of the Syrian and Persian culture as well as Persian methods of government, and ushered in "the golden age." Three speculative thinkers—notably all three Persians, al-Kindi, al-Farabi, and Avicenna—combined Aristotelianism and Neoplatonism with other ideas introduced through Islam.

Greatly influenced by Baghdad's Greek heritage in philosophy that survived the Arab invasion, and especially the writings of Aristotle, Farabi adopted the view—eminently heretical from an Islamic viewpoint—that reason is superior to revelation. He saw religion as a symbolic rendering of truth, and, like Plato, saw it as the task of the philosopher to provide guidance to the state. He indulged in rationalistic questioning of the authority of the Kuran, and rejected predestination. He wrote more than 100 works, notably *The Ideas of the Citizens of the Virtuous City*, which belongs to "Islam" just as much as Voltaire belongs to "Christianity."

The Muslim mainstream, on the other hand, emphasized the Kuranic orthodoxy but tried to deploy Greek philosophy and science in asserting its authority: "They were rationalists in so far as they fell back on Greek philosophy for their metaphysical and physical explanations of phenomena; still, it was their aim to keep within the limits of orthodox belief. In this they bore a close resemblance to the first Schoolmen of Christian Europe."[131] From the conflict of these two divergent forces there arose, about the ninth century, the tendency of thought represented by the philosophers of Islam. But when the thinkers went too far in their free inquiry into the secrets of nature, paying little attention to the authority of the Kuran, they aroused suspicion of the rulers both in North Africa and Spain, as well as in the East. Persecution, exile, and death were frequent punishments suffered by the philosophers of Islam whose writings did not conform to the canon.

At this time Sufism also arose as a reaction against philosophy. It rejected all philosophical inquiry, condemned the use of Greek philosophy even within the limits of orthodoxy, and taught that whatever truth there is can be attained by reverent reading of the Kuran and meditation on the words of the sacred text. Sufism was a mystical rebellion against the spiritual rigidity of Islam that sought to find divine love and knowledge through direct personal experience of Allah. This, to orthodox Islam, was not only impossible but heretical, and Sufism cannot be regarded as a properly "Islamic" sect. It is akin to mystical sects elsewhere. The practices of Sufi orders and suborders vary, but most include the recitation of the name of Allah or of certain phrases from the Kuran as a way to loosen the bonds of the lower self, enabling the soul to experience the "higher reality" toward which it naturally aspires.

On the other side of the Empire, in Spain, Averroës exercised much influence on both Jewish and Christian thinkers with his interpretation of Aristotle. While mostly faithful to Aristotle's method, he found the Aristotelian "prime mover" in Allah, the universal First Cause. His writings brought him into political disfavor, and he was banished until shortly

---

[131] *The Catholic Encyclopaedia.*

194

before his death, while many of his works on logic and metaphysics were consigned to the flames. He left no school, and the end of the dominion of the Moors in Spain, which occurred shortly afterwards, turned the current of Averoism completely into Hebrew and Latin channels, through which it influenced the thought of Christian Europe down to the dawn of the modern era.

Averroes advocated the principle of twofold truth, maintaining that religion has one sphere and philosophy another. Religion, he said, is for the unlettered multitude; philosophy for the chosen few. Religion teaches by signs and symbols; philosophy presents the truth itself. In the mind, therefore, of the truly enlightened, philosophy supersedes religion.

From Spain, the Arabic philosophic literature was translated into Hebrew and Latin, which contributed to the development of modern European philosophy. In Egypt around the same time, Maimonides—not a Muslim but a Jew—and Ibn Khaldun made their contribution. A Christian, Constantine "the African" and a native of Carthage, translated medical works from Arab into Latin, thus introducing Greek medicine to the West. His translations of Hippocrates and Galen first gave the West a view of Greek medicine as a whole. Overall, the years between 900 and 1200 in Spain and North Africa were a sort of Judeo-Christian Renaissance that arose from the fusion of different worlds. People could learn to be astronomers, philosophers, scientists, and poets, regardless of their background. Their ability to remain safe in their knowledge, or their identity, was never guaranteed, however.

Visual, literary, and musical arts of the lands conquered by Islam from the seventh century had to be largely nonrepresentational (in religious art strictly so). The "golden age" of Islamic art lasted from A.D. 750 to the mid-eleventh century, when ceramics, glass, metalwork, textiles, illuminated manuscripts, and woodwork flourished. Lustered glass became the greatest Islamic contribution to ceramics. Manuscript illumination became an important and greatly respected art, and miniature painting flourished in Iran. Calligraphy, an essential aspect of written Arabic, developed in manuscripts and architectural decoration.

In the exact sciences, the contribution of Al-Khwarzimi, mathematician and astronomer, was considerable. Like Euclid, he wrote mathematical books that collected and arranged the discoveries of earlier mathematicians. His *Book of Integration and Equation* is a compilation of

195

rules for solving linear and quadratic equations, as well as problems of geometry and proportion. Its translation into Latin in the twelfth century provided the link between the great Hindu mathematicians and European scholars. A corruption of the book's title resulted in the word *algebra;* a corruption of the author's own name resulted in the term *algorithm.*

Whatever flourished, it was not by reason of Islam, it was *in spite of Islam.* In Islam's "golden age," there was a lot of speculation and very little application; and for almost a thousand years, even speculation has stopped. The periods of civilization under Islam, however brief, were predicated on the readiness of the conquerors to borrow from earlier cultures, to compile, translate, learn, and absorb. Islam *per se* never encouraged science, meaning "disinterested inquiry," because the only *knowledge* it accepts is religious knowledge.

It is said that when the Caliph Umar conquered Alexandria in the seventh century, he had its huge library burned, saying that if the writings contained within were in agreement with the Kuran, then they were redundant and therefore useless; if they disagreed with the holy book of the Muslims, then they were blasphemous and must be burned. Modern Muslims delight in debunking this apocryphal story as anti-Islamic slander; yet it was not invented by Christians or Jews, but by Umar's twelfth century successors to justify the end of critical inquiry, *ijtihad,* exemplified in the burning of works by Ibn al-Haitham, who dared claim that the earth was spherical.

Nine hundred years later, in 1993, the supreme religious authority of Saudi Arabia, Sheik Abdel-Aziz Ibn Baaz, issued an edict, declaring that the world is flat: anyone of the round persuasion does not believe in God and should be punished. "Among many ironies of this *fatwa* is the fact that the lucid evidence that the Earth is a sphere, accumulated by the second-century Graeco-Roman astronomer Ptolemaeus, was transmitted to the West by astronomers who were Muslim and Arab."[132] For many long centuries, philosophy, natural history, medicine, and astronomy were looked upon with particular suspicion, and occasionally with open hostility. They were seen as a threat to Islam, as they came largely from non-Muslim sources.

---

[132] Carl Sagan, *The Demon-Haunted World,* 1996.

A number of medieval thinkers and scientists living under Islamic rule, by no means all of them Muslims either nominally or substantially, have played a useful role of transmitting Greek, Hindu, and other pre-Islamic fruits of knowledge to the West. They contributed to making Aristotle known in Christian Europe; however, in doing this, they were but transmitting what they themselves had received from Christian sources; and, moreover, the Aristotle who finally gained recognition in Christian Europe was not the Arabian Aristotle, but the *Greek* Aristotle, who came to Western Europe by way of Constantinople, largely via Byzantine Greeks fleeing the Ottoman onslaught. In the end it was the *Westerners* who were able to make good use of them, thanks to their ability to pursue intellectual inquiry that has grown increasingly independent of the Church. *Their* assertions were subjected to rigorous testing by a recognized adversarial method of proof. *They* were thus able to proceed to "the invention of invention," the institutionalization of research, resulting in the exponential growth of knowledge.

Most social and political thinkers in the Muslim world, following the paths opened in the fertile variety of European mind, have run the risk of being deemed heretical by Islamic standards—and the crime of heresy is still punishable by death in Islamic nations. Their endeavors were respectable but short of even approximating the genius of their original sources of inspiration, the glory that once was Hellas, and the majesty of Rome. By claiming that it is otherwise, we are not doing us—or them—any favors. Oriana Fallaci has finally got it right: those who evade the truth about our two civilizations out of weakness or lack of courage or habitual fence-straddling are just masochists:

> It bothers me to even talk about "two of them": to put them on the same plane as though they were two parallel realities of equal weight and equal measure. Because behind our civilization we have Homer, Socrates, Plato, Aristotle, Phydias, for God's sake. We have ancient Greece with its Parthenon and its discovery of Democracy. We have ancient Rome with its greatness, its laws, its concept of Law. Its sculptures, its literature, its architecture. Its buildings, its amphitheaters, its aqueducts, its bridges and its roads. We have a revolutionary, that Christ who died on the cross,

197

who taught us (too bad if we didn't learn it) the concept of love and of justice.[133]

Yes, I know—Fallaci says—there's also a Church that gave me the Inquisition, the torture and the burning at the stake. But it also made a great contribution to the History of Thought, and inspired Leonardo, Michelangelo, and Raphael, the music of Bach, Mozart, and Beethoven, on and on through Rossini and Donizetti and Verdi, and science that cures diseases, and has invented the train, the car, the airplane, the spaceships, and changed the face of this planet with electricity, the radio, the telephone. Fallaci offers a resolute reply to "the fatal question" of what is behind the other culture: "We can search and search and find only Mohammed with his Kuran and Averroe with his scholarly merits, his second-hand Commentaries on Aristotle"—all worthy but second-rate stuff, *really*. Well, yes, numbers and math; but even on this one, there's far less than meets the eye. As Bernard Lewis explains, the Muslim Empire inherited "the knowledge and skills of the ancient Middle East, of Greece and of Persia, it added to them new and important innovations from outside, such as the manufacture of paper from China and decimal positional numbering from India."[134] The decimal numbers were thus transmitted to the West, where they are still mistakenly known as "Arabic" numbers, honoring not their Hindu inventors but their Muslim transmitters.

For many centuries, cross-fertilization of elements from diverse regions and traditions became increasingly difficult: Islam was accepted or rejected in its entirety, regardless of local custom or tradition. An unprecedented rigidity was introduced into the relations between civilizations, reflecting the fundamental tenet of Islam—accurately restated a decade ago by Bosnia's president, Alija Izetbegovic, in his *Islamic Declaration*—that "there can be no peace between Islam and other forms of social and political organization." Most social and natural scientists, whose work demands certain assumptions about the nature and history of man, society, institutions, and the universe, would be deemed heretical by Islamic standards, and "for them garments of fire shall be cut and there shall be poured over their heads boiling water whereby whatever is in their

---

[133] "Anger and Pride" by Oriana Fallaci, *Corriere della Sera*, September 29, 2001.
[134] Bernard Lewis, *What Went Wrong?*, OUP, 2002, p. 6.

bowels and skins shall be dissolved, and they will be punished with hooked iron rods."[135]

The result is a climate of intolerance that inhibits the development of the Muslim world to this day. The intellectual foundation of Islam nurtures "a curious tendency to believe that non-Muslims either know that Islam is the truth and reject it out of pure obstinacy, or else are simply ignorant of it and can be converted by elementary explanations; that anyone should be able to oppose Islam with a good conscience quite exceeds the Muslim powers of imagination, precisely because Islam coincides in his mind with the irresistible logic of things."[136] The main victims, for now, are the non-conforming Muslims themselves, like Sudanese theologian Mahmud Muhammad Taha, a practicing Muslim who dared try to reform the Shari'a there. He was found guilty of apostasy, temporarily escaped death sentence long enough to see his works destroyed, and was finally publicly hanged in Khartoum in 1985 at the age of 76.

The Golden Age of Islam was "golden" only on its own terms. No self-respecting Western Islamophile would ever admit to this. Each and every one, on the other hand, felt duty-bound to be ambiguous, pained, agonized, if not outright supportive, of the fatwa passed on Salman Rushdie two decades ago. They came up with a stream of statements effectively blaming Rushdie for bringing the sentence onto himself by writing *The Satanic Verses*. John Esposito, an American academic Islamophile, claimed he knew "of no Western scholar of Islam who would not have predicted that [Rushdie's] kind of statements would be explosive."

Some writers included condescending asides about understanding the hurt felt by the Muslims. A British historian, Professor Trevor-Roper, even gave the tacit approval to the brutish call for the murder of a British citizen: "I would not shed a tear if some British Muslims, deploring his manners, should waylay him in a dark street and seek to improve them. If that should cause him thereafter to control his pen, society would benefit and literature would not suffer." Nowhere in any of these articles is there any criticism of the call to murder. Even worse, a recommendation was made that Rushdie's book be banned or removed from circulation. Astonishingly, there was no defense of one of the fundamental principles of democracy,

---

[135] 22.9.
[136] *Stations of Wisdom* by Frithjof Schuon.

the principle without which there can be no human progress, namely, the freedom of speech. One would have thought that this was one principle that writers and intellectuals would have been prepared to die for.[137]

Some political pressure has been brought to bear on Iran to get this rescinded, but not by the intellectuals. The ulema know the power of inflexibility, even if governmental hints that nothing will be done to implement the fatwa have any meaning. To make the life of poor Rushdie miserable, and to make the Western cultural establishment scamper about in consternation, was the principal object of the exercise. Militant Islam threatened the secular conscience; the sentence has been left on the books.

DECLINE WITHOUT A FALL

After the brief period of flourishing, first in Baghdad and then in Spain, the history of Islam has been that of a long decline without a fall. What started as a violent creed of the invaders from the desert soon ran out of steam, but the collective memory of earlier successes lingered on. It was still invoked as the proof of the divine approval and superiority. The fact that history was no longer on the side of Islam was for centuries blurred by the success of Turkish arms. It was not until 1683 that the menace to Europe was finally crushed at the gates of Vienna, but for long before that the Islamic world had little interesting to say, or do, at least measured against the enormous cultural melting pot it had made for itself and its unrivalled opportunities between East and West. Not even a prime location at the crossroads of the world could supply an antidote to the slow poison of Islamic obscurantism. The Ottoman interlude concealed and postponed the latent tension between the view of world history as the fulfillment of Islam and its triumph everywhere on the one hand, and the reality of the squalor and decadence on the other.

The nature of the problem has always been spiritual. Like all totalitarian ideologies, Islam has an inherent tendency to the closing of the mind. The spirit of critical inquiry essential to the growth of knowledge is completely alien to it. All known episodes invoked to counter this simple fact happened in spite of Islam, not thanks to it.

---

[137] Ibn Warraq, 1995, p. 9.

When the Ottomans realized that something was seriously wrong, tentatively in the eighteenth century and explicitly in the nineteenth, their view of knowledge remained that of a commodity that could be imported and used. Western engineers, military officers, and doctors trained their Muslim students, but the latter never managed to produce more than what was imparted to them. The problem was insoluble: the Sublime Porte wanted the fruits of Western culture, but not the culture itself. Western discipline, cohesion, ingenuity, and prosperity were rooted in the individual pride of free and egalitarian Greek hoplite squares, Swiss pikemen and German *Landsknechts*, and echoed in the war cries of Napoleon's Old Guards. Instant gratification—inherent to the Muslim mindset ever since Muhammad resorted to divine intervention in his lust for his daughter-in-law—could not be gratified so easily in this instance. Getting the results— gunboats, computers, life-saving drugs—but avoiding the undesirable trappings of democracy, of the spirit of critical inquiry and debate, has been the impossible task of despots ever since. In subsequent decades Stalin, Mao, Castro, and their ilk were no better at squaring the circle than the Sultan and his advisors in the 1850s. In the Crimea, Turkish regiments acquired field guns, steamboats plied the Bosphorus, and one could travel by rail from Istanbul to all corners of Europe, but there was no creative spark from within that could use foreign novelties to transform the society and jumpstart it into modernity.

The contrast with Japan in the period of Meiji Restoration is startling, but the Japanese could make it because even without "democracy"—as Athens of old, or Paris, London, and Philadelphia of the modern age have known it—it possessed a culture inured to discipline, approving of delayed gratification and self-restraint. Bernard Lewis points out that Islam, fatalistic, hypersensual, and still puzzled by its own failures, was struggling even to limp along:

> Muslim modernizers—by reform or revolution—concentrated their efforts in three main areas: military, economic, and political. The results achieved were, to say the least, disappointing. The quest for victory by updated armies brought a series of humiliating defeats. The quest for prosperity through development brought in some countries impoverished and corrupt economies in recurring need of external aid, in others an unhealthy dependence on a single resource—oil. And even this

was discovered, extracted, and put to use by Western ingenuity and industry, and is doomed, sooner or later, to be exhausted, or, more probably, superseded ... Worst of all are the political results: the long quest for freedom has left a string of shabby tyrannies, ranging from traditional autocracies to dictatorships that are modern only in their apparatus of repression and indoctrination.

The contrast between Japanese success and Islamic failure is aptly illustrated in their differing attitudes to Western music. Without giving up their sense of uniqueness and even understated superiority, the Japanese readily admitted that Western music expressed their emotions far better than anything in their own tradition. As he left French soil, writer Nagai Kafu (1879–1959) pondered the magnificence of French culture:

No matter how much I wanted to sing Western songs, they were all very difficult. Had I, born in Japan, no choice but to sing Japanese songs? Was there a Japanese song that expressed my present sentiment—a traveler who had immersed himself in love and the arts in France but was now going back to the extreme end of the Orient where only death would follow monotonous life? ...
I felt totally forsaken. I belonged to a nation that had no music to express swelling emotions and agonized feelings. [138]

Kafu here describes emotions almost entirely unknown to Muslims, or—in the same spirit—to the Bolshevik of Bolsheviks: Lenin once explained to Gorky that he refused to listen to music because "it makes you want to say stupid, nice things and stroke the heads of people who could create such beauty while living in this vile hell."[139] Lenin had a kindred soul in Ayatollah Khomeini, who expressed similar views in an interview with Oriana Fallaci:

K: Music dulls the mind, because it involves pleasure and ecstasy, similar to drugs. Your music I mean. Usually your music has not exalted the spirit, it puts it to sleep. And it destructs our

---

[138] Quoted in Daniel Pipes, "You Need Beethoven to Modernize," *Middle East Quarterly,* September 1998.

[139] Quoted in Paul Johnson, *Modern Times,* London, Phoenix, 1996, p. 51.

youth who become poisoned by it, and then they no longer care about their country.

Q: Even the music of Bach, Beethoven, Verdi?

K: I do not know these names.[140]

Khomeini allowed for the possibility that if "their" music does not dull the mind, it would not be prohibited: "Some of your music is permitted. For example, marches and hymns for marching. . . . Yes, but your marches are permitted." So, perhaps the late Ayatollah and the pro-Nazi Grand Mufti al-Husseyni would both find *Die Fahne Hoch* to their musical taste.

Other Muslims have joined Khomeini in approving the ecstasy that Western music can create is if it helps march youth to their deaths.[141] Across the Gulf, in Saudi Arabia,

> The government censors all forms of public artistic expression and prohibits cinemas and public musical or theatrical performances, except those that are considered folkloric. The authorities prohibit the study of evolution, Freud, Marx, Western music, and Western philosophy. Informers monitor lectures and report to government and religious authorities.[142]

The depth of ignorant zeal unaware of the existence of Bach and Beethoven but certain of the need to eradicate them illustrates the task facing a narrow segment of urban intelligentsia in the Muslim world that seeks to reform Islam into a matter of personal choice separated from the State and distinct from the society. This has always remained a minority view in the world of Islam, and even its apparent triumph in Turkey under Mustafa Kemal remains tentative at best: the simmering Islamic volcano in the villages of Anatolia and in the poor neighborhoods of the sprawling cities makes us wonder not "if" but "when." If and when Turkey becomes a fully-fledged democracy, that instant it will become Islamic and anti-Western.

---

[140] Oriana Fallaci, "An Interview with Khomeini," *The New York Times Magazine*, 7 October 1979, p. 31.

[141] Daniel Pipes, "You Need Beethoven to Modernize."

[142] U.S. Department of State, *Saudi Arabia: Country Reports on Human Rights Practices—2000*. Released by the Bureau of Democracy, Human Rights, and Labor, February 23, 2001.

In Egypt, secularization has run out of steam; half a century after Cairo led the way in the intellectual quest for an authentically Arab response to the challenge of modernity, its leading writers are forced into exile, silenced, or tried for atheism. "I have an opinion, and I expressed my opinion in these books," Salaheddin Mohsen told a state security court in Cairo.[143] That opinion was skeptical of Islam, and therefore enough to bring charges of "propagating extremist ideas to provoke strife and damage national unity." In 1996, Egypt's top appeals court pronounced Cairo University professor Nasr Abu Zeid an apostate on the basis of his writings and forcibly divorced him from his wife.

The Egyptian example indicates that the predominant response of the Muslim world to the crisis caused by western superiority has been the clamoring for "Islamic solutions." Both traditionalists and fundamentalists postulate the superiority of their faith and its divinely ordained world leadership, and both regard the early success of Islam as a natural result of the strict and uncompromising observance of all tenets of that faith. The subsequent decline and the temporary superiority of the unbelievers is both resented—creating the culture of anti-Western otherness—and feared. The failure of the umma was understood as a consequence of the failure of the Muslim world to be "truly Islamic." The solution, therefore, remained in the revival of religious fervor and in the transformation of Muslim societies not into the copies of the hated heathen West but into "genuine" umma. This was an inherently anachronistic approach, and it demanded "nullification of the historicity of meaning as subject to the political, economic, and cultural metamorphoses of society. . . . The Muslim cognitive system is essentially mythical."[144]

The only difference between Muslim "conservatives" and misnamed "fundamentalists" concern the methods to be applied, not the final objectives, which are the same: to rekindle the glory that was Islam under the prophet and his early successors. The difference is that the traditionalists would probably allow for the inclusion of the fruits of the "golden age" in the legacy that remains yet to be revived, while the fundamentalist position explicitly rejects them as the corrupting influence

---

[143] Reuters, June 18, 2000.
[144] Arkoun, Mohammed, *Rethinking Islam: Common Questions, Uncommon Answers*, Boulder, Colo., Westview Press, 1994, p. 99.

by a few converted or, worse still, faithless Greeks, Syrians, and Jews. Either way,

> It is in the myth of the complete and Perfect Man, and not in the corpus or in History, that one can read the universal, that all knowledge adds up and that the return to the golden age—the time of the prophet—is foreshadowed. It is with this mystical conception of knowledge that the new [Islamist] intellectual completes his homemade construction.[145]

The revival of the model of early Islam in a modern form absolutely mandates the reaffirmation of uncompromising animosity to non-believers and the return to violence as a means of attaining political ends. Islamic terrorism, far from being an aberration, became inseparable from modern-day jihad. It is legitimized by it, and it is its defining feature. The late medieval redefinition of jihad as spiritual battling with the evil impulses of the soul—a rendering endlessly repeated by Islam's apologists in the Western world—is quite properly rejected by today's Islamic activists not only as theologically incorrect (which it is) but also as a dangerous and harmful distraction from the path of divinely ordained struggle. The cult of martyrdom, always present in Shi'ite Islam, was fully revived by the Muslim brotherhoods in the early twentieth century and their different modern incarnations throughout the Islamic world and the Muslim diaspora in the West. What distinguishes "fundamentalists" and "conservatives" from "ordinary" Muslims as far as reference to the "golden age" is concerned is that "the former blot out history in favor of the reactivation of the founding myth, while the latter accommodate themselves to the history of Muslim societies."[146]

While it would be simplistic to claim that Islamists routinely cheat in representing their history to the rest of us, it is closer to the mark to say that they are prone to construct an invented reality for themselves. To understand the reality of Islam's record with its non-adherents, one should not compare it to Judaism or Christianity but match it against modern totalitarian ideologies, notably Bolshevism and National Socialism. Each

---

[145] Roy, Olivier, *The Failure of Political Islam*, Cambridge, Mass., Harvard University Press, 1996, p. 148.

[146] Kepel, Gilles, *Muslim Extremism in Egypt: The Prophet and the Pharaoh*, Berkeley, University of California Press, 1993, p. 228.

explicitly denied the legitimacy of any form of social, political, or cultural organization other than itself. In the name of Allah and Islam, more people were killed in one year of Khomeini than during the preceding quarter-century of the shah. It is easy to eliminate enemies who have been dehumanized. When Khomeini announced, "In Persia no people have been killed so far, only beasts," he was following in the footsteps of the architects of the Holocaust and the Gulag. "The beasts" may be Jews, Gypsies, Slavs, or all real, imagined, or potential enemies of "socialism," or mortal sinners and apostates; the principle is the same. Hitler's or Stalin's *forma mentis* was different from that of Khomeini only in quantity, not in quality. The latter's statement that the Muslims have no choice but to wage "holy war against profane governments" until the conquest of the world has been accomplished—an eminently orthodox and "mainstream" statement of Islamic world outlook, different only in its frankness from the pitch of Muslim apologists in the West—had a familiar ring to it. It was Nikita Khrushchev's "We shall bury you" wrapped in green instead of red. The Kremlin ruse called "peaceful coexistence" was but jihad under another name.

Islam and Communism differ from Nazism only in their inability to create a viable economy. Always reliant on the plunder of its neighbors and robbery of its non-Muslim subjects, Islam was unable to create new wealth once the conquerors had run out of steam and reduced the vanquished to utter penury. Pre-Islamic Egypt was the granary of Europe, just like the pre-Bolshevik Ukraine; now both have to import food. Pre-Islamic Syria and Asia Minor suffered a similar fate under Umar to the highly developed and prosperous East Germany and Czechoslovakia after 1945. Both Islam and Communism oppose the preconditions for successful economic development in principle as well as in practice. In both cases, attempts to copy Western methods of production failed because they were not accompanied by the essential changes of social, political, and legal structure; the problem of Ottoman experiments with modernization were remarkably similar to the tinkering with various "models of socialism" a hundred years later. According to the World Bank, the total exports of the Arab countries (other than fossil fuels) amount to less than those of Finland, a country of 5 million inhabitants. There are at least 50 Arabs to each Finn.

206

Islam starts with a simple profession of a simple faith. It ends by demanding complete, total, absolute allegiance of each individual to Muhammad and his successors. Anything less is disbelief, punishable by eternal torment: "they can have no (real) Faith, until they make Thee judge in all disputes between them, and find in their souls no resistance against Thy decisions, but accept them with the fullest conviction."[147] Total control is claimed, over every aspect of public and private life. Islam is revolutionary in outlook, extremist in behavior, totalitarian in ambition. To this day, Shari'a does not differentiate between rituals, legal codes, ethics, and good manners. Prayer and pilgrimage have been incorporated into national law, while affairs of state—such as taxes and warfare—are written into the Kuran. Wherever this is not the case, corruption and abomination are inevitable in the view of any true Muslim:

> As one of their spokesmen put it as long ago as 1951, "there is no one town in the whole world where Islam is observed as enjoined by Allah, whether in politics, economics or social matters." Implied here is that Muslims true to God's message must reject the status quo and build wholly new institutions.[148]

In seeking undivided control over its subjects, Islam has found its sole niche of "modernity" in being akin to twentieth century totalitarian ideologies. Grand Mufti al-Husseyni placed himself at the disposal of National Socialism. On the other side of the Suez Canal, Gammal Abdel Nasser ultimately placed his policy on Pan-Arabist socialism at the disposal of the Soviet Union. Islam, Communism, and National Socialism have all sought an eschatological shortcut that would enable the initiated to bypass the predicament of a seemingly aimless existence. All three did so by explicitly rejecting natural morality and replacing it with the gnostic mantras of *umma*, or *classless society*, or *Volksgemeinschaft*.

The fruits of attempted escape from the shackles of natural morality are as predictable as they are grim, for the Muslims no less than for their victims: both are enslaved, brutalized, and dehumanized by Islam. The all-pervasive lack of freedom is the hallmark of the Muslim world. Discrimination against non-coreligionists and women of all creeds, racism,

---

[147] 4:65.

[148] Daniel Pipes, "There Are No Moderates: Dealing with Fundamentalist Islam," *National Interest*, Fall 1995.

slavery, virulent anti-Semitism, and cultural imperialism can be found—individually or in various combinations—in different cultures and eras. Islam alone has them all at once, all the time, and divinely sanctioned at that. There is no presumed equality of different people's claim to life, liberty, or any pursuit at all in Islam. The fruits of Muhammad's adage that "only Muslims' blood is equal" is the curse that cannot be eradicated, short of a bold reform from within that seems no more likely today than at any time in the past 14 centuries.

Alexis de Tocqueville has expressed many opinions that have retained their prescient freshness in our own time. It is therefore unsurprising that his final word on the subject of Islam is as valid today as it was when first written over a century and a half ago:

> I studied the Kuran a great deal. . . . I came away from that study with the conviction that by and large there have been few religions in the world as deadly to men as that of Muhammad. As far as I can see, it is the principal cause of the decadence so visible today in the Muslim world, and, though less absurd than the polytheism of old, its social and political tendencies are in my opinion infinitely more to be feared, and I therefore regard it as a form of decadence rather than a form of progress in relation to paganism itself.

CHAPTER FIVE
Western Appeasement

Not a single Moslem state is a democracy. When there is serious internal opposition to a Moslem ruler, his rivals sometimes demand "democracy" during their bid to topple him, but never maintain it if they gain power. So there is an obvious contradiction between promoting democracy and supporting Moslem states. The contradiction between supporting globalism with ostensibly equal rights for all races, religions, or nations and across-the-board support for Moslem territorial and cultural expansion should be no less obvious. These contradictions are a grave American weakness, as ideological confusion hamstrings the ability to act logically and firmly.

> Yohanan Ramati, *The Islamic Danger to Western Civilization*

There are foreign policy strategists in Washington who have sought for decades to turn militant Islam into a tool of policy. This is not a flight of critical fancy: it is a well documented fact; it is not challenged as an accusation, but it is not unduly admitted either. In the beginning those strategists, or their predecessors, may have underestimated the danger of "blowback," but over the years they have bound good men to bad policy, and they have reinforced failure with gold. "Blowback" is the apt metaphor: poison gas blowing back from its intended victims to choke one's own soldiers in their trenches. The strategy of effective support for Islamic ambitions in pursuit of short-term political or military objectives of the United States has helped turn Islamic radicalism into a truly global phenomenon.

The underlying assumption was that militant Muslims could be used and eventually discarded—like Diem, Noriega, the Shah, and the Contras. The Kaiser lived to regret giving passage to Lenin on that sealed train in 1917, but in Washington the lesson remains unknown. In his now famous interview with *Le Nouvel Observateur* in January 1998, former National Security Advisor Zbigniew Brzezinski described how the Carter

209

Administration had instigated Islamic resistance to the pro-Soviet government in Afghanistan and thus maneuvered Moscow into military intervention.[1] Asked if he had any regrets about the consequences of that operation almost two decades later, Dr. Brzezinski was indignant:

> B: Regret what? That secret operation was an excellent idea. It had the effect of drawing the Russians into the Afghan trap and you want me to regret it? The day that the Soviets crossed the border, I wrote to President Carter that we now have the opportunity of giving to the USSR its Vietnam War. Indeed, for almost ten years, Moscow had to carry on an unsupportable conflict that brought about the demoralization and finally the breakup of the Soviet empire.
>
> *Q: And neither do you regret having supported the Islamic fundamentalism, giving arms and advice to future terrorists?*
>
> B: What matters more to world history, the Taliban or the collapse of the Soviet empire? Some stirred-up Moslems or the liberation of Central Europe and the end of the Cold War?
>
> *Q: Some stirred-up Moslems? But isn't Islamic fundamentalism a world menace today?*
>
> B: Nonsense! There is no global Islam.

The rest, as they say, is history. Let us start by noting the almost hysterical exaggeration in Brzezinski's conceited claim. Afghanistan was not the graveyard of the Soviet system. Most fighting was Afghan on Afghan: the Soviet commitment was limited; the casualties were not very serious on an annual basis and were certainly not regime-threatening. The Afghan blunder was bad for military morale and expensive, but that was all. If there was a war that bled the Soviet system of economic options, it was the one fought in Vietnam, where they supported the winning side. It is more reasonable to assert that all the conviction had leached out of the Kremlin well before Brezhnev was dead. The USSR was the husk of a dying system before a single Soviet soldier crossed the Afghan border. Brzezinski could not know this in 1979, but he should have known better by 1998.

---

[1] French original is on archives.nouvelobs.com/voir_article.cfm?id=33731&mot= brzezinski.

In the event, President Carter secretly authorized $500 million (closer to a billion in today's money) to help create an international network that would spread Islamism in Central Asia and "destabilize" the Soviet Union. The CIA called this "Operation Cyclone," and in the following years poured over $4 billion into setting up Islamic training schools in Pakistan (hence the "Taliban" movement, which means "student"). Young fanatics were sent to training camps paid for by the U.S. taxpayer, where future members of Al-Qaeda were taught "sabotage skills" (i.e., terrorism). In Pakistan they were directed by British MI6 officers and trained by the SAS.

The result, contrary to Dr. Brzezinski's quip, was considerably more formidable than "a few stirred up Muslims." He would probably choose his words more guardedly today, but it is a matter of amply documented record that, despite the Islamic revolution in Iran that had taken place only months earlier, the policy makers in Washington had not treated Islamic fundamentalist ideology in adversarial terms until it started attacking America. It failed to take note of the change of mood taking place in the Islamic world, thanks to Afghanistan: "By 1989, the jihadists thought that they had destroyed the Soviet Union, and that militant Islam was a force that could prevail against any enemy, forgetting that what really drove the Russians out of Afghanistan was the Stinger antiaircraft missiles given to them by the United States," says French Islamologist Gilles Kepel. "This led them to believe that they could triumph everywhere."[2]

The enlistment of militant Islam in the destruction of Communism was an error compounded by simultaneous Muslim mass immigration. Leeds and Leicester have acquired the sights and sounds of Peshawar and Rawalpindi, Marseilles and Toulon the suburbs of Dakkar or Algiers, Berlin and Stuttgart a growing slice of Istanbul or Adana. This social experiment—Britain's Roy Jenkins, a liberal Home Secretary in the mid-sixties, admitted slyly that his contemporaries "might have considered matters more carefully"—antedated America's Cold War expedients, but the consequences of the experiment and the expedient have fused.

The assumption all along has been that the Islamic genie released by Dr. Brzezinski's "excellent idea" could be controlled through its eventual reduction to yet another humanistic project in self-celebration, through its adherents' immersion in the consumerist culture, and through their

---

[2] *The New York Times*, January 27, 2002.

children's multicultural indoctrination by state education. How well it has worked we can see in the swelling ranks of British, French, and American-born jihadi volunteers for martyrdom.[3] Few Westerners saw the essence of the problem before it got out of hand:

> Do you remember those bearded men with the gowns and the turbans who, before firing their mortars shouted "Allah akbar! Allah akbar!" I remember them very well. I used to shiver hearing the word "Allah" coupled with the shot of a mortar. . . . Well, the Russians left Afghanistan . . . and from Afghanistan the bearded men of the most-bearded Osama bin Laden arrived in New York with the unbearded . . . nineteen kamikaze.[4]

Greed and politics of oil have played a key role throughout. "Globalization" as a means of promoting economic profits and political hegemony was the basis of both immigration and the peculiar love-hate relationship between Washington and the Muslim world:

> The decision to allow Moslem states to assume full sovereign rights over their oil and natural gas resources and expropriate them in part or sometimes *in toto* was thus primarily a U.S. gamble based on the hope that these states would cooperate with American oil companies, leaving them effective control and a lion's share of the profits. In practice, effective control duly passed to the Moslem states concerned, which also appropriated a steadily growing share of the wealth energy produced. Though there is no shortage of oil and never has been, restrictions on output and the fact that (apart from the U.S. itself) communist USSR and China were the two other biggest oil producers, enabled the Moslems—and particularly the Arabs—to use oil embargoes as a political weapon.[5]

The effectiveness of that weapon meant that in the conflicts that inevitably define the line between Islam and its neighbors, Washington

---

[3] "We will replace the Bible with the Kuran in Britain," in the British weekly *Observer*, November 4, 2001.

[4] "Anger and Pride" by Oriana Fallaci, *Corriere della Sera*, September 29, 2001.

[5] Yohanan Ramati: *The Islamic Danger to Western Civilization,* www.westerndefense.org/special/TwinTowers2001.htm.

almost invariably supported the Muslims. By January 1996, Jacob Heilbrunn and Michael Lind of *The New Republic* approvingly wrote in *The New York Times* of the U.S. role as the leader of Muslim nations from the Persian Gulf to the Balkans, with the Ottoman lands becoming "the heart of a third American empire."[6] What they overlooked was that all across that empire, "all around the edges of the Muslim world, tension is growing in communities divided by religion. Clashes, shootings, and massacres have highlighted the atavistic suspicions of those who live in the borderlands where the tectonic plates of the world's two largest faiths overlap."[7] The Heilbrunn-Lind mindset prompted George Will to claim on *This Week* in 1999 that "the unpleasantness over Kosovo was an Orthodox Slav population, the Serbs, brutalizing to an extraordinary degree, a small Muslim state of Kosovo, and that's exactly what's happening today with Chechnya."[8] Quite apart from the multiple lie of the statement itself, the reverse notion—that America should go to war to defend the Christians of Cyprus, Armenia, Sudan, Egypt or Timor against "extraordinary brutalization" by their Muslim neighbors—is simply unimaginable.

SLAUGHTER IN THE ISLANDS

The precursor of it all was the murderous terror of Indonesian Muslims against Christians in East Timor, unknown in America although Washington tolerated ex-President Suharto's carnage on a scale worthy of Pol Pot. By 1989, Amnesty International estimated that Indonesia had murdered 200,000 East Timorese, out of a population of 600,000–700,000.[9] Suharto was not a devout Muslim but he nevertheless used Islamic fanatics as allies in various campaigns: notably against Chinese communists and their alleged accomplices that killed over 500,000 people, many of them Christians, in 1965.

---

[6] Jacob Heilbrunn and Michael Lind, "The Third American Empire," *The New York Times,* January 2, 1996.

[7] Michael Binyon in *The Times* of London, January 4, 2002.

[8] Cf. *New York Press*, Vol. 12, No. 52, www.nypress.com/content.cfm?content_id= 972.

[9] The same estimate was made by Human Rights Watch in 1989—proportionately more deaths than the simultaneous campaign of Khmer Rouge in Cambodia.

Indonesia's treatment of religious minorities had already been tested in West Papua. Suharto's anticommunist credentials enabled him to preserve the support of the U.S. government while he terrorized the inhabitants of Dutch New Guinea, which was handed over to Indonesia in 1962 and its name changed to Irian Jaya. The tribal people of West Papua had nothing in common with Indonesia, except that both had previously been ruled by Holland. They are Melanesians and not Indo-Malays, and Christians or animists. Under Suharto the army rounded up all the children from the missions and forced them to attend state schools. Passive resistance to Indonesian control was widespread, and zealous Muslim officers responded by ordering soldiers to kill the villagers' pigs, an important element in their basic economy. They soon proceeded to killing people: by September 1973, over 30,000 civilians had been killed by Indonesian troops, the number rising to an estimated 100,000 by 1990. The story was unreported in the U.S. media, and uncommented upon by the Nixon Administration.

East Timor came on the agenda with the disintegration of the Portuguese colonial empire. Indonesia did not have any valid claim to it, but President Gerald Ford and Secretary of State Henry Kissinger, who were visiting Jakarta, nevertheless approved the Indonesian invasion of the former Portuguese on December 7, 1975. They only asked that the attack be delayed until after their departure. Kissinger told reporters that "the United States understands Indonesia's position on the question of East Timor," and the U.S. abstained in the subsequent U.N. vote condemning the invasion. "The United States wished things to turn out as they did and worked to bring this about. The Department of State desired that the United Nations prove utterly ineffective in whatever measures it undertook. This task was given to me, and I carried it forward with no inconsiderable success."[10] Suharto was delighted to have received U.S. support for the invasion because of the Indonesian army's reliance on American weaponry that, by U.S. law, could only be used for defensive purposes. Washington continued to supply arms to Indonesia that were obviously not meant for general defense purposes, but specifically chosen to meet the needs of a counterinsurgency campaign. At the same time Indonesian military forces linked to the carnage in East Timor were trained in the United States under

---

[10] Daniel Patrick Moynihan, then-U.S. Ambassador to the United Nations, in a cable to Secretary of State Henry Kissinger on January 23, 1976.

a covert program sponsored by the Clinton Administration, which continued until 1998. It was codenamed "Iron Balance," and hidden from legislators and the public when Congress curbed the official schooling of Indonesia's army after a massacre in 1991. Principal among the units that continued to be trained was the Kopassus, an elite force with a bloody history. Amnesty International described it as "responsible for some of the worst human rights violations in Indonesia's history."

Through two and a half subsequent years of that campaign—leading to the death of about a third of the population—*The New York Times* ran only two brief stories about "the problem of East Timorese refugees." The startling hypocrisy was seldom remarked upon in the mainstream media:

> If East Timor was Kosovo, we all know what would have happened by now. U.S. President Bill Clinton would have gone on national television to denounce Indonesian president B.J. Habibie as a new Hitler and a threat to world peace. There would have been American-led cries . . . to indict Indonesia's army generals for war crimes. The media would be referring to what is now happening in East Timor as a "new Holocaust." The reason none of this is happening is obvious. The United States, the key player in both conflicts, regards Serbia as a pariah state and Indonesia as a valued trading partner. . . . [It] pursued its interests by minimizing Indonesian atrocities and portraying the Indonesian military and political leadership as positively as possible. In both cases, of course, the dead are still the dead.[11]

In the motivation, patterns, and perceptions of the actors on the ground—killers and victims alike—East Timor was an Islamic jihad against Christian infidels, identical in form and purpose to other tragedies caused by Islam's insatiable appetite for other people's lands, property, bodies, and souls. Dili's bishop, Mgr. Coste Lopez, later stated: "The soldiers who landed started killing everyone they could find. There were many dead bodies in the streets." They had been told that they were fighting a jihad, and whole villages—for example, Remexio and Aileu— were slaughtered. In Dili, hundreds of Chinese were shot and thrown off the wharf into the sea. In Maubara and Luiquica, the entire Chinese

---

[11] Lorrie Goldstein: "Our selective morality," *The Toronto Sun,* September 14, 1999.

populations were wiped out. Nineteen ships were moored in Dili harbor to remove looted cars, radios, furniture, tractors, and whatever else could be ransacked. Churches and the seminary were looted and their books burnt. Australian Consul to East Timor, James Dunn, reported that East Timorese refugees were not even safe in West Timor: 2,000 men, women, and children had been burned or shot to death at Lamaknan. At the concentration camp on Atauro island, the prisoners were given one small can of corn per person per week. Punishment for listening to foreign broadcasts or for speaking Portuguese included beatings, burning with cigarettes on face and genitals, electric shock, water immersion, and the removal of toenails. Many priests had moved to the hills with their flocks and were able to report on the massacres of children in Lospalos, Viqueque, Amoro, and Sumalai. Priests were beaten, churches invaded, and their congregations arrested.[12] By November 1976, the death toll had reached 100,000. The military focused on the more educated strata of Timorese seminarians, teachers, nurses, and public officials.

Once East Timor was out of the way, the next target was the Christian minority in Indonesia itself. In 1999–2000 the persecution, destruction of property, and killing of Indonesia's Christians amounted to a deliberate campaign of religious cleansing, abetted by the Indonesian military, which is overwhelmingly Muslim. Independent television footage illustrated numerous instances of soldiers and police taking sides.[13] The worst atrocities were committed on the island of Ambon, where an upsurge in violence followed the arrival of 2,000 Laskar Jihad—a militant Muslim force determined to join the "holy war" against the Christians on the island—who sent its warriors from Java and South Sulawesi. Indonesian soldiers sent to the Molucca Islands were fighting alongside militant Muslims, leading to calls by the Christians for a neutral U.N. peacekeeping force. Most of the fighting took place around the city of Ambon.[14] Violence in North Halmahera has resulted in up to 100,000 people fleeing their homes for the jungles and mountains; the Christian communities were in

---

[12] "The Harassment of the Church in East Timor," *Catholic Leader* (Brisbane), August 1984.

[13] *The Guardian Weekly*, 13–19 January 2000.

[14] *Jane's Defense Weekly*, 19 July 2000; *The Guardian Weekly*, 20–26 July 2000; *The Guardian Weekly*, 13–19 July 2000.

disarray.[15] The campaign of anti-Christian violence finally abated in 2001, after Muslim migrants from the overpopulated islands of Java and Sulawesi had been well established in the homes and on the lands of expelled Christians.

Indonesia's northern neighbor Malaysia is another "pro-Western" Muslim state, and it is often quoted by Western experts on Islam as an example that the Muslim religion is capable of reform, progress, and economic development. It is insufficiently known that Malaysia is not a "Muslim" state but a multi-ethnic, multi-religious state in which state-sponsored Islamization is proceeding at the expense of the non-Muslim communities. Fewer than half of Malaysians are Muslim, while Christians comprise a tenth of the population, Buddhists 17 percent, Hindus 7 percent, Confucians and Taoists 12 percent. The non-Muslims are responsible for the bulk of Malaysia's economic progress, contributing over three-quarters of the country's GNP. Nevertheless, Islam is the official religion in Malaysia, and a number of laws give it precedence over the others. The import and sale of the Bible in Malay is prohibited as it is "considered prejudicial to the national interest and security of the Federation." Conversion of Muslims is illegal, but a non-Muslim minor can convert to Islam. Non-Muslim schools can only give religious instruction out of school hours, and yet a non-Muslim "may not object to his children receiving lessons in Islam in the public school because in so doing they are instructed in the ideology of the state."

BALKAN CONNECTION I: BOSNIA

The Bosnian crisis started in the aftermath of the first post-communist election (fall 1990) when three main ethnic political parties representing Serbs, Croats, and Muslims formed a coalition government. The breakup of that coalition was caused by Alija Izetbegovic, the Muslim leader, who reneged on an agreement brokered by the European Union that provided for continued power-sharing in Sarajevo, rather opting for an unilateral declaration of independence; in making this decision, he was supported by the U.S. Ambassador in Belgrade, Warren Zimmerman.

---

[15] *The Globe and Mail*, 8 August 2000.

The crisis was greatly aggravated by President Slobodan Milosevic of Serbia. A cynical *apparatchik* devoid of convictions, he sent in his paramilitaries, who triggered ethnic cleansing. Milosevic in Serbia and President Franjo Tudjman in Croatia were both busy establishing a quasidictatorial post-communist regime and saw their brutal involvement in Bosnia as a means of enhancing their power base at home. Their respective struggles to impose themselves on their own republics may explain more about the war in Bosnia than the confused and variable goals of any of the Bosnian leaders.

The numeric advantage lay with the Muslims, however, who were able to win in the end with international help. At the beginning of the Balkan conflict, Acting Secretary of State Lawrence Eagleburger made it clear that a goal in Bosnia was to mollify the Muslim world and to counter any perception of an anti-Muslim bias regarding American policies in Iraq.[16] The subsequent portrayal in the American media of the Muslims of Bosnia as innocent martyrs in the cause of multicultural tolerance concealed the fact that the war was primarily religious in nature. Before the first shots were fired, the Bosnian Muslim leader, Alija Izetbegovic, proudly proclaimed, in his "Islamic Declaration" (1974; republished 1990) that "there can be no peace or coexistence between the Islamic faith and non-Islamic societies and political institutions":

> The Islamic movement should and must start taking power as soon as it is morally and numerically strong enough not only to overthrow the existing non-Islamic power structure, but also to build a great Islamic federation spreading from Morocco to Indonesia, from tropical Africa to Central Asia.[17]

This is hardly an unusual viewpoint for a sincere and dedicated Islamist, and Mr. Izetbegovic should have been commended for his frankness. Nevertheless, it should have been obvious in the West that the Bosnian-Muslims did not want to establish a multiethnic liberal democratic society. The U.S. Army Foreign Military Studies Office saw the situation more clearly than the politicians: "Such ideals may appeal to a few members of Bosnia's ruling circles as well as to a generally secular

---

[16] Eagleburger's MacNeil/Lehrer PBS NewsHour interview on October 6, 1992.

[17] For pean to Izetbegovic from a Western Muslim source cf., www.youngmuslims.ca/biographies/display.asp?ID=2.

populace, but President Izethbegovic and his cabal appear to harbor much different private intentions and goals."[18]

The demonization of the Serbs proceeded nevertheless, a school text case of media-induced pseudo-reality in the service of the Washingtonian foreign policy "community" which—by the end of 1991—had decided to side with Islam in the Balkans. An orchestrated campaign soon followed to contextualize the brutalities of the Balkans with the horrors of the Holocaust. This worked wonders for the Bosnian Muslims. In a complex conflict with confusing and contradictory pieces, Americans were offered a powerful package that simplified the equation into a clear-cut morality play: "Looking for a frame for Bosnia, Westerners could so easily have found meaning in terms like 'fascist' and 'Islamic radical': they actually found it in 'genocide' and 'holocaust'—leaving no room for compromise or even debate." Saving the Muslims would thus expiate for not saving the Jews of Warsaw or Budapest fifty years earlier. Mr. Izetbegovic's Western apologists could dismiss his "Islamic Declaration" as a passing indiscretion. His apologists included former Marxists previously apologetic of Moscow, Peking, Castro, Che, and Ho. The Parisian ex-communist "philosophe" Bernard Henry-Levy calmly declared that Izetbegovic's policy "has been demonstrably against the establishment of an Islamic state. The government of Sarajevo is mixed, with a strict parity of the Muslim, Croat, and Serb ministers."[19]

More than a decade later, we know that Mr. Izetbegovic meant business.[20] President Clinton was still in the White House when a classified State Department report warned that the Muslim-controlled parts of Bosnia were a safe haven for Islamic terrorism.[21] It said that hundreds of foreign mujaheddin, who had become Bosnian citizens and remained there after fighting in the war, presented a major terrorist threat to Europe and the United States. Among them were hard-core terrorists, some with ties to

---

[18] "Selling the Bosnia Myth to America: Buyer Beware," Lieutenant Colonel John E. Sray, USA, U.S. Army Foreign Military Studies Office, Fort Leavenworth, KS, October 1995.

[19] www.npq.org/issues/v102/p60.html.

[20] For a critique of the "Declaration" from a Bosnian-Muslim source opposed to fundamentalism, cf. "Alija Izetbegovic: The Portrait of a Tolerant Totalitarian" (in Serbo-Croat), www.bhdani.com/ arhiv/2000/143/t432a.htm.

[21] *The Los Angeles Times,* October 7, 2001, www.latimes.com/news/nationworld/ nation/ la-100701terror.story.

Osama bin Laden, who were protected by the Muslim government in Sarajevo. (This was confirmed in November 2001, when Afghanistan's northern alliance forces found two Bosnian passports among documents in a house vacated in Kabul by the fleeing Taliban.[22])

The findings of the report were summarized in the words of a former State Department official: Bosnia was "a staging area and safe haven" for Islamic terrorists. The magnitude of the problem was revealed in a subsequent report quoting Israeli intelligence sources that "about 6,000 fighters in Bosnia and Herzegovina, Kosovo, Albania, and Macedonia are ready to do Bin Laden's bidding," and that "a nucleus of Bin Laden followers in the Balkans could balloon into an army of about 40,000 men," mostly local Muslims from Bosnia, Kosovo, and Albania.[23]

The core of Bin Laden's Balkan network are the veterans of El Moujahed brigade of the Bosnian-Muslim army. It was established in 1992 and included volunteers from all over the Islamic world whose passage to Bosnia was facilitated by Al-Qaeda. The unit was distinguished by its spectacular cruelty to Christians, including decapitation of prisoners to the chants of *Allahu-akbar*.[24] El Moujahed was the nursery from which an international terrorist network spread to Europe and North America. After the end of the Bosnian war, many Muslim volunteers remained.[25]

The potential threat of Islamic fundamentalism in Europe persuaded the U.S. and other Western nations to oppose the presence of foreign mujahedeen in Bosnia as part of the November 1995 Dayton peace agreements, which specifically called for the expulsion of all foreign fighters. But the Muslim-controlled Bosnian government circumvented the rule by granting Bosnian citizenship to several hundred Arab and other Islamist volunteers—eliminating their "foreign" status before the accord took effect. Many of them had taken over the former Serbian village of

---

[22] AP, November 21, 2001.

[23] European edition of the U.S. forces' weekly newspaper *Stars & Stripes,* September 30, 2001.

[24] www.balkanpeace.org/wcs/wct/wcts/wcts19.shtml.

Such gruesome spectacles were duly videotaped and circulated through the network of Islamic centers and stores and Internet sites in the West.

[25] "Foreign Muslims Fighting in Bosnia Considered 'Threat' to U.S. Troops," *The Washington Post*, November 30, 1995.

Bocinja Donja, near the city of Zenica in central Bosnia; elsewhere they took over properties and married local women, sometimes by force.[26]

The results followed swiftly. On December 18, 1995, a car bomb prematurely exploded in Zenica. It was apparently meant for American troops stationed nearby, as revenge for the sentencing of Sheikh Omah Abdel Rahman for the WTC bombing.[27] Two months later, in February 1996, NATO-led units raided the training center of the Bosnian government's secret police AID near the city of Fojnica and found out that instructors from the Middle East were teaching AID officers how to disguise bombs as toys and ice-cream cones.[28]

Iran had already obtained a foothold of its own in Bosnia, when the Clinton Administration asked for—and obtained—Teheran's help in supplying the Muslim army with weapons.[29] This was done in violation of the arms embargo initially demanded by the U.S. and behind the back of its European allies.[30] The CIA and the Departments of State and Defense were kept in the dark until after the decision was made.[31] Along with the weapons, Iranian Revolutionary Guards and VEVAK intelligence operatives entered Bosnia in large numbers.

In March 1996, just before a Group of 7 summit in Lille, French police discovered a terrorist plot to attack the Western heads of states or governments by a group of local Muslims who had fought in the Balkans. All of their weapons and explosives were smuggled from Bosnia. The French thus uncovered what they called "the Bosnian Connection."[32] They

---

[26] "Mujaheddin Remaining in Bosnia: Islamic Militants Strongarm Civilians, Defy Dayton Plan," *The Washington Post*, July 8, 1996.

[27] www.balkanpeace.org/our/our02.shtml.

[28] "NATO Captures Terrorist Training Camp, Claims Iranian Involvement," Associated Press, February 16, 1996; "Bosnian government denies camp was for terrorists," Reuters, February 16, 1996.

[29] "Clinton-Approved Iranian Arms Transfers Help Turn Bosnia into Militant Islamic Base," U.S. Senate Republican Policy Committee, January 16, 1997, www.senate.gov/~rpc/releases/1997/iran.htm.

[30] See "Fingerprints: Arms to Bosnia, the real story," *The New Republic*, October 28, 1996.

[31] "U.S. Had Options to Let Bosnia Get Arms, Avoid Iran," *The Los Angeles Times*, July 1, 1996.

[32] For an account of *l'affaire de Roubaix* see: www.lavoixdunord.fr/vdn/journal/dossier/justice/gang/resume.shtml. For a recent summary in *Le Monde,* see: www.lemonde.fr/article/0,5987,3226--229239-VT,00.html.

were upset that Osama Bin Laden's links to the Bosnian Muslims, and in particular his supplies of weapons in 1992–1993 to the Izetbegovic government, were known to the Clinton Administration and quietly tolerated by it.[33] Three months after the Lille incident, even *The Washington Post*—normally supportive of the Administration's Balkan policy—confirmed that "the Clinton Administration knew of the activities of Bin Laden's so-called Relief Agency, which was, in fact, funneling weapons and money into Bosnia to prop up the Izetebegovic Muslim government in Sarajevo."

The following year, the Bosnian Connection resurfaced following the bombing of the Al Khobar building in Riyadh, Saudi Arabia: several suspects had served with the Bosnian Muslim forces and were linked to Osama Bin Laden.[34] From that point on, the U.S. had complained periodically and ineffectually to the Muslim authorities in Sarajevo about the continued presence of the mujahadeen in Bosnia, but to little avail.

In 1999 the U.S. law enforcement authorities discovered that several suspects linked to Bosnia were associated with a terrorist plot to bomb the Los Angeles International Airport on New Year's Day. Some months earlier, Abdelkader Mokhtari, an Algerian with Bosnian citizenship, tried to help smuggle military C-4 plastic explosives and blasting caps to a group plotting to destroy U.S. military installations in Germany.[35] Washington tried to force his deportation from Bosnia, but only when the U.S. threatened to stop all economic aid Izetbegovic agreed to do so. The measure was not permanent: he was back within a year, moving in and out freely and spending part of his time in Afghanistan with the leadership of the Al-Qaeda group.

Izetbegovic stepped down in 2000, but many hard-liners remain in Bosnia's bureaucracy, and they are suspected of operating their own rogue intelligence service that protects Islamic extremists. In 2002, six Algerian-born naturalized Bosnian citizens belonging to Bin Laden's network plotted to capture aircraft at an airstrip at Visoko, just north of Sarajevo, and use them to attack American peacekeepers at NATO bases in the city of Tuzla—Camp Eagle, with some 3,000 U.S. personnel—and a smaller base, Camp Conor, near Srebrenica. After the group was arrested, the NATO

---

[33] *L'Express*, December 26, 1996.
[34] *The New York Times*, June 26, 1997.
[35] *The Los Angeles Times*, October 7, 2001.

Secretary-General Lord Robertson himself linked them with Al-Qaeda.[36] Their leader, Bensahay Balkatsem, had made 70 calls to Afghanistan in September and October 2001. However, a court in Sarajevo refused to accept evidence because the phone taps had been carried out "illegally" on its soil. The six men were ordered released; the U.S. apprehended them as they left the prison in Sarajevo to fly them to Guantanamo Bay in Cuba, amidst violently anti-American demonstrations by thousands of outraged Bosnian Muslims.

In addition to being a terrorist base, Bosnia has become a staging post for illegal Muslim immigrants from the Middle East making their way into Western Europe. Most of them are economic migrants, but European officials fear that many terrorist operatives and their potential recruits are slipping in. A senior United Nations official who watched another planeload of Iranians fly into Sarajevo airport on an almost daily smuggling run commented: "There should be a sign on the tarmac saying 'Welcome to Bosnia—the open backdoor to Fortress Europe." [37] In 2000 up to 10,000 migrants a month were arriving there by air and road, and then smuggled through Bosnia's border into Croatia on their way to the main European capitals.

Senior Muslim politicians in Sarajevo were not interested in stopping this trade in human cargo, and they had no reason to try. To most Bosnian Muslims, and especially to their political class nurtured on Izetbegovic's ideology, it is a great and good thing to help as many of their Middle Eastern co-religionists as possible settle in the infidel West.

BALKAN CONNECTION II: KOSOVO

While an intricate Islamic terror network was maturing in Bosnia, Osama bin Laden was busy looking for fresh opportunities in the Balkans. During the NATO war against Serbia, in May 1999, U.S. Sen. Jim Inhofe warned that if American troops go into Kosovo "they'd be fighting alongside a terrorist organization—the KLA [the Albanian separatist

---

[36] "Bosnian conspiracy" by Gaby Rado, Channel Four News (UK), January 17, 2002.
[37] *The* (London) *Times* "Bosnia opens the door to Europe for Iranian illegal immigrants," August 31, 2000.

"Kosovo Liberation Army"]—that is, Bin Laden's partner."[38] European and Israeli sources warned that after Bosnia, Kosovo promised to be the second Islamic bastion. The Clinton Administration ignored the warnings.[39] This reflected a shift in U.S. policy that facilitated Bin Laden's work. At first the Clinton Administration's then-special envoy for Kosovo, Robert Gelbard, had little difficulty in condemning the KLA (also known by its Albanian initials, UCK) in terms comparable to those he used for Serbian police repression. "The violence we have seen growing is incredibly dangerous," Gelbard said. He criticized violence "promulgated by the (Serb) police" and condemned the actions of an ethnic Albanian underground group Kosovo Liberation Army (UCK), which has claimed responsibility for a series of attacks on Serb targets. "We condemn very strongly terrorist actions in Kosovo. The UCK is, without any questions, a terrorist group."[40]

Mr. Gelbard's remarks came just before a KLA attack on a Serbian police station, which led to a retaliation that left dozens of Albanians dead, leading in turn to a rapid escalation of the cycle of violence.[41] Responding to criticism that his earlier words might have been seen as Washington's "green light" to Belgrade that a crack-down on the KLA would be acceptable, Mr. Gelbard told the House Committee on International Relations that while it has committed "terrorist acts," it has "not been classified legally by the U.S. Government as a terrorist organization."[42] By the end of that year, the policy was fully reversed: "It doesn't mean we don't condemn other types of violent behavior . . . but we are restricted by the laws that we're required to report on."[43]

Once the sustained NATO bombing of civilian targets in Serbia forced the withdrawal of Serbian forces from Kosovo, the province was swiftly cleansed of its non-Albanian inhabitants. Once the Christian people were out, the zeal of the victorious Muslims was immediately transferred to the centuries-old Christian churches and monasteries:

---

[38] The Daily Oklahoman, May 28, 1999.

[39] The Jerusalem Post, September 14, 1998.

[40] Agence France Presse, February 23, 1998.

[41] Cf. "The Kosovo Liberation Army: Does Clinton Policy Support Group with Terror, Drug Ties? From 'Terrorists' to 'Partners,'" U.S. Senate Republican Policy Committee, March 31, 1999, www.senate.gov/~rpc/releases/ 1999/fr033199.htm.

[42] The New York Times, March 13, 1998.

[43] usinfo.state.gov/regional/ar/us-cuba/ellis30.htm.

The Church of Saints Cosma and Damian was built in 1327. It is now a ruin of broken stone, yellowed by the centuries that the sanctuary endured. Four other, newer buildings where the monks lived and worked were not blown up. They were gutted by fire instead, and scorched pieces of religious icons lie among the ruins. . . . The Zociste monastery is one of at least 60 Serbian Orthodox churches and other religious sites that have been looted, burned, or, in at least 21 cases, blown up since the NATO-led peacekeeping force, known as KFOR, began to take control of Kosovo.[44]

Thus the KLA earned its spurs in the eyes of its Islamist partners. The relationship was cemented by the zeal of some KLA veterans who joined Bin Laden's network in Afghanistan:

Perhaps most telling about the minds of those who trained here is a document found at the [Al-Qaeda] camp. "I am interested in suicide operations,'" wrote Damir Bajrami, 24, an ethnic Albanian from Kosovo, on his entry application in April. "'I have Kosovo Liberation Army combat experience against Serb and American forces. I need no further training. I recommend (suicide) operations against (amusement) parks like Disney."[45]

In December 2001, NATO troops raided the offices of a U.S.-based charity in Kosovo that links two large Muslim charities based in Chicago to Bin Laden and his network. They raised millions of dollars each year for Muslim causes, including Kosovo Albanians, but according to NATO were in fact "directly involved in supporting worldwide international terrorist activities [and] involved in planning attacks against targets in the U.S.A. and Europe." Tasia Scolinos, a spokeswoman for the Treasury Department, subsequently confirmed that Global Relief Foundation and Benevolence International Foundation "are both linked financially with funneling funds to Al-Qaeda and other associate groups."

---

[44] Paul Watson, "Christian Sites Being Decimated in Kosovo," *The Los Angeles Times*, September 22, 1999.

[45] *USA Today,* November 26, 2001, on documents found at an Al-Qaeda training camp.

The KLA's rehabilitation in Washington went hand-in-hand with its growing links with the Islamic radicals. Iranian Revolutionary Guards had joined forces with Osama bin Laden to support the Albanian insurgency in Kosovo, hoping "to turn the region into their main base for Islamic armed activity in Europe."[46] By the end of 1998, when Bin Laden's terrorist network in Albania started sending units to fight the Serbs in Kosovo, the U.S. drug officials complained that the transformation of the KLA from terrorists into freedom fighters hampered their ability to stem the flow of Albanian-peddled heroin into America.[47] By that time the NATO bombing of Serbia was in full swing, however, and the mujaheddin were once again American allies: "Al-Qaeda has both trained and financially supported the KLA. Many border crossings into Kosovo by 'foreign fighters' also have been documented and include veterans of the militant group Islamic Jihad from Bosnia, Chechnya, and Afghanistan."[48]

All along, the Clinton Administration was positively elated about the shift in alliances and attitudes displayed by the Kosovo intervention:

> Insofar as Kosovo emerged as a unique case of U.S. support for a Muslim population against an avowed Christian state and led to an alliance with a Muslim guerilla army, it is something of a watershed event. The breakthrough in Kosovo also came about at the tail end of major changes in the international and domestic politics of Muslim societies over the course of the preceding decade. Policymakers are challenged to respond to those changes in order to bring American foreign policy in line with the reality of Islam's place in domestic, regional, and international politics. Given the importance of Islam to international affairs and the sheer number of Muslims who live in areas that affect Western and U.S. interests, rethinking America's foreign policy on Islam may be a welcome development.[49]

In the light of past latitude, it is unsurprising that Bin Laden has established a presence in Macedonia. The NLA—the KLA subsidiary in

---

[46] *The Sunday Times* of London March 22, 1998.

[47] *The Washington Times*, May 4, 1999.

[48] Ibid.

[49] *Georgetown Journal of International Affairs*, cfdev.georgetown.edu/publications/journal/vol1_1/1_2.htm.

Macedonia—is mainly dependent on the drug trade, but "in addition to drug money, the NLA also has another prominent venture capitalist: Osama bin Laden."[50] In March 2002, Macedonian security forces announced to have liquidated seven mujaheddin planning attacks on the American, German, and British embassies in Skopje. The men—including at least two Pakistanis—were found with multiple weapons, Arabic prayer-books, and NLA uniforms. The police action was precipitated by the earlier capture of two Jordanians and two Bosnians in front of the German Embassy. According to the records seized from captured or killed NLA guerillas, one of their units included a special group of 25–30 mujaheddin, under the direction of one Sabedini Selmani, a theology graduate from a Saudi school, and a Bosnian war veteran. In the end, "the mujaheddin presence in Macedonia will come at the peril not only of the Macedonians, not only the Westerners—but even of the Albanians."[51] American and other foreign peacekeeping forces in Kosovo and Macedonia are in danger from attacks by Albanian Muslims, and U.S. officials are fully aware of this.[52]

Where does a decade of U.S. involvement leave the Balkans? "The small jihad is now finished and we have—some of us—survived the war. The Bosnian state is intact. But now we have to fight a bigger, second jihad," says Mustafa Ceric, the Reis-ul-Ulema in Bosnia-Herzegovina (educated at Al-Azhar and the University of Chicago).

The American intervention in the Balkans—humanitarian bombings, multicultural Muslims, and all—was the Clinton team's exercise in counter-realism. Its end result is the strengthening of an already aggressive Islamic base in the heart of Europe that will not go away.

AMBIGUITY IN CHECHNYA

When in November 2001 President Bush repeated his call on European officials to help fight the "dark threat" represented by Al-Qaeda and Afghanistan's Taliban regime, Russian President Vladimir Putin warned that "double standards" in the international fight against terrorism could split the global coalition. "There cannot be good and bad terrorists,

---

[50] *The Washington Times*, June 22, 2001.
[51] Christopher Deliso in www.antiwar.com/orig/deliso36.html.
[52] *Stars and Stripes,* September 30, 2001.

our terrorists and others," Putin said.[53] He meant Chechnya, of course, where for the best part of the previous decade the U.S. government and the array of Western "NGOs" had followed an ambiguous policy.

In Chechnya, like in the Balkans, Islamic fundamentalism is a substitute for genuine nationhood. Islam was not firmly established there until the late eighteenth and mid-nineteenth centuries. Its traditional Sufi brotherhoods survived Stalin's expulsions but were unable to resist the well-financed incursion of Wahabism in the post-Soviet period. Echoing Bosnia and Kosovo, in Chechnya gangsterism and radical Islam went arm-in-arm. Drug trafficking and crime syndicates financed a bogus "national liberation" struggle.[54] Just as the KLA expanded into Macedonia after NATO brought it to power in Kosovo, Chechens led by Shamil Basayev and his Jordanian ally, Khabib Abdel Rahman Khattab, invaded Dagestan, proclaimed their intention to "liberate" their fellow Muslims from the rule of Moscow and help them establish an Islamic state.[55] Since 1996, hundreds of Westerners and Russians—including women and children—have been taken hostage. Ransom is extracted through the use of videos that record torture and dismemberment: "The grisly highlights include the beheading with a knife of a hostage in Chechnya and a prisoner being tortured with a sizzling piece of metal. Another close-up shows a victim's tongue being cut out."[56] Hostages are bought and sold among the various clans like commodities. The Chechens, like the Bosnian Muslims and Albanians, enjoyed the support of Islamic militants from abroad, including an active branch of Osama bin Laden's network.

The Clinton Administration supported the Chechens even to the extent of blocking a proposed $500 million loan guarantee from the U.S. Export-Import Bank to a Russian oil company that was going to be used to purchase American-made equipment.[57] In 1997–1998 the U.S. repeatedly expressed "concern" that Russia was granting the Orthodox Church

---

[53] His statement came at an off-the-record briefing after a meeting with the Indian prime minister, who could share the sentiment vis-à-vis Pakistan's actions in Kashmir: www.stratfor.com/ home/0111082200.htm.

[54] Cf. *The Russia Journal*, November 1, 1999, www.russiajournal.com/ weekly/article. shtml?ad=1644.

[55] www.en.monde-diplomatique.fr/1999/11/07taliban.

[56] *The Sunday Times* (London), December 30, 2001.

[57] *New England International & Comparative Law Annual*, www.nesl.edu/annual/ vol5/mccarthy.htm.

allegedly privileged status among the country's religious faiths, but it made no statement about the introduction of Shari'a in Chechnya.

The proponents of a tough line on Moscow in Washington—notably Secretary of Defense Rumsfeld and his deputy Wolfowitz—were able to establish the continuity of policy on Chechnya under the Bush Administration. They rejected any strategic paradigm shift in the light of terrorist attacks and, within weeks of September 11, the U.S. ambassador in Moscow, Alexander Vershbow, was instructed to declare that the overall U.S. agenda remained unchanged. The U.S. would push ahead with its missile defense program, he said, it will push for NATO expansion, and it would continue opposing Russian policies in Chechnya.

Such rhetoric did abate for the last three months of 2001, while Moscow's full cooperation was needed in the "war against terrorism"— above all to enlist Mr. Putin's help in getting the Central Asian republics on board. The logistical network for the war against Afghanistan was soon secured: after Mr. Putin's famous telephone call to President Bush immediately following the attacks, and their subsequent meeting at the Texas ranch, they comported themselves not just as allies, but also as friends. The biggest diplomatic concession to Moscow was the State Department's public admission that Chechen "freedom fighters" were linked to the Osama bin Ladin group. It seemed that the U.S. finally realized that it is impossible to fight Bin Ladin and be soft on Basayev.

As soon as the first phase of the war in Afghanistan was over, however, the old ambiguity was back. Exactly four months after the attacks, State Department spokesman Richard Boucher accused the Russian forces in Chechnya of "disproportionate use of force against civilian facilities" and "further human rights violations." While re-deploying human rights rhetoric against Russia, the Administration abrogated a Cold War-era bill that placed conditions on former Soviet republics' trade relations with the U.S. based on their human rights records. The countries exempt from human rights requirement included the predominantly Muslim Central Asian republics of Azerbaijan, Kazakhstan, Tajikistan, Turkmenistan, and Uzbekistan—but not Russia.[58] State Department officials received Ilyas Akhmadov, self-styled foreign minister in Chechnya's separatist leadership. The Russians expressed "amazement"

---

[58] *The Washington Post*, January 6, 2002.

that the officials would meet with the people "whose direct links with Osama bin Laden and Al-Qaeda are being proven with constantly emerging, irrefutable evidence."[59]

Harmful ambiguity of U.S. policy on Chechnya was reflected in the unfinished job further east in Afghanistan. After the fall of the Taliban regime, the country was left in the hands of hard-line Islamists, different from their predecessors in degree but not in kind. The new, "pro-Western" prime minister Hamid Karzai said that his government would continue to impose the Shari'a. His Justice Minister Karimi promised that it would do so "with less harshness." Judge Ahamat Ullha Zarif gave the details: public executions and amputations would continue, but there were to be changes: "The Taliban used to hang the victim's body in public for four days. We will only hang the body for a short time, say 15 minutes."[60] He also promised that Kabul's sports stadium, financed by the IMF—the site of public executions and amputations under the Taliban—would no longer be used for the same purpose.

PAKISTAN, A NUCLEAR ROGUE STATE

Pakistan was the first modern state to be established on openly Islamic principles, and even its name, the "Land of the Pure," implies that only the "pure" ones—Muslims, that is—are its true citizens. It was carved out of India, in which there never was a complete Islamic conquest. Although the Muslims ruled much of North India until the early eighteenth century, the Mahrattas and the Sikhs destroyed Muslim power and created their own empires before the advent of the British. European rule introduced the New Learning of Europe, to which the Hindus were more receptive than the Muslims:

> Muslim insecurity led to the call for the creation of Pakistan. It went at the same time with an idea of old glory, of the invaders sweeping down from the northwest and looting the temples of Hindustan and imposing faith on the infidel. The fantasy still lives: and for the Muslim converts of the subcontinent it is the

---

[59] *Agence France Presse*, January 24, 2002.
[60] "Wild Justice" by Alexander Cockburn, *New York Press*, www.nypress.com/15/3/news&columns/wildjustice.cfm.

start of their neurosis, because in this fantasy the convert forgets who or what he is and becomes the violator.[61]

Unlike India, Pakistan has never been a functional democracy. It allows discrimination against Christians and other religious minorities, it surreptitiously aids and abets terrorists in Kashmir. And yet its self-appointed president Pervez Musharraf, described in a thousand American editorials as "a key ally in the U.S.-led fight against terror," was warmly welcomed by President Bush at the White House in February 2002. He came to Washington asking for money, arms, and political support in the territorial dispute with India, while declaring his goal to turn his country into "a modern, progressive Islamic state."

The visitor thought it was payback time: After the September 2001 attacks, Musharraf allowed America to use Pakistani air bases and air space, winning praise from Bush and obtaining an improvement in U.S-Pakistani relations that had deteriorated since the end of the Cold War. The U.S. has dropped long-standing economic sanctions resulting from Pakistan's nuclear program, committed up to $600 million in credits and aid, and encouraged the IMF to give Pakistan a major loan. The subsequent abduction and murder of *Wall Street Journal's* Daniel Pearl only temporarily threw a spanner in Musharraf's work of portraying his country as "progressive" and not beholden to Islamic extremism.

While Mr. Musharraf's cooperation was helpful to the military campaign in Afghanistan, the Pakistani Army's deliberate failure to block Al-Qaeda's escape routes ensured that all the big fish have safely slipped away. The Pakistani military were loath to risk firefights with their erstwhile Taliban clients and allies, and never went into the remote border areas.

It was wrong to assume either that Musharraf is turning into a Pakistani Kemal Ataturk, or that Pakistan itself was a stable and reliably responsible partner of the United States, let alone an "ally" in the way Britain is, or Russia could be. Concerns over the Musharraf regime's double game in Afghanistan were reflected in the 2001 Senate confirmation hearings of the U.S. Ambassador-designate to Pakistan, Wendy Chamberlain, months before the September attacks.[62] The Chairman of the

---

[61] V.S. Naipaul (1998).
[62] Senate Foreign Relations Committee, June 26, 2001.

Sub-Committee on South Asian Affairs, Senator Paul Wellstone, said that Musharraf's decision "to anoint himself as president, apparently without the knowledge of his own foreign minister, is a troubling development" and deplored "the cruelty of the Taliban regime that Pakistan itself helps maintain in power."

Indeed, not only Taliban but most other Islamic extremist and terrorist movements all over the world were born out of ideas conceived in the battlefields of Afghanistan—Dr. Brzezinski's "excellent idea" of the 1980s—but subsequently matured and spread from Pakistan's political, military, and religious establishment. These movements enjoyed the support of the Pakistani military-intelligence structures, and most notably its powerful, 40,000-strong Inter-Service Intelligence Agency (ISI).[63] It grew rich and mighty, thanks to the U.S. role in helping Islamic fundamentalists fight their Soviet foe in the last decade of the Cold War.

The ethos of the Pakistani military may be better understood from the preface to "The Qur'anic Concept of War" by Brigadier S.K. Malik:

> But in Islam war is waged to establish supremacy of the Lord only when every other argument has failed to convince those who reject His Will and work against the every purpose of the creation of mankind. . . . Many Western scholars have pointed their accusing fingers at some of the verses in the Qur'an to be able to contend that world of Islam is in a state of perpetual struggle against the non-Muslims. . . . The defiance of God's authority by one who is His slave exposes that slave to the risk of being held guilty of treason."

It is therefore "necessary to remove such cancerous malformation, even if it be by surgical means, in order to save the rest of humanity," the good Brigadier concludes. It was in such spirit that the officers of the ISI were steeped when the CIA subcontracted to the ISI the arm-them-to-their-teeth policy on the mujaheddin. The ISI's past and current loyalties were, at best, uncertain. It was hedging its bets during the 2001 Afghan war, and probably arranged the murder of Afghan opposition leader Abdul Haq. The U.S. intelligence admitted to having no idea "which side of the street

---

[63] Cf. "The Unseen Power" by Michael Schaffer, *U.S. News & World Report*, November 12, 2001; also see, e.g., *Asia Times,* "America's Pact with the Devil," September 18, 2001, www.atimes.com/ind-pak/CI18Df02.html.

they're playing on," an opinion unwittingly echoed by former ISI chief Hamid Gul—now a vociferous defender of the defeated Taliban—who freely admitted that "it is unnatural to expect the ISI to act against what it knows are Pakistan's best interests [in upholding the interests of the Islamists against the U.S.] and be as motivated as it was before."[64]

For decades Pakistan has waged its own war by proxy against India through its Kashmiri surrogates controlled by the ISI, even while denying any links with or control over them.[65] Bombings at the Srinagar legislature and the Delhi parliament in 2001, which killed dozens of people and brought two countries to the brink of war, were terrorist acts *par excellence* by Muslim groups with Pakistani connections. They were heinous crimes that should make the perpetrators, and their protectors, a legitimate target of Mr. Bush's pledge in his State of the Union address to wage global war against terror.

The future of Pakistan's nuclear program should be of even greater concern to the United States, but on this front we also encounter denial and make-believe optimism that has characterized Washington's relations with the Muslim world for decades. Before leaving Pakistan at the end of his official visit in November 2001, Secretary of Defense Donald Rumsfeld declared that Washington was not concerned about the potential for misuse of Pakistan's nuclear weapons. Whether his soothing words reflected political expediency or wishful thinking, the problem of Pakistan's capability and its potential misuse will not go away. In 1972, following its third war with India, Pakistan secretly started a nuclear weapons program. It was ostensibly peaceful—that's how they all start—and Canada supplied a reactor, heavy water, and a production facility. But in 1974, Western suppliers embargoed nuclear exports to Pakistan, suspecting its true agenda, and in 1976, Canada stopped supplying nuclear fuel. The following year the U.S. halted economic and military aid to Islamabad over what was by then known to be Pakistan's nuclear weapons program.

Following the Soviet invasion of Afghanistan, the Reagan Administration radically changed its policy, however. It lifted sanctions and provided generous military and financial aid because of Pakistan's help to Afghan rebels battling Moscow. By 1983, the CIA strongly suspected

---

[64] *U.S. News*, op.cit.

[65] See *Patterns of Global Terrorism during 2000*, released by the Counter-Terrorism Division of the U.S. Department of State, April 2001.

that China had supplied Pakistan with bomb design, but the White House looked the other way. On Capitol Hill this was deemed a matter of great concern, and in 1985 Congress passed the Pressler amendment, requiring economic sanctions unless the White House certified that Pakistan was not embarked on a nuclear weapons program. Islamabad was certified every year until 1990. That year, however, Pakistan made cores for several nuclear weapons, and the Bush Administration—under the Pressler amendment—imposed economic and military sanctions against Pakistan. The government in Islamabad nevertheless managed to complete a 40-megawatt heavy-water reactor that, once operational, provided the source of plutonium-bearing spent fuel that was not subjected to international inspections. The process reached its logical conclusion on May 28, 1998, when Pakistan detonated a string of nuclear devices and became the first Islamic country to join the nuclear club. The United States imposed sanctions, as it had on India.

When the jubilant masses poured to the streets of Pakistan to cheer the news, they shouted *Allah Akbar!* They carried models of the *Hatf*—Pakistan's nuclear missile—marked "Islamic bomb." In Friday prayers, mullahs stressed that the tests are a "triumph for Islam."

The question vexing the U.S. intelligence community now is not so much whether there will be a nuclear exchange between Pakistan and India, but what will happen if some of Pakistan's assets—two dozen warheads, not counting fissure material—fall into the wrong hands. Elite U.S. and Israeli units were reportedly being trained to "take out Pakistan's nuclear weapons to make sure that the warheads do not fall into the hands of renegades" if Pervez Musharraf is toppled.[66]

In 2001, U.S. intelligence officers were alarmed over the disclosure that two retired Pakistani nuclear scientists have had connections to the Taliban. Both men, Sultan Bashiruddin Mahmood and Chaudry Abdul Majid, had spent their careers at the Pakistan Atomic Energy Commission, working on weapons-related projects. This indicates that extremist sympathies extend beyond the Pakistani Army into the country's supposedly highly disciplined nuclear-weapons laboratories. "They're retired, but they have friends on the inside," a U.S. intelligence officer commented. "My sense is that the problem of an insider or insiders making

---

[66] The *New Yorker,* October 29, 2001.

off with fissile material is probably greater than somebody making off with an actual weapon," according to George Perkovich, author of *India's Nuclear Bomb*. Designing a simple, gun-type device is not difficult once the enriched uranium is at hand. As little as three kilograms could be turned into a weapon of nearly half the power of the bomb that was dropped on Hiroshima at the end of World War II. If detonated in a major metropolitan area, even such a crude weapon—of the sort that could be transported in a van—could kill hundreds of thousands of people and render hundreds of square miles uninhabitable for years. Because such tragedy *may* happen, it is necessary to contemplate the timely means of its prevention; and this has to include a cool assessment of the role of Pakistan.

At the time of the Partition, it came into being as an avowedly Muslim state, and to this day it suffers from the many defects inherent in such origins. It is divided by caste, with the highest status reserved for the alleged, imagined, and perhaps a few real descendants of Arab conquerors, called *ashraf.* This social structure predicated upon the supposed superiority of Islamic imperialism in itself suggests that Islam is the cause, or at least an aggravating feature in the array of problems of underdevelopment, illiteracy, oppression, poverty, disease, and rigidity of thought. For as long as the country's Islamic character is explicitly upheld, Pakistan cannot evolve into a democracy, an efficient economy, or a civilized polity without undermining the religious rationale for its very existence. For as long is it remains an "Islamic Republic," it will remain a country in which girls as young as five are auctioned off to highest bidders and where women who accuse a man of rape are in turn condemned to death for adultery .[67]

Always on the verge of bankruptcy, Pakistan has been for most of its 55 years of existence under military dictatorships. None of its leaders has ever left power voluntarily. Some were executed on trumped-up charges, notably the democratically elected Prime Minister Bhutto. His executioner, the ultra-pious Islamist General Zia ul-Haq, was the military dictator of Pakistan from 1977 until 1988. He had strong links with the Jamaat-e-Islami and Shari'a was reintroduced after a bogus referendum, but Zia was enlightened enough to allow doctors to be present so that the whipping of

---

[67] "Sale of children thrives in Pakistan" by Andrew Bushel. *The Washington Times*, January 21, 2002. "In Pakistan, Rape victims Are 'Criminals'" *The New York Times*, May 17, 2002.

transgressors stopped short of death. Smelling salts were often administered if the victim lost consciousness before receiving his allotted number of lashes. Nevertheless, Zia had maintained Pakistan's special relationship with the United States. Despite human rights abuses, Pakistan was a "front-line state" helping to fight a jihad against Communism. He received over $500 million a year in economic and military aid from the U.S.A., plus whatever did not reach the mujaheddin forces in Afghanistan. The U.S. Under-Secretary of State James Buckley testified before the Senate Foreign Relations Committee that elections "were not in the security interests of Pakistan."

Benazir Bhutto promised a new dawn for Pakistan in the 1980s, but in the end had to make compromises with the religious groups. She may have thought that they would accept the legitimacy of her credentials in spite of her sex, but she was wrong. Her career is not a demonstration that women may succeed in Islam, but, quite the contrary, that they are unwelcome at the top. The civilian government of Prime Minister Nawaz Sharif was overthrown on October 12, 1999, by General Musharraf—who is now a self-anointed president. That was the first military coup in a major country since the end of the Cold War, and the first ever in a country with nuclear weapons.

Pakistan has a constitution that guarantees religious freedom, but murders, endemic discrimination, and constant harassment of Christians is persistent. Any dispute with a Muslim—most commonly over land—can become a religious confrontation; Christians are frequently accused of "blasphemy against Islam," an offense that carries the death penalty. Pakistan has some of the strictest blasphemy laws in the Muslim world. Charges of blasphemy can be made on the flimsiest of evidence—even one man's word against another, and since it is invariably a Muslim's word against that of a Christian, the outcome is preordained.

The ease with which blasphemy charges can be made to stick has led to a spate of accusations against Christians, mostly malicious complaints motivated by personal enmity and greed, especially for the Christians' land. Some 2,500 people are said to be in jail or to face charges for blasphemy. Muslim rioters in Rahimyar Khan, a town in southern Punjab, burned a dozen churches in 1997 after attacking Christians they accused of throwing torn pages of the Kuran into a mosque. This turned out to be a fabrication invented by the surrounding Muslims as the pretext to occupy their land.

Christians charged with blasphemy have been murdered by fundamentalists before their cases reached the courts. Musharraf decided against amending the law, and under his regime the Christian minority has continued to live in fear.

That fear is fully justified, judging by the grenade attack on a Christian church in the capital, Islamabad, on March 17, 2002, which killed five people, including a U.S. embassy administrator and her daughter. It was preceded by the slaughter on October 28, 2001, in a church in Behawalpur, when two Kalashnikov-brandishing Muslims massacred 18 Protestants. The only surprise for the survivors was that the attack "did not come sooner," following the beginning of the bombing of Afghanistan.[68]

Pakistani-born Patrick Sookhdeo, who grew up as a Muslim, converted to Christianity, and eventually became an Anglican priest, laments the fact that the West prefers to deny the suffering of Christian communities at the hands of Muslims:

> We can rescue Kuwait because there is oil, but why should we want to rescue black Sudanese Christians? And the church opted for inter-religious dialogue. They desperately wanted a relationship with the Muslims. So it meant the Christian minorities had to be sacrificed on the altar of community relations.[69]

WHITHER TURKEY?

A century ago the Ottoman Empire was moribund, the Sick Man on the Bosphorus whose hold on the far-flung provinces in the Balkans, North Africa, and the Middle East was growing more tenuous by the day. Its precarious survival in the century before the Great War was due entirely to the inability of Europe to agree on what to do with the spoils, and the intractable "Eastern Question" remained on the European diplomatic agenda until the Great War.

The emergence of Mustafa Kemal's Republic coincided with the final curtain for the Christians of the Ottoman Empire. Between 1915 and 1922,

---

[68] *The Independent*, 29 October 2001.
[69] *The Washington Times*, January 16, 2002.

most of the Armenian and Greek Christians in Asia Minor were exterminated or ethnically cleansed. It is this reality that should be the focus of any consideration of modern Turkey. That the "modern" descendants of the Ottomans are perhaps among the least tolerant nations in the world—as is evinced by Turkey's continuing persecution of not only fellow Muslims such as Kurds and Alawites but of Greeks, Cypriots, Assyrians, and Armenians as well—gives us a small insight into what the Eastern Christians must have endured.

This crime against humanity is continuing to this day in the form of an ambitious and well-funded campaign of genocide denial by the Turkish government and its supporters in the Western world. Stanley Cohen, Professor of Criminology at Hebrew University in Jerusalem, has called it the nearest successful example of "collective denial" in the modern era: "This denial has been sustained by deliberate propaganda, lying and cover-ups, forging documents, suppression of archives, and bribing scholars. The West, especially the United States, has colluded by not referring to the massacres in the United Nations, ignoring memorial ceremonies, and surrendering to Turkish pressure in NATO and other strategic arenas of cooperation."[70]

An example is the pressure exerted by the Microsoft Encarta Encyclopedia editors on its contributing scholars to cast doubt on the occurrence of the Armenian genocide because "the Turkish government had threatened to arrest local Microsoft officials and ban Microsoft products unless [the] massacres were presented as topics open to debate."[71] As a result of the ensuing negative coverage, Encarta was shamed into reversing its acquiescence to Turkey's near-successful attempt at genocide denial.

Today's Turkey nevertheless is presuming to be accepted as a fully fledged member of the "international community" and respected as a major player in its own right. It is indeed a regional power and the U. S. ally in Eastern Mediterranean, the Middle East, and Central Asia. Its population will exceed that of Russia in 30 years if today's demographic trends continue. Its influence is on the rise in its old holdings in the Balkans as well as throughout the former Soviet Central Asia. Turkey is aggressively

---

[70] *Law and Social Inquiry*, Winter 1995, pp. 13–14.
[71] *The Chronicle of Higher Education*, "The Other Side of Genocide," August 18, 2000.

pursuing its European Union candidacy, while resisting even feeble Western demands to end its brutal war against the Kurds in the eastern part of the country, which has been going on for almost three decades and has claimed some 30,000 mostly civilian lives.

No less egregious is Turkey's refusal to make any concessions on Cyprus—invaded in July 1974 with the U.S.-made and supplied weapons, and partly occupied by 35,000 Turkish soldiers ever since. Over the past 28 years, Turkey has flooded the occupied northern part of the island with settlers from the mainland; their numbers by now exceed the number of native Turkish Cypriots, about 115,000 in 1974, as opposed to just over half a million Greeks. They occupied two-fifths of Cyprus and, in the best tradition of the Prophet and "rightly guided" caliphs, ordered Greeks inhabiting the area to leave within 24 hours. Greek houses and businesses were handed over to Turkish Cypriots. Greek villages and towns were attacked indiscriminately, but in cities with mixed populations targets were selected: Christian churches were the first to go up in flames, or be converted into mosques. The final toll was 4,000 men, women, and children dead, 1,619 missing and undoubtedly dead; virtually the entire Greek population of the Turkish-occupied part of the island was exterminated or ethnically cleansed. Nearly 40 percent of the island, including 65 percent of the arable land, 60 percent of all its water resources, two-thirds of its mineral wealth, 70 percent of its industries and four-fifths of tourist installations came under Turkish rule.

While other countries would be condemned, embargoed, or bombed for similar transgressions, Turkey's status as a bona fide member of NATO and the pillar of U.S. strategy in the eastern Mediterranean, and the bridgehead of influence in the oil-rich Caspian basin, was never in doubt. Its position as an essential U.S. ally, and its ability to get away with murder, was further reinforced in 1979 when the entire U.S. position in the Middle East was thrown into disarray with the fall of the Shah. This was an event to which President Carter's Administration made a considerable contribution with its heavy-handed attempt to appease the radical Islamic movement by forcing concessions from Reza Pahlevi.

Almost a quarter of a century later, the axiom in Washington that Turkey will remain "secular" and "pro-Western" looks tenuous. It behooves us to examine the validity of those assumptions. What will happen if history repeats itself, if Ankara goes the way of Teheran, cutting off America's access to the oil-rich Caspian region and bringing into its orbit America's new clients in Sarajevo, Tirana, and Pristina? Is it possible, or likely, or even imminent? Can the U.S. afford to be caught by surprise yet again? What can it do to prepare for such eventuality?

The lack of a coherent "Turkish" strategy in Washington was apparent in June 1997, when the Turkish army forced the resignation of Necmettin Erbakan, the country's democratically elected prime minister. This was hailed by the Clinton Administration as a welcome event, a defeat for "Islamic fundamentalists" of Erbakan's Refah party and the victory for the "pro-Western" camp led by the army and supported by some "secular" parties. Such posture mirrored the U.S. reaction to the military coup in Algeria that prevented the establishment of a pro-Islamic government following the victory of radical Muslims at the polls.

In established democracies, the army does not replace elected governments, of course, but the propriety of political acts is judged in Washington on the basis of the desirability of their outcome, not on any lofty principle. To this day the Turkish army is regarded by the U.S. foreign policy establishment as the reliable guarantor of Ankara's permanently "pro-Western," secular orientation. But in the Middle East, "secularism" does not coincide with "democracy"—the regimes in Iraq and Syria provide a vivid example. If we are to have a serious debate on America's long-term interests in eastern Mediterranean, the Middle East experts in Washington should stop pretending that Turkey is democratic. At present it is, at best, a "guided democracy" in which no institution—judicial or civil—is independent of the State, nor the State from the army. Its abysmal human rights record is well documented and beyond dispute.

Turkey is a polity based on an Islamic ethos, regardless of its political superstructure. It inherited its Islamic legacy from the Ottoman Empire. With the establishment of the Turkish nation state in 1923 by Mustafa Kemal "Ataturk," the project introduced a secular concept of nationhood, but the establishment of the multi-party political system in 1945 gave political Islam an opportunity to reassert itself. Popular Islamic political movements of the past three decades have produced a "Turkish-Islamic synthesis"—an Islamic concept of nationhood that has Ottoman roots and seeks to re-establish an Ottoman-Islamic concept of Turkish nationhood. They are explicit in their rejection of the contemporary Western way of life, values, and ideology. Their success is due to the fact that an

240

overwhelming majority of Turks are Muslims in their beliefs, values, and world outlook. Just as enormous oil revenues could not resolve the problem in Iran, there is no reason to believe that the proposed massive injections of foreign liquidity will do the trick in Turkey. The Kemalist dream of strict secularism has never penetrated beyond the military and a relatively narrow stratum of urban elite centered in Istanbul.

The fact that political Islam had found such fertile ground in Turkey came as a shock to many, revealing the ultimate dependence of the political system on the army. The CIA's 1997 "State Failure Task Force" report identified Turkey as a nation in danger of collapse. The resulting erosion of the ruling stratum's self-confidence has led to increased oppression. Journalists now risk fines, imprisonment, bans, or violent attacks if they write about "the role of Islam in politics and society" or "the proper role of the military in government and society."[72]

The lack of cultural rootedness of Turkey's political elites remains as serious a problem today as it was in Ataturk's times, and in many minds the question about the dormant Islamic volcano is not *if*, but *when*. The Kemalist ruling class rules Turkey by the grace of the West and the will of the army. The same dynamics that have swept it away in Teheran may apply in Ankara. The parallel with Iran is alarming. The United States may yet discover that "democratization" of Turkey would mean its irreversible Islamization. America needs alternative scenarios to cover such an eventuality.

WITH FRIENDS LIKE THESE: SAUDI ARABIA

Austere mosques, women relegated to the background, and a puritanical faith that rejects change. A brand of Islam that drives the Taliban and influenced the young American who fought by their side has taken root in the Mecca of modernism, America.[73]

The mosques and women in question are in Dearborn, Michigan, the fruits of America's "special relationship" with the most rigid totalitarian

---

[72] Human Rights Watch, 1999.

[73] "Fundamentalist form of Islam taking root in America," by Ron Kampeas, Associated Press, December 10, 2000.

dictatorship in the world. Welcome to the Saudi connection, one of the best-kept secrets inside the Beltway.

In the early decades of the twentieth century, interaction between Islam and the West started as a serious challenge to Islam, and by the turn of the millennium it has turned into a threat to the West. Two centuries after revolutionary France proclaimed complete religious equality and freedom of movement to the Muslims, massive migratory process is now accompanied by a well-financed and coordinated effort to spread Islam through planned missionary activities.

The moving spirit behind the project is in Muhammad's homeland, and the fuel that makes it possible is oil. The Muslim World League was founded in Mecca in 1962, and a decade later the Organization of the Islamic Conference—a kind of Islamic Comintern—with its headquarters in Jeddah. Both organizations, and a myriad of ostensibly private charities devoted to Islamic proselytism, are richly endowed by the petrodollars from Saudi Arabia's narrow, ultra-rich ruling elite. Its members provide aid to countries willing to follow the path of Islamization, and build mosques wherever they can. They send missionaries, provide literature, and run electronic media. The MWL runs the world's largest printing presses, producing tens of millions of copies of the Kuran every year for worldwide distribution.

The Kingdom of Saudi Arabia also remains the most intolerant Islamic regime in the world. Within Saudi Arabia, the practice of any religion besides Islam is as strictly prohibited now as it was in Muhammad's lifetime. While the Saudis continue to build mosques all over the world, thousands of Christians among the hundreds of thousands of foreign workers from India, Europe, America, and the Philippines must worship in secret, if at all. They are arrested, lashed, or deported for public display of their beliefs.

American citizens can be detained indefinitely at the pleasure of their Saudi Muslim father who kidnapped them from their American mother. This happened to Patricia Roush, whose daughters Alia and Aisha are now clad from head to toe in the black abaya.[74] Alia was married off to one of her father's cousins, and Aisha is the next on whom the purdah will fall.

---

[74] Our "friends" in Riyadh hold two American citizens prisoner, *The Wall Street Journal*, December 21, 2001.

The State Department directed the U.S. embassy in Riyadh to remain "impartial." Ray Mabus, ex-U.S. ambassador to Saudi Arabia, deplores the pressure from the State Department that makes diplomats feel they should be working on the "big stuff," which is appeasement by another name. His efforts to repatriate the Roush girls were thwarted by Washington, lest our Saudi "friends" be offended.

The "big stuff" for Western policymakers also means seeking to restrict media freedom in their own countries. In July 1977, an Englishman with a miniature camera was able to take photographs that shocked the world. He recorded the public execution in Jeddah of Princess Mishael bint Fahd bin Mohammed, a young married but separated mother, and her boyfriend, Khalid Muhallah. She was shot six times in the head, he was beheaded. The photographs became part of Anthony Thomas' TV documentary, "Death of a Princess." The news threw the Saudis into a fit of rage, and Western governments hurried to suppress the showing of the film. In 1980, the Carter Administration strenuously opposed the program being shown on PBS.

A month earlier, the showing of the same film on British TV had led to a crisis in diplomatic relations between Saudi Arabia and Britain, and heavy pressure was exerted by the Foreign Office and Prime Minister Margaret Thatcher on the ITV to drop the show. (Only months later, then-Prime Minister Margaret Thatcher's son Mark brokered the £20 billion Al Yamamah arms deal with Saudi Arabia, the biggest in history until that time.) In the United States, government pressure on PBS to drop the program went so far that the State Department formally "appealed" to the network to refrain from showing the executions. Commercial pressures followed: Exxon withdrew their sponsorship of public television.

Over two decades later, nothing much has changed: "Saudi Arabia is a good and dependable friend to the civilized world," Britain's Tony Blair declared during a tour of the Middle East in 2001. "Civilization" is a relative term to a high priest of postmodernism like Mr. Blair, but his enthusiasm for the House of Saud may be easier to understand if we consider that Britain's arms merchants have their most lucrative buyer in the desert kingdom. In only six years (1991–1997) there were $23 billion worth of arms agreements between the United States and Saudi Arabia.

Saudi Arabia is the source of most Al-Qaeda fighters, funding, and instigator of Islamic agitation all over the world, but it is also a major source of oil, and its royal cleptocracy owns large chunks of major American corporations—and that is the "big stuff."

The focus on the "big stuff" allowed thousands of young Saudis easy access to American visas under various pretexts, many of them hell-bent on fighting the Jihad against the unbelievers across the ocean. The Saudi authorities issued them exit visas with full knowledge of what they were up to. They were keen to get rid of the potentially troublesome hotheads who could stir up trouble at home. Worse still, they may have considered the resulting mayhem, exemplified in the predominantly Saudi suicide teams of September 11, as not necessarily undesirable. Rather than prevent young Saudis from enlisting in military ventures abroad or silence the sheiks encouraging them, some officials say Saudi Arabia has mostly tried to deflect the problem outside its borders. "Alarm bells should have rung," said Wyche Fowler Jr., the former U.S. ambassador in Saudi Arabia and himself a major proponent of the "special relationship" with the Kingdom. "Someone should have said, 'Wait a minute, we can't have people marching off to choose their own jihad, without examining the foreign policy and security repercussions.'"

In anticipation of such a development, alarm bells have rung in Riyadh. On September 12, 2001, Crown Prince Abdullah ibn Abdulaziz, the Saudi leader, and his oil minister, Ali Nuaimi, decided to break a recent promise to other OPEC nations to cut oil production. They arranged for a quick delivery of an additional 9 million barrels of oil to the United States instead, which helped reduce the price from almost $30 a barrel before 9-11 to under $20 only weeks later. This was a preemptive gesture by people with a guilty conscience. They knew that someone, somewhere in the United States would put two and two together: that whenever there are Islamic terrorists bringing death, destruction, and havoc to the non-Muslim world, there are Saudis lurking in the background, either as masterminds, or direct participants, or as bankrollers.

The questioning of the Saudi connection is only beginning, and for now it tends to focus on the questionable ability of the members of the royal family—whose numbers add up to an incredible 30,000—to break away from their addiction to a lifestyle of parasitic idleness and institute reforms:

> U.S. policymakers and analysts also express concern about the
> ability of the Saud family to handle what may be a rapid turnover

of kings in the next few years and its political resolve to undertake pressing domestic reforms judged critical to Saudi Arabia's future stability. "The mass murder of September 11 . . . has raised many questions in the minds of Americans and others about Saudi Arabia and our relationship to it," said Chas. W. Freeman Jr., a former U.S. ambassador to Riyadh, who is now president of the Middle East Policy Council. "Is there something rotten in the Kingdom of Saudi Arabia? Is it still stable enough to be a reliable partner of the United States in the future?"[75]

The Saudi establishment, interestingly, refuses to acknowledge that its nationals were the primary culprits for that "mass murder." The Saudi government-controlled daily newspaper *'Ukkaz* and other media have repeatedly raised "strong suspicions" about the involvement of "the Jews" in general and Israel's Mossad in particular in the terrorist attacks. This fits the strongly anti-Semitic outlook of the country's rulers.

In the aftermath of 9-11 Saudi Prince Mamdouh bin Abd Al-Aziz, president of the Saudi Center for Strategic Studies, wrote in the London daily *Al-Hayat* that the *Protocols* were based on a number of other genuine documents.[76]

"The veil has been lifted, and the American people see a double game," declared Samuel Berger, National Security Advisor during the Clinton Administration, who noted that the Saudi regime is repressive with respect to the extremists that threaten them "but more than tolerant— indeed, the more we find out, beneficent—to the general movement of extreme Islamists in the region." He was alluding to tens of thousands of able-bodied Saudi males sound of mind and devout Muslims, who have completed terrorist training or received combat experience abroad since 1979. Saudi Arabia is not nearly as populous as its Muslim brethren in Indonesia, Pakistan, Egypt, Bangladesh, or Nigeria, but their initiated jihadi volunteers are proportionately over-represented everywhere. At home, they planted a bomb in Riyadh that killed 5 Americans and wounded 37 in November 1995. In June 1996, they bombed an air base in the eastern city of Al Khobar, killing 19 American airmen and wounding hundreds more.

---

[75] "Severe Tests Loom for Relationship," by David B. Ottaway and Robert G. Kaiser, *The Washington Post,* February 12, 2002.

[76] *Al-Hayat*, September 24, 2001.

Abroad, from Chechnya to Kosovo, from the Philippines to Bosnia, there is a distinct Wahhabi imprint on the proceedings, such as the ritual decapitation of 26 Serb POWs captured on videotape in the mountains of Bosnia. In the attack on the U.S. Embassy in Nairobi, one of the attackers was a Saudi, and the bombing in Yemen of the destroyer *Cole* in October 2000 was masterminded by another Saudi, Tawfiq al-Atash, who lost a leg in Afghanistan. All along the Islamic "charities" that financed terrorists included prominent members of the royal family on their boards.

The United States is still reluctant to read the riot act to the Saudis. Secretary of Defense Donald Rumsfeld, normally not a mealy-mouthed man, on a visit to Saudi Arabia in the aftermath of terrorist attacks appeared strangely evasive on the issue of Saudi funds for Islamic terror and admitted that he had not asked the Saudis to freeze the assets of people and groups linked to Mr. Bin Laden, even though the United States had asked all countries to do so:

> We understand that each country is different, each country lives
> in a different neighborhood, has a different perspective and has
> different sensitivities and different practices, and we do not
> expect every nation on the face of the earth to be publicly
> engaged in every single activity the United States is.

The limits of Saudi Arabia's engagement are strict and narrow: not until October 2001, and the beginning of the U.S. military campaign in Afghanistan began, did Saudi Arabia detain its young men trying to join that fight. Choosing accommodation over confrontation, the government shied away from a crackdown on militant clerics or their followers, a move that would have inflamed the religious establishment, the disaffected returnees from other wars, and a growing number of unemployed in this economically and socially dysfunctional society. Saudi Arabia has 18 million citizens (and 6 million foreign workers), growing at over 4 percent a year from 1980 to 1998. The average Saudi family now has between six and seven children. Per-capita income has collapsed from a peak of $19,000 in 1981 to $7,300 in 1997. Unemployment is rampant, but young people don't want the lower-paying jobs held by foreigners. The government can no longer support the generous social welfare system it created at the height of the oil boom. From a peak of $227 billion in 1981, oil revenue is down to under $50 billion.

246

The only expanding, local Saudi industry is that of Islamic extremism. In 1966, the vice president of the Islamic University of Medina complained that Copernican theory was being taught at Riyadh University. Three hundred years after the Christian theologians had to concede that the Earth went around the Sun, the geocentric theory was reaffirmed in the centers of Saudi learning. In 1967, segregation of the sexes at schools was set at age nine, which was the age for girls to start to wear the veil. That year the king was forced to sack the minister of information for "offensive" TV programs: apparently a cartoon passed the censors in which Mickey Mouse gave Minnie a little peck.

The opinions of the *ullema* are the only internal check and balance on the ruling family; and it can halt them in their tracks, even when they try to be bold. Just outside the city of Riyadh there is a magnificent concert hall seating 3,000 known as the King Fahd Cultural Center. Shortly before his death in 1975, King Faysal approved the building of this center as part of the recreational facilities to turn his capital into a handsome modern city. Completed in 1989 at a cost of $140 million (a quarter of a billion dollars in today's money), it boasts the finest marble and precious woods, a state-of-the-art laser lighting system, and a hydraulic stage:

> But the hall has never staged an event. A foreign diplomat who managed to visit the mothballed facility found that a full-time staff of 180 has for almost a decade maintained the building and its gardens in mint condition. This has meant not just tending the flower-beds, but air-conditioning the facility all year around so that the delicate woods on the interior do not deteriorate. Why is the cultural center not used? Because it offends the strict Islamic sensibilities prevalent in Saudi Arabia. According to one report, on hearing about Western-style music played by mixed casts (meaning men and women) to mixed audiences, the country's religious leaders "went berserk." [77]

Those "religious leaders" are a self-perpetuating lot. Saudi Arabia's five Islamic universities produce thousands of clerics, many more than will

---

[77] Daniel Pipes, "You Need Beethoven to Modernize," *Middle East Quarterly,* September 1998.

ever be hired to work in the country's mosques and religious institutions. Many end up spreading and promoting Wahhabism at home and abroad:

> It appears to have been a miscalculation of global proportions, Western diplomats now say. As they look back to examine the roots of the Sept. 11 attacks, officials in Saudi Arabia, Europe, and the United States describe a similar pattern. In country after country, Al-Qaeda's networks took hold, often with the knowledge of local intelligence and security agencies. But on the rare occasions that countries did address the terrorist threat, they chose to deal with it as a local issue rather than an interlocking global network.[78]

For Osama bin Laden's most audacious strike against the Great Satan, Europe was his forward base, Saudi Arabia provided his pool of recruits and most of the money, the United States a vulnerable target. As the Western world braces for more attacks, Saudi Arabia is still managing to square the circle of its ostensible "partnership" with the United States, while maintaining its leading role as the promoter and bankroller of Islamic interests in the outside world. In that sense, the fruits of their labor are not a "miscalculation" but a foreseeable and acceptable risk.

The ability of the inherently fanatical and mendacious (as well as profligate and corrupt) rulers of the desert kingdom to square any circles at all is entirely due to its oil reserves, which account for up to one-fifth of all U.S. imports. The Saudis are perfectly aware that this is their only, albeit enormously powerful, trump card, and have embarked on a multimillion-dollar public relations campaign to try to restore confidence in the Saudi-American "special relationship," post September 11.

In reality, the rulers of Saudi Arabia differ from their prodigal sons in the caves of Afghanistan only in degree, not in kind. Their response to the outrage of September 11 illustrates the point. The reactions throughout the Muslim world have been less concerned by the fact of those terrorist attacks than by the alleged Islamophobia of the West. Saudi religious establishmentarians in particular have repeatedly said that extremists have "distorted Islamic teachings," but beyond these now-familiar declarations that the attacks were "not Islam," there has been mostly silence. There has

---

[78] *The New York Times*, December 27, 2001.

been no public repudiation of those, like Hamoud Shuaebi, who has called on Muslims to wage war against Americans, and has warned that "those who help the infidels are infidels themselves." The response from prominent, establishment clerics like Saleh al-Sheikh, the Saudi minister of Islamic Affairs, has been almost tepid. "The problem of extremism comes when some people surrender to emotions but don't use their brain," Mr. al-Sheikh was quoted as saying in the *Ukkaz*. The reality behind this ambiguity is that the Saudis and their co-religionists do not object to terrorism—unless, of course, it is directed against their rulers:

> Every successful act of terrorism against unbelievers enhances the prestige and following of terrorist movements among the Moslem masses. Most Western policymakers are aware of this, and sometimes indirectly admit it in public. Yet they and their tame media were always ready with excuses. . . . The rulers of the Arab states, even when they do not identify with the terrorists personally, know that their acts enjoy widespread support in their own countries.[79]

The Taliban in Afghanistan and Islamist terrorism in Algeria and the states of the former USSR have been funded, aided, and abetted from Saudi Arabia. The Western press has lamentably failed to peer inside the black box of the U.S.-Saudi relationship. Short of an extraordinary humiliation, the Washingtonian policymakers will continue to insist that they "need" Saudi Arabia even more than they "need" Pakistan.

For the time being, the Saudis and their co-religionists have no reason to doubt that the talk about promoting democracy is propaganda for internal consumption, and that the U.S. prefers to deal with autocratic rulers, who are much easier to bribe. The end result, for now, favors an oppressive plutocracy without elected representative bodies, light-years and worlds apart from all that America and the rest of the Western world hold near and dear. It cannot be otherwise, because Saudi Arabia is defined, and exists, as an Islamic polity based on the virulently intolerant and aggressive brand of what is already an intolerant and aggressive religion.

---

[79] Yohanan Ramati, *The Islamic Danger to Western Civilization,* www.western-defense.org/special/TwinTowers2001.htm.

It cannot be said often enough that the Bin Laden phenomenon is above all about the future of Saudi Arabia. To examine in detail what the Saudis have done—and were allowed to get away with—has become urgent, essential work for Western intelligence services. The Saudi regime has been a model of what appalls us about Islamic discipline; it is a playground of staggering wealth protected by a large investment in theocratic excess, the patron of fanaticism. It must not be allowed to continue its old game because it is "a valued ally" of the United States.

America and the rest of the West urgently need to set themselves free from the need to pander to Saudi whims, including the nonexistent and unreciprocated "right" of its government to bankroll thousands of mosques and Islamic "cultural centers" around the world—including in the United States—that teach hate and provide the logistic infrastructure to Islamic terrorism. The ability to break free from the Saudi connection is predicated upon the liberation from Middle Eastern oil imports. That liberation is possible and necessary. It only requires political will and monetary investment into the development of new technologies. This is, and has always been, the crucial prerequisite to the development of a meaningful anti-terrorist strategy.

BETRAYAL IN AFRICA

During his two days in Nigeria in August 2000 then-President Clinton tried—in his own words—to encourage the "struggling new democracy." His visit was meant to symbolize America's blessing on Africa's most populous country, which was pointedly bypassed during Clinton's previous African tour, two years earlier, while it was still under military rule.

The performance was remarkable: Mr. Clinton had managed to visit Nigeria, talk about "democracy," and not mention its most acute human rights problem that has claimed thousands of lives. He remained silent on the brutal oppression and suffering of the millions of Christians inhabiting the north of the country by their Islamic rulers. It is as if a visitor to Ulster talked of peace and democracy, but avoided any reference to "the Troubles," or a visitor to New York's Ground Zero kept politely quiet about the late unpleasantness.

Nigeria, an ethnically and religiously heterogeneous country, has been plagued by all the standard African post-colonial experiences, from a

250

bloody civil war and a procession of corrupt and brutal military dictatorships to many bouts of intercommunal strife rooted in the clashing tribal-religious loyalties of its more than 100 million people. Its oil riches have been squandered, stolen, or mismanaged. Its countless economic and social problems would test the abilities of its rulers, even without the specter of a religious conflict.

Enter militant Islam. Only about half of all Nigerians are Muslim, but they are a majority in several northern states. Nigeria's corrupt military rulers also came from the north. For years they treated the rest as occupied territories, theirs to plunder at will. They also sought to give an Islamic stamp to the country as a whole—to the point of joining the Islamic Conference Organization, and thus creating the impression that Nigeria is "Muslim" in its entirety.

Their long-term strategy is apparent from the opening communiqué of the Islam in Africa Organization, founded at a conference in Abuja, in northern Nigeria in November 1989. It insists on "re-instating a strong and united Umma" in Africa and on "restoring the use of Arabic script in the vernacular."[80] In addition, "the Conference notes the yearning of Muslims everywhere on the continent who have been deprived of their rights to be governed by the Shari'a and urges them to intensify efforts in the struggle to reinstate the application of the Shari'a."

The implication is that once there had been an Umma in Africa, within which the local languages were written in Arabic lettering, and that Africans were under Shari'a law. This is not true. Finally, in the best Islamic tradition, the Conference also demanded "the appointment of only Muslims into strategic national and international posts of member nations." It pledged "to eradicate in all its forms and ramifications all non-Muslim religions in member nations (such religions shall include Christianity, Ahmadiyya[81] and other tribal modes of worship unacceptable to Muslims)" and "to ensure that only Muslims are elected to all political posts of member nations." The members pledged to pursue those objectives not only in Islamic states, but also in those with Muslim minorities.

---

[80] www.islaminafrica.org/backG.htm.

[81] A sect named after M. Ghulam Ahmad, who preached in British India that Jesus feigned death and escaped to India, and that jihad is a peaceful battle against nonbelievers. Ahmadis are zealous missionaries, preaching Ahmadi beliefs as the one true Islam.

The IAO had huge funds at its disposal from the very first day, including $21 billion that was "generously donated" by the "government and people of Nigeria" for the "Islamic Development Fund." (In the same year, 1989, the Nigerian head of state, General Ibrahim B. Babangida, had a balance at the Arab-African International Bank of $57.48 billion. His chief of the army and two cabinet ministers—all Muslims—had $5.2, $17.8, and $24.9 billion respectively.)

Unhappy with the loss of power following the collapse of Babangida's military regime, traditional rulers of predominantly Muslim states in northern Nigeria are now seeking to apply the IAO communiqué at the level of their own communities, most visibly by introducing the Shari'a. In late 1999, the state of Zamfara, whose 2 million people are predominantly Muslim, was the first to adopt a bill to introduce Shari'a. Its devoutly Muslim state governor, Alhaji Ahmed Sani, approved it in spite of the objections of the Christian minority in Zamfara and protests from the rest of the country. Within weeks all bars were closed, cinemas and video parlors were shut down, and boys and girls were divided into separate schools. The rest of the novelties are familiar to any visitor to the Middle East: women now must cover themselves; amputations of limbs, stonings to death and beheadings are on the statute book for a variety of offenses; consumers of alcohol in any form are "severely flogged" if caught drinking. Governor Sani has asserted that he would replicate the Shari'a code used in Saudi Arabia. "Shari'a will only apply to Muslims and consenting Christians," he claims, but it is already clear that the ability of "non-consenting" Christians to claim exemption will be severely curtailed.

The consequences were predictable. Muslim fanatics were emboldened to demand Shari'a in all northern Nigerian states where they have a majority. Resulting clashes in mixed areas included two bouts of bloody riots, in February and May 2000, in which over 2,000 people were killed when another northern Nigerian state, Kaduna, tried to introduce Shari'a there. Dozens of Christian churches have been burned and desecrated all over northern Nigeria.

Christians have been told not to fear Islamic law. "Islam," declared Usman Bugaje, Secretary General of the Islam in Africa Organization, based in Nigeria, "has a great capacity for tolerance." But he left his peculiar meaning of "tolerance" unclear; it is limited to those who believe in the principles of Shari'a to start with (i.e., Muslims). Nigerian proponents of Shari'a say that nonbelievers must be persuaded by argument, dialogue, and example. Central to their argument, however, is the thesis that all people should eventually adhere to the tenets of Islam. Like their co-religionists everywhere, they hold that Islam must unify Muslims over and beyond the confines of the nation state and provide one single center of authority. Africa "craves for Islam," says Usman Bugaje, as a part of its quest for "cultural freedom" and search for "an alternative world view that can stand up to challenge the West."

The impulse motivating sub-Saharan Islamists has little to do with any desire for a "moral revivification and renewal": theological analysis and ethical reflection have disappeared from the Muslim intellectual domain in Africa long ago, and in the equatorial part of the continent they have never developed. Contemporary African Islam is an anti-Western flight from ethical concern with explicitly political objectives: the human swath of the faithful prostrated outside the mosques is less an expression of fervor than an act of aggressive political protest. Nothing new under Allah's sun, perhaps, and that is what the demand for Shari'a is all about. The consequences of its introduction in the mixed areas of Africa were obvious in Sudan. In Khartoum, the military regime of General Omar Hassan al-Bashiri upheld Shari'a law in 1989. This move immediately pitted the northern Sudanese Arabs against the Christians and animists of the south and caused the long-running civil war in which at least 2 million Christians have been killed.[82] Tragic as it was for the people of Sudan, the resulting mayhem was welcomed by some Arabic countries—often America's Middle Eastern "allies"—that are actively promoting and funding the Islamic onslaught in black Africa.

One of them, Egypt, supposedly a friend of the United States and the second largest recipient of the U.S. taxpayers' largesse, failed to convict a single murderer following the January 2000 massacre of 21 Coptic Christians in the village of Al-Kosheh, 300 miles south of Cairo. The court convicted only four of 96 defendants, and only on lesser charges. All four men convicted were Muslims; not one was convicted for murder, but two for "accidental homicide and illegal possession of a weapon" and the other two were each sentenced to one year in prison for damaging a private car.[83]

---

[82] 107th U.S. Congress, 1st Session (H. CON. RES. 113), "Regarding human rights violations and oil development in Sudan."

[83] Associated Press, February 5, 2001.

From the outset, the government of Egypt had sought to cover up the gravity of the case and to avoid the political minefield of punishing Muslims for the murder of Christians. After the verdict, Egypt's Christians have cause to fear for their lives.

The worst offender in Africa, however, is the richly endowed non-African center of Islamic agitation, Saudi Arabia. Already in 1983, Saudi Arabia exerted pressure on Sudan to declare itself an Islamic state. It ensures that those who join the Islamic Conference Organization are given speedy access to the funds of the Islamic Development Bank and the Arab-controlled "Bank for Economic Development in Africa." Just as the Arab proselytizers of Islam were unconcerned about the welfare of black Africans when they ventured to hunt them, mutilate them, and sell them into slavery centuries ago, their heirs see them but as canon fodder in the project of global Islamic expansion, or else simply deny their existence. Mauritanian Muslim-dominated regimes in particular are notorious for denying the existence of the black majority in the country, while simultaneously keeping it enslaved. Its ex-President Ould Taya once declared that "Mauritania cannot be in the process of Arabization as it is already an Arab country."[84]

At the same time, according to *Africa Watch* (1990), there was not a single Arab among the 200,000 Mauritanian citizens who were deported to Senegal or Mali. While black Mauritanians were being driven out of their homes to refugee camps, Arab refugees from Senegal, Mali, or West Sahara were welcomed into Mauritania, where they were given citizenship and resettled on land whose rightful owners were deported. Slavery is practiced exclusively by Arab Mauritanians and Sudanese on non-Arab citizens in both countries, and upon the introduction of Shari'a laws in Mauritania and Sudan, respectively in 1980 and 1983, savage punishments like amputation and flogging have been applied mainly on non-Muslim blacks by exclusively Arab-Muslim judges. As a result, there is "an undeclared war simmering at the western end of the line dividing Arab North Africa from the African sub-Sahara." [85] Racially and religiously motivated incidents are occurring regularly; in 1990 alone, hundreds of blacks were slaughtered in Mauritania and 300,000 more were driven south

---

[84] *Jeune Afrique,* January 1, 1990.
[85] *Newsweek,* 12.2. 1990.

as Arabic speakers rushed north from Senegal to take over their homes and lands.

The Rt. Rev. Bullen Dolli, an Episcopal bishop from Sudan, was puzzled by the cold reception when he came to Washington in October 2001 to talk about the predicament of his much-abused flock under Islam. "It is a militant religion," he said at a scantily attended press conference, and warned on behalf of the victims against those who act as its character witnesses. He pointed out that Sudan's death toll is larger than the combined fatalities suffered in Bosnia, Kosovo, Afghanistan, Chechnya, Somalia, and Algeria. Twice as many Sudanese have perished in the past two decades than all the war-related deaths suffered by Americans in the past 200 years.[86] But hardly anyone listened. The bishop's hosts could not get him a slot on NPR, on the networks, or any other high-profile venue previously so eager to accommodate any itinerant mullah praising the "Religion of Peace and Tolerance."

To Bishop Dolli, it may seem incomprehensible that the U.S. has intervened militarily and politically to "save" the Muslims in Bosnia and Kosovo from alleged genocides perpetrated by their Christian neighbors while it remains indifferent to the very real genocide of Christians that has been perpetrated by the ruling Muslims in Sudan for two decades. He does not understand that his flock's very Christianity barred them from certified victimhood in the eyes of the ruling Western elites.

ANY LESSONS?

Decades of covert and overt support for "moderate" Islamic movements, countries, and regimes, whenever they were deemed useful to Western foreign policy objectives—and especially if they have lots of oil, or prove willing to make peace with Israel, or both—have been an unmitigated moral and political disaster.

Egypt, Saudi Arabia, Jordan, Turkey, Pakistan, Morocco, the Gulf states, Bosnia-Herzegovina, Nigeria, Indonesia, and a few others have become the darlings of U.S. policy, valued as

---

[86] Testimony of Roger Winter, Executive Director, U.S. Committee for Refugees on America's Sudan policy to the U.S. House of Representatives Committee on International Relations, March 28, 2001.

supposed bulwarks against "fundamentalism" of the Iranian variety (Iran itself having lately been a member of the favored assembly). Operationally, this means not only overlooking the radical activities of the supposedly "moderate" Muslim states—for example, Saudi Arabia's and Pakistan's support for the Taliban regime in Afghanistan . . . and assistance by virtually all Islamic nations to the thinly disguised radical regime in Sarajevo—but also a consistent American bias in favor of the Muslim party in virtually every conflict with a Christian nation.[87]

Saudi Arabia and, beyond the Arab world, the unlovely examples of Afghanistan and Pakistan suggest that Islamist intolerance can flourish on the back of American support, or—in the case of Iran—as a reaction against it. These are the societies most affected by America's experiment in Islamic management since the lamentable CIA/SIS coup against Mossaddeq in 1953—in short, the disaster zone.

Appeasement of Saudi Arabia in particular, and the string of related little despotic sheikhdoms along its eastern rim, is continuing even in the aftermath of September 11. It is as detrimental to peace and democracy in all affected regions as it is detrimental to the long-term security of North America, Africa, Asia and Europe. It does nothing to help the Muslim world come out of its state of deep denial about its responsibility for the worst terrorist outrage of all time, the denial as irrational as the culture that breeds it: in early 2002, according to a Gallup poll of 10,000 Muslims throughout the Middle East, 61 percent denied an Arab role on September 11 (including a staggering 89 percent in Kuwait), while only 18 percent believed Arabs were at the controls; only 9 percent of those polled considered military action against Afghanistan morally justified.[88]

The beneficiaries of three decades of Western appeasement have been Osama bin Laden, his ilk, and his co-religionists all over the world. Conceivers and executors of "excellent ideas" paved the way for September 11 by failing to grasp Islam's inherent link with violence and intolerance. The unspoken assumption of the architects of failed Western policies, that generosity would be rewarded by loyalty, is mistaken: loyalty to unbelievers is not a Muslim trait, but pragmatism is—and, as Yohanan

---

[87] James Jatras, *Chronicles* (1999), op. cit.
[88] *The Washington Times*, March 8, 2002.

Ramati has remarked, "pragmatism prescribes that when dealing with fools, one milks them for all one can get, demoralizes them until they are incapable of protecting their interests, and then deprives them of any influence they have left":

> The Moslem world today has no love and very little respect for the Western powers in general, and the United States in particular. It was for many years a bitterly divided world, where individual rulers competed with each other for wealth, influence, and sometimes territory. This was why the wealthy states of the Gulf Cooperation Council were ready to accept protection from American and other Western forces. But four decades of prattling about decolonization and "globalism" have made their mark. If globalism is a good reason for uniting Europe, preventing it is a better reason for uniting Moslem states (which have much more in common than the Europeans) on a policy to wrest power from the unbelievers.[89]

The Muslim states are aware of Western greed and its political repercussions, Ramati concludes, and they still trust that they will not be hindered in increasing their military, political, and economic capacity to a point at which they can blackmail the West into accepting their political, cultural, or religious demands. After September 11, they are hoping that the U.S. will settle for destroying Bin Laden and the Taliban and gradually resume its oil-dictated pro-Muslim policies. Such policies, drastically manifested in the "great game" under Presidents Carter and Reagan, has had its apologists in each subsequent American administration. In the team of George Bush, Sr., it was summarized in a statement by then Assistant Secretary of State for Near East and North African Affairs, Edward Djerejian, who declared that the United States did not regard Islam or Islamic movements as the enemy and recognized their right to participate in the political process.[90] The spirit of the statement was reiterated and expanded upon by his successor, Robert Pelletreau, under Clinton. Pelletreau lamented in 1996 the fact that the "image of Islam in the minds of the average newspaper reader is often one of an undifferentiated

---

[89] Ramati: *The Islamic Danger to Western Civilization*, www.westerndefense.org/special/TwinTowers2001.htm.

[90] dosfan.lib.uic.edu/ERC/briefing/dispatch/1993/html/Dispatchv4no 21.html.

movement hostile to the West and ready to use violence and terrorism to achieve its ends."[91] He distinguished the many "legitimate, socially responsible Muslim groups with political goals from Islamists who operate outside the bounds of law."

The continuation of such policy is heartily cheered by the "experts." The legions of Islam's character witnesses and fellow-travelers in the academy today represent the mirror image of the Duranties and Shaws six or seven decades ago. They are insistent that Americans "must become aware that these people are not our enemies, but our partners and potential friends, who can be talked to and who can be understood."[92] Bringing the Islamists into the tent and opening dialogue with them will result in their moderation; in the writings of today's Western apologists for "understanding" Islam, Islamists seem not much different from the Methodists down the street.

The standard establishmentarian view—in this case summarized by the Islamophile *par excellence* John Esposito, director of the Center for Muslim-Christian Understanding at Georgetown University—remains as rose-tinted as it is disdainful of any opposing view:

> Contemporary Islam is more a challenge than a threat. It challenges the West to know and understand the diversity of the Muslim experience. . . . Contrary to what some have advised, the United States should not, in principle, object to the implementation of Islamic law or involvement of Islamic activists in government. Islamically oriented political actors and groups should be evaluated by the same criteria that are applied to any other potential leaders or opposition party.[93]

This argument is simply wrong. The United States has no business intervening militarily to prevent the establishment of Islamic law in some remote desert wasteland, but "object" it must, on principle and for selfish reasons of self-preservation. To treat "Islamically oriented" actors the same as others will not buy their benevolence, much less respect; there will never be an "Islamic Democracy." Continued appeasement can only encourage

---

[91] www.usis-israel.org.il/publish/press/state/archive/august/sd2_8-28. Htm.

[92] www.danielpipes.org/articles/win9596.shtml.

[93] John L. Esposito, *Islam and U.S. Policy*, msanews.mynet.net/books/threat/6.11. html.

radical Islam to hone its skills at playing at "democracy," which it will do with gusto for as long as it is insufficiently strong to reveal its true character. As Daniel Pipes has noted, even within the same countries, Turkey and Algeria, the radical Islamic movement may have a "legitimate" wing taking part in elections, and the terrorist wing pursuing the same objectives through the barrel of the gun:

> Like Hitler and Allende, who exploited the democratic process to reach power, the fundamentalists are actively taking part in elections; like the earlier figures, too, they have done dismayingly well. Fundamentalists swept municipal elections in Algeria in 1990 and won the mayoralties of Istanbul and Ankara in 1994. They have had success in the Lebanese and Jordanian elections and should win a substantial vote in the West Bank and Gaza, should Palestinian elections be held.[94]

There is "democracy" of sorts in Iran, for instance, for all participants in the political process have to subscribe to the principles of the Islamic revolution. Only candidates (including non-Muslims) who subscribe to the official ideology may run for office, as under former Communist countries. Cabinets and legislatures may change; the regime cannot.

A generation ago it was understandable, even excusable, for bone-headed, God-fearing CIA bosses of the low-church Protestant kind to work up a hatred of atheism and enjoy dealing with believers. They used Muslims in just the way they used the Church of Rome in the early 1950s in their fight against the Communists. But appeasement by their feeble successors in our own time only breeds the contempt and arrogance of the radicals and fuels their ambition. Changing the self-defeating trend demands recognition that the West is in a war of religion, whether it wants that or not, and however much it hates the fact.

On the Islamic side this war is being fought with the deep and unshakeable belief that the West is on its last legs. The success of the demographic deluge enhances the image of "a candy store with the busted lock," reinforced by the evidence from history that a civilization that loses the urge for biological self-perpetuation is indeed finished. Falling

---

[94] Daniel Pipes, "There Are No Moderates: Dealing with Fundamentalist Islam," *National Interest*, Fall 1995.

birthrates in Europe and the need to support European welfare entitlements with a host of "guest-workers" and immigrants seem to make it inevitable that the colonization of Europe by Islamic peoples will continue.

Even after its unfinished victory in Afghanistan, America is viewed as a paper tiger, with F-16s and dollars to be sure, but no strong heart and no long-term stamina. Indeed, it is uncertain that anything significant has taken place in Afghanistan: the Afghan Taliban were forced to change their coats as one set of Islamists took a lot of money for replacing another. Moreover America's borders are still open to the continuing flow of immigrants from hostile Islamic countries.

Western policy toward Islam will remain on a path to disaster for as long as its response excludes any notion of self-definition other than liberal platitudes about "tolerance," "democracy," "human rights," or "opportunity." To face the war of religion that has been imposed on it, the West also needs to rediscover its own religion, or at least to stop denying its value. The sooner it faces this reality, the better for all concerned—including the Muslim world that may be otherwise tempted to overplay its hand and suffer cataclysmic consequences.

American leaders such as President Bush may have been hoping to domesticate Islam under the aegis of the nondenominational deism that is professed in their rhetoric. The attempt will continue to fail. So far this failure has not been admitted. Hence the enduring fantasy of an American-Islamic alliance against extremism.

The West cannot wage "war on terror" while maintaining its dependence on Arab oil, appeasing Islamist aggression around the world, turning a blind eye to the Islamic destruction of peoples who are animists, Hindus and Christians, and allowing mass immigration of Muslims into its own lands. It risks being the star actor of a Greek tragedy in which the gods make the unfortunate rulers mad before they destroy them; as Yohanan Ramati put it: "Waiting to be hit by Moslem nuclear bombs because one does not wish to be ruthless with states sponsoring terrorism, to shift to non-oil energy, or to interfere with the profits of tycoons who do not even care for the economies of their own countries is no prescription for the survival of Western civilization." To reverse the failed strategy, specific policy reversals are called for:

> Islamic terrorism has been thriving because the existing policy is
> perceived as a sign of Western weakness. . . . The real problem

facing the United States and Western democracy is not how the Moslems will respond to a policy hostile to their interests, but whether the West still has the moral strength to adopt any policy causing its power-wielders temporary financial losses. Curbing their greed is a prerequisite for maintaining US superpower status and for success in the inevitable conflict with Islam.[95]

Just as in 1936, the author concludes, checking appeasement requires a revolution in the West's political thinking and a realization that safeguarding Western power-wielders' economic interests from Muslim encroachment or confiscation may become impossible if such encroachments continue to be tolerated or encouraged. It also requires understanding that Islam regards lies, violence, and threats of violence as legitimate means of gaining political ends and that the only capacity Islam respects in an unbeliever is the capacity to use diplomacy or military force successfully against it.

Of course, it would be preferable to have a reformed Islam as our global neighbor, rather than the grim variations on the same theme that currently prevail in Iran, Pakistan, Sudan, Libya, Saudi Arabia, and elsewhere, but Islam's ability to reform itself is undermined by the appeasement of Islamism. It will only enhance a downward spiral of hate and spite, rage and self-pity, poverty and oppression that may culminate sooner or later in yet another bout of alien domination.

Muslims, as Christians once did, tend to sympathize with each other in a familiar and more or less nationalist fashion. If this tendency goes unchecked it produces a lunatic account of world affairs in which Muslim societies are always victims of the West and always innocent. It is not just the extremists who believe that in Palestine, Chechnya, Bosnia, Kosovo, and Kashmir, the Muslims are entirely in the right: at present, almost every Muslim thinks so. The "politically correct" Westerners accept the Muslim judgment. But this is extremely dangerous, as the West cannot afford to concede such a large measure of moral approval to so self-conscious and agitated a force in world affairs.

To encourage the Muslim sense of pure victimhood is to feed the minds of suicide bombers with a political pap that nourishes their anger. The recent record of Islamist misrule and mischief must become more

---

[95] Ramati, op. cit.

familiar: for misrule we could start with the Sudan and Saudi Arabia and, for Islamist mischief, look at the Balkans and Nigeria. The obstacle to doing so is often the alliances, apologetics, and the tradition of appeasement of American policy. For their sake, and ours, appeasement must stop. Pandering to Islam's geopolitical designs, and sacrificing smaller Christian nations—Timorese and Sudanese yesterday, Serbs and Orthodox Cypriots today, Bulgars and Greeks tomorrow—is counterproductive: such morsels will only whet the Islamic appetite, paving the way to a major confrontation some time in this century.

CHAPTER SIX
Jihad's Fifth Column

Islam is today the fastest growing faith in the Western world, and nearly 20 million inhabitants of the European Union are self-avowedly Muslims. If present trends continue, by 2020, Muslims will account for 10 percent of the overall population of Europe and exceed 10 million in America. This population is expanding by immigration and an enormous birth rate that far exceeds that of the indigenous population.

What is happening today is nothing like the wave of immigration to America that took place in the 1880s and 90s. That was not clandestine. It was not based on the presumed right of the newcomers to bully the citizens of the United States into submitting to their worldview—and killing them if they proved reluctant to do so soon enough. Under McKinley, the business was regulated by acts of Congress. But today, there has never been any act of any Western legislature inviting, let alone urging, illegal Muslim immigrants to come. "What occurred was not an immigration, it was more of an invasion conducted under an emblem of secrecy—a secrecy that's disturbing because it's not meek and dolorous but arrogant and protected by the cynicism of politicians who close an eye or maybe even both."[1]

Most Muslim migrant workers initially expected to spend only a brief period of their lives in the non-Muslim industrial West. The old reluctance to submit to life under the unbelievers was overcome by the lure of economic opportunity. In 30 years, the Muslim population of Great Britain rose from 82,000 to 2 million. In Germany there are 4 million Muslims, mostly Turks, and over 5 million in France, mostly North Africans. There are 1 million Muslims each in Italy and the Netherlands, and 500,000 in Spain—that is more than in the last two centuries of the Caliphate of Cordoba. Almost a tenth of all babies born in EU countries are Muslim, and in the moribund Brussels the figure was over 50 percent. With the expanding numbers and the creation of distinctly Muslim neighborhoods in Western, primarily European cities, the initial detachment of culture from territory has been reversed, and the bold notion of conquest by demographic rather than military means entered the activists' minds. The

---

[1] "Anger and Pride" by Oriana Fallaci, *Corriere della Sera*, September 29, 2001.

blueprint was developed over two decades ago, in 1981, when the Third Islamic Summit Conference of Kaaba adopted the "Mecca Declaration." It stated:

> We have resolved to conduct Jihad with all the means at our disposal so as to free our territory from occupation.
> We declare that the oppression suffered by Muslim minorities and communities in many countries is a flagrant offense against the rights and dignity of man.
> We appeal to all states in which there are Islamic minorities to allow them full liberty.
> We are convinced of the need to propagate the precepts of Islam and its cultural influence in Muslim societies and throughout the world.

In the ensuing two decades, a new mosque was opened somewhere in the Western world twice every week. As far as the activists in Mecca were concerned, this did not mean that the Muslims in those countries were not "oppressed," however. In Islam, Muslim minorities are oppressed as long as they are not governed by Shari'a, which is the only "full liberty" possible. Demands for freedom from "oppression" and pledges to propagate Islam were advanced, irrespective of the fact that the signers of the Declaration openly oppressed non-Muslim communities in their own lands, or prevented them from being established at all.

The number of Muslims in the United States has grown threefold since the Mecca Declaration, to about 3 million. (We can disregard, for now, the inflated claims of 6, 7, or even 10 million, made by various Islamic activists.) That number is rising, overwhelmingly through immigration rather than conversion. Some are legal, and others are "undocumented workers"—equivalents of what the Italian liberals call "manual-labor-for-which-there-is-demand." Already at the time of the first World Trade Center attack in 1993, it was obvious that belligerent Islam had a firm foothold within the Muslim diaspora in the United States. That foothold has grown in numbers, power, and savvy over the ensuing decade.

Nevertheless, over the years the U.S. government has been unfathomably lax in allowing entry not only to hundreds of thousands of Muslim immigrants—many of them from countries considered risky or openly unfriendly to U.S. interests—but also to supporters and propagators

264

of radical Islam, or agents of terrorist regimes and organizations. It allowed terrorists and their supporters to enter the United States on fraudulently obtained student visas that camouflaged their true purpose. Worse still, some really come for education, specialist technical training unobtainable at home—so that they could go back and develop their countries' nuclear, chemical, or biological weapons programs. Others come and go for shorter periods, including clerics and leaders of radical Islamic groups, who attend conferences organized by militant groups in the U.S. but whose real purpose is to recruit new members, raise funds, coordinate strategies with other militant leaders, indoctrinate new "foot soldiers" and even participate in training sessions.

A decade and several thousand American lives later, President Bush restated the failed politically correct orthodoxy during a visit to a mosque on September 17, 2001: "America counts millions of Muslims among our citizens, and Muslims make an incredibly valuable contribution to our country. Muslims are professionals, as well as moms and dads." Two days later, he added that "there are millions of good Americans who practice the Muslim faith who love their country as much as I love the country, who salute the flag as strongly as I salute the flag." The President and the oilmen around him are willfully blind to Islamic extremism no less than the prophets of globalization once grouped around Clinton. Bush's post-9-11 theological assurances about Islam-as-Peace show how stubborn the conciliatory gambit is.

Islam may be forced into a quietist mode, as we have seen in the aftermath of World War I, but a religion born in holy war and spread largely by conquest deserves to have its traditions and record taken seriously. Perhaps Mr. Bush should see the popular Iranian film *Not Without My Daughter,* in which an immigrant father assures his little girl that he is as American as an apple pie, yet he could revert at any moment to being as strict a Muslim as any Ayatollah.

HOSPITALITY ABUSED

The consequences of the delusion reflected in Mr. Bush's words, and accepted for many years as orthodoxy, have been grave. By early 2000, the United States and Canada had become the home for a wide spectrum of international Islamic terrorist groups as well as indigenous groups, which are the primary threat of international terrorism on American soil. They have set up fundraising operations, political headquarters, military recruitment, and sometimes even command and control centers.[2] The entire spectrum of Islamic terrorist groups operated on American soil, including Hamas, Hezbollah, the Algerian Armed Islamic Group, the Egyptian Al Gamat Al Islamiya, the Palestinian Islamic Jihad, the Islamic Liberation Party, and Al-Qaeda. They all share the outlook frankly stated during his FBI interrogation by Siddiq Ibrahim Siddiq Ali, one of the suspects in the first World Trade Center bombing:

> Of course, don't forget God said in the Kuran, in times like this, everything is lawful to the Muslim, their money, their women, their honors, everything. . . . Infidels must be killed . . . and the Muslim when he dies, it is the way to heaven. He becomes a martyr. A Muslim will never go to hell by killing an infidel."[3]

The pattern was set over the preceding decade and has its model in the *Tawheed*—Muslim conquest of Arabia—and the *Fatah,* the early Muslim expansion. It was then that the concept of "dodging the threat," *Al-Taqiya,* was developed. It encouraged Muslims to use subterfuge to defeat the enemy. They were ordered to infiltrate the enemy's cities and plant the seeds of discord and sedition. Sometimes they argued that Jihad is not aimed at the people about to be conquered, that they are not targeted. Taqiya in our own time is reflected in the attempts by Muslim activists in the West to present Islam favorably, replete with tolerance and peace, faith and charity, equality and brotherhood. The "misunderstood Muslims" tell us that Jihad is really the "striving for Allah" and "inner struggle." They quote the abrogated Meccan verses and keep quiet about the later, Medinan ones. They accuse those who question Islam of being racist. This fact alone should arouse suspicion when it is noted that in the United States four-fifths of the Arabs are Christians, many of whom have fled persecution by Islamic governments. The critique of Islam's encroachment in the West is certainly not "anti-Arab" but rather opposed to an inherently intolerant ideology that seeks to undermine Western democratic values.

---

[2] United States House of Representatives: House Subcommittee on Immigration and Claims, Hearing on International Terrorism and Immigration Policy, January 25, 2000, Testimony of Steven Emerson.

[3] UPI, August 23, 1993.

An early proponent in the U. S. was Ismail Al-Faruqi, a Palestinian immigrant who founded the International Institute of Islamic Thought and taught for many years at Temple University in Philadelphia, was also the first contemporary theorist of the Islamic Caliphate of America. He declared in 1983 that "nothing could be greater than this youthful, vigorous, and rich continent [North America] turning away from its past evil and marching forward under the banner of *Allahu Akbar.*" In December 1989, several extremist leaders attended a rally at Chicago, including Bashir Nafi, the funding member of Islamic Jihad, and Abdul Aziz Odeh, its spiritual leader. Two years later, Omar Abdel Rahman—the blind sheikh and head of the Egyptian Al Gamat Al Islamiya, later convicted of planning a "day of rage" by blowing up New York buildings—called on Muslims with perfect impunity to "conquer the land of the infidels." He was a legal resident alien in the U.S. at that time.

Echoing his words, Siraj Wahaj, an African American convert to Islam, a "highly respected community leader" and the first imam to deliver a Muslim prayer for the U.S. House of Representatives in 1991, declared in 1997 that Muslims will eventually elect the president and replace the constitutional government with a caliphate. "If we were united and strong, we'd elect our own emir and give allegiance to him. Take my word, if 6–8 million Muslims unite in America, the country will come to us." In 1995, he was a character witness for Omar Abdel Rahman at his trial, assuring the court of the defendant's "peaceful" and kindly disposition. For his part, Zaid Shakir, formerly the Muslim chaplain at Yale University, declared that Muslims could not accept the legitimacy of the existing political, social, and constitutional order in the United States.

After meeting with that noted Muslim "heretic" Louis Farrakhan in 1996, Libyan president Muammar Kaddafi said: "We are used to facing the United States as a fortress from the outside. Now we are finding a breach to penetrate the country and confront it from within."[4] When the leader of the Nation of Islam visited Iran on the anniversary of the fundamentalist revolution, he declared that "God will destroy America by the hand of the Muslims. God will not give this honor to Japan or to Europe. It is an honor that He will reserve for the Muslims." One year later in Harlem, Farrakhan declared, "A decree of death has been passed on America. The judgment of

---

[4] *Le Monde*, February 26, 1996.

God has been rendered, and she must be destroyed."[5] He never repudiated his well-known utterances in 1984 about Judaism being a "gutter religion" and calling Hitler a "very great man." The Nation of Islam distributes the *Protocols* at its events. In 1991 it published *The Secret Relationship between Blacks and Jews* that purports to show that Jews were primarily responsible for the slavery of blacks and the trans-Atlantic trade. Unlike other anti-Semitic groups, it has an organized paramilitary force in dozens of cities, and even has managed to win federal grants.

The visitors who arrive on visas issued by the U.S. embassies and consulates are as bellicose as the resident Muslim activists. Ahmad Nawfal, a Jordanian who was a frequent speaker at Islamic rallies throughout the United States in the 1990s, drew cheers for saying that America has "no thought, no values, and no ideals" and declaring that if Muslims stand up, "it will be very easy for us to preside over this world once again." In June 1991, the innocuously named United Association for Studies and Research (UASR), based in Virginia and operated by Musa Abu Marzook, one of the top three officials of Hamas, co-sponsored one of the largest gatherings of Islamist militants ever held in the U.S. It included Kamal Hilbawi, the leader of the Muslim brotherhood of Egypt, who openly advocated terrorist attacks.[6] Bassam Al-Amoush, a top pan-Islamist leader and Member of Parliament from Jordan, who used similar rhetoric in Chicago in 1994, subsequently had meetings at the State department and on Capitol Hill—courtesy of the Council on American-Islamic Relations (CAIR). Throughout this period, two fanatics were working the U.S. lecture circuit, Sheikh Ghuniem from Egypt and Yusuf Qaradawi, a militant cleric living in Qatar and ideologue of Hamas, who openly preaches violence on his website. The latter told a huge audience meeting in Kansas City in 1989, "On the hour of judgment, Muslims will fight the Jews and kill them." Qaradawi also praises Sudan as a model for the Muslim world. Ghuniem was the star speaker at a conference in Brooklyn organized by pan-Islamist groups on May 24, 1998.

At many of these meetings, the speakers routinely call on their audience to help eliminate Israel; the announcement of a fresh suicide bombing arouses unrestrained cheering. A connected theme concerns the

---

[5] *New York Amsterdam News*, August 14–20, 1997.
[6] commdocs.house.gov/committees/judiciary/hju64355.000/ hju64355 _0.htm.

need to gain more clout than the Jews. And finally, the overall strategic objective is to convert America, to turn it into an Islamic country and thus to save it from itself. The list goes on, and justifies the conclusion of a witness at the House of Representatives hearing on terrorism and immigration in January 2000:

> As water seeking its own level, terrorists will gravitate to those areas that give them the greatest freedom to maneuver. Unless choked off and stopped along the different points of entry— ranging from the visa granting process overseas to the hundreds of unmanned border crossing points between Canada and the United States—terrorists will continue to come to the United States.[7]

The unpleasant truth is that mosques throughout America and around the Western world are being used to teach hate. In the first instance, they promote the most outwardly visible form of Islamic piety, the one that focuses on Islamic ritual and practice in the immigrants' daily lives. Traditional dress, beard, headscarf or even complete veil, strict observance of prayers and dietary prohibitions, are a sure means of differentiating the diaspora in the Western world from the host society. For younger members of the second and third generation of Muslim immigrants to the West, Islamic appearance and lifestyle provides the much-needed means of enhancing group identity, loyalty, and self-respect.

The next step is to use the pool of outwardly pious to recruit the foot-soldiers of radical Islam, sometimes mistakenly referred to as "fundamentalists." They join the considerable ranks of the former Middle Eastern secularists who have been disappointed both in the Marxist failed god and in the futile dead-end of Third World nationalism symbolized by Ataturk, Nasser, Assad, or Saddam. In radical Islam, both find a common ground in their opposition to Western democracy, secularism, and value system on one hand, and, on the other, to many regimes throughout the Muslim world, which they regard as collaborationist and treasonous to traditional Islamic teaching. They see political parties as mere "traps for

---

[7] House Subcommittee on Immigration and Claims, Hearing on International Terrorism and Immigration Policy, January 25, 2000, Testimony of Steven Emerson.

hunting votes, which ensure the wielding of power for a few people's benefit"—in other words, democracy is really a form of dictatorship.[8]

OSAMA'S FELLOW-TRAVELERS

Radical Muslims dominate the Islamic life in the United States to the point that moderates hardly have a voice. Radical Muslims control every major Muslim organization, including the Islamic Association for Palestine, the Islamic Circle of North America, the Islamic Committee for Palestine, the Islamic Society for North America, the Muslim Arab Youth Association, the Muslim Public Affairs Council, and the Muslim Students Association. They also control a growing majority of mosques, weekly newspapers, and communal organizations. They are funded by the Iranians, Libyans, and Saudis, who have for years helped the most extreme groups. The moderates do exist, but they tend to go out into the world to avoid confronting the fanatical "community leaders." Islamist groups found they could manipulate the American public and politicians hiding under non-profit "religious charities," self-defined religious umbrellas and the politically correct buzzword of *human rights*.[9] Their friends and allies have even managed to join the armed forces of the United States and continue their subversive activities not only from within America but also from within its defense establishment.[10]

Prior to September 11, the Islamic vanguard in the United States had grown confident—even cocky. The Council of American-Islamic Relations (CAIR), the American Muslim Council (AMC), and the Muslim Public Affairs Council (MPAC) all protested the U.S. designation of Hamas, Islamic Jihad, and Hezbollah as terrorist organizations. According to the *Muslim World Monitor,* the groups said that characterization was wrong, because "Palestinian resistance organizations such as Hamas and Islamic Jihad have never committed any act outside of occupied Palestine and have only fought forces of the Israeli occupation." This was at the time when a spokesman for Hamas openly declared that "there are no such terms as

---

[8] Daniel Pipes: "Are Today's Islamic Movements Compatible with Democracy?" *Insight*, August 14, 2000.

[9] www.geocities.com/Athens/Crete/3450/terrorists.html.

[10] www.newsobserver.com/monday/front/Story/831377p-821059c.html, October 21, 2001, "Al-Qaeda terrorist duped FBI, Army."

compromise and surrender in the Islamic cultural lexicon": if the only alternative is destruction and death for the enemies of true Islam, so be it. Hezbollah's spiritual leader, Muhammad Husayn Fadlallah, concurred.

CAIR had even started to organize street protests against news organizations that dared report on the history of militant Islam, going to the point of lambasting anyone who referred to "fundamentalist Islam" or to the concept of jihad in Islam as guilty of "defaming Islam."[11] CAIR has called the verdict in the 1993 World Trade Center bombing "a travesty of justice" because it "represents the degree to which an anti-Muslim venom has penetrated into society."

CAIR, AMC and MPAC joined forces at a rally in Lafayette Park, in front of the White House, at which Abdurahman Alamoudi, former executive director and current member of the board of directors of the AMC, said, "We are all supporters of Hamas. Allahu Akbar! I am also a supporter of Hezbollah."[12] All three groups also condemned the August 1998 retaliation against Osama bin Laden in the aftermath of the bombings of two U.S. embassies in Africa.

In its statement about the August 8, 2001, bombing of a Sbarro pizzeria in Tel Aviv that killed 15 young Israelis, MPAC described it as "the expected bitter result of the reckless policy of Israeli assassinations. . . MPAC holds Israel responsible for this pattern of violence."[13]

In 1996 CAIR was incensed when the Nike Corporation, a leading sneaker manufacturer, presented a new model with the word *Air* written in stylized lettering. CAIR charged that the logo resembled the Arab script for "Allah." Instead of dismissing the "issue" as being on par with sinful subliminal messages in videos and on rock-'n'-roll albums, Nike was scared into paying for the construction of a playground next to a mosque in suburban Northern Virginia and recalled the sneakers. That was not good enough for CAIR, however. It demanded that the firm should submit to a "sensitivity training."

---

[11] Daniel Pipes, "How Dare You Defame Islam," *Commentary*, November 1999.

[12] 'Mainstream' Muslims? *New York Post* June 18, 2002

[13] This statement was originally posted on the organization's website, **www.mpac.org/news/news** -- but it was removed after September 11. Unfortunately for MPAC, it was cashed by Google and other search engines.

271

In 1999 CAIR objected to the season premiere of *Touched by an Angel*, which featured a story line about slavery in Sudan and forced conversions of Christians living in the south of the country. A CAIR official said the show was tantamount to "thinly disguised anti-Muslim propaganda and political partisanship."[14] Later that same year, American Muslim groups called for a boycott of Disney theme parks and merchandise to protest the Jerusalem exhibit at Disney World's EPCOT, claiming Disney ignored the city's significance to Islam.

CAIR's 1999 annual report on Muslim civil rights stated that American public schools are a "major area in which Muslim apprehension about the lack of religious accommodation is growing." It cited progress in Chicago, where alternative foods are available when pork is served; Fairfax County, Virginia, where a "pig" sign on school menus indicates items that include pork; and in Paterson, New Jersey (the scene of much public rejoicing by immigrant residents on September 11), where the school district cancels classes on two Muslim holidays.

When Argenbright Security (infamous for letting through the Nepalese illegal immigrant with seven knives and a stun-gun at O'Hare) fired seven Muslim women a few years ago—including four from the Sudan, listed as a terrorist state by the U.S. government—the EEOC made the firm rehire the women; the EEOC complaint was drafted by a lawyer for CAIR. [15] At a benefit dinner organized by the Muslim American Society and CAIR, just two days before the WTC attacks, an American convert to Islam, Sheikh Hamza Yusuf Hanson, told the crowd: "This country [America] unfortunately has a great, great tribulation coming to it. And much of it is already here, yet people are too illiterate to read the writing on the wall." [16]

In the best Stalinist tradition, both CAIR and MPAC have been busy airbrushing their past record since the World Trade Center and Pentagon attacks. They used to keep archives of all their past public statements, activists' speeches, etc. on the web, but after September 11 most of them have mysteriously disappeared.

---

[14] Richard John Neuhaus in First Things, No. 111 (March 2001)

[15] Cf. Thomas Fleming in *ChroniclesExtra* (November 18, 2001):
http://www.rockfordinstitute.org/HardRight/HardRight.htm

[16] "John Walker's Brothers and Sisters" by Anthony York, *Salon.com*, 12/21/2001

Corruption attracts corruption: Muslim leaders are courted by politicians—primarily those belonging to the Democrat camp—who are no more squeamish about their client-base than Unocal executives. On at least two occasions, Hillary Clinton hosted receptions organized by the aforementioned Muslim Public Affairs Council (MPAC), a group that has promoted the activities of Hamas, Turkey's fundamentalist Welfare Party, and the Muslim Brotherhood. Its officials have defended Hezbollah, while publicly insisting that they condemn terrorism. They raise tens of millions of dollars a year, much of it through nonprofit organizations, and much of that money is then funneled to overseas radical Islamic groups. Ms. Clinton had to return $50,000 received from MPAC—the Jewish vote in New York was at risk—but she justified her contacts by claiming that she was trying "to promote a framework for peace," that included "lines of communication to many different groups and many different individuals."[17]

The courting of such people has continued even after September 11. While it is understandable that the president was keen to demonstrate that the war on terrorism is not also a war on Islam, but his choice of Muslim leaders in America to be received at the White House or met elsewhere was unfortunate. One of them was MPAC's executive director, Salam al-Maryati, who had previously told a public radio interviewer in Los Angeles on September 11 that Israel should be considered a prime suspect in the World Trade Center and Pentagon attacks.[18]

Another was Muzammil Siddiqui, the former president of the Islamic Society of North America and imam of the Islamic Society of Orange County, California, who was also invited to the Oval Office on September 26 so that the president could thank him for his participation in the national day of mourning and remembrance. Imam Siddiqui had soothing and reassuring words for the president: "The Muslim community has unanimously condemned and deplored the crime committed on September 11, 2001. It was a most horrible crime against our nation and against humanity." In reality, Mr. Siddiqui, like all his true co-religionists, puts his Islamic loyalties first. Only a year earlier, at a Jerusalem Day rally in Washington, this same Imam Siddiqui warned his presumably adopted country, America, that if it remained on the side of injustice, the wrath of

---

[17] "Hillary's Outreach" by Steven Emerson. *Jewish World Review* November 6 , 2000
[18] Strange Bedfellows by Eric Fingerhut, Washington Jewish Week
http://www.jewsweek.com/politics/031.htm

Allah—who is watching everyone—would come.[19] To believe that he was shocked, terrified, and disgusted by September 11 defies belief.

For his part, Sheikh Muhammad Gamei'a, formerly both Al-Azhar University's representative in the United States and imam of the Islamic Cultural Center and Mosque in New York City, declared that "all the signs indicate that the Jews have the most to gain from an explosion like that."[20]

But even if one allows for the unlikely event that Muslims carried out the September 11 attacks, according to a leading Muslim cleric, "terrorism" must be differentiated "from the struggle of peoples for their acknowledged national causes and the liberation of their territories."[21] The key is supposedly "the intention of the perpetrator and the general acceptability of his act is *Din* with all its spirit, laws and concepts," not his act as such. "Terrorism" does not apply to "acts of national resistance . . . resistance against racial discrimination":

> It is indeed comical that the United States of America, the mother of international terrorism and the source of all the circumstances of oppression and subjection of peoples . . . should seek to convene symposia on combating *terrorism* (i.e. any act that conflicts with its imperialist interests). . . . Islam does not omit to lay down a comprehensive, realistic, and flexible code of sanctions that deals with facts according to their social effects.[22]

This is the acceptable face of Islam presented to international forums and the media. One is led to wonder what "extremist" Islam must be like. Some of those organizations may have an "American" adjective, but all of them share an agenda that harks to Medina circa A.D. 628.

---

[19] Cf. comprehensive study of Islamic extremism in the U.S. by AVOT, http://www.empower.org/docs/avot/jihad.pdf

[20] In an interview on October 4, 2001. Middle East Media Research Institute, http://www.memri.de/uebersetzungen_analysen/laender/aegypten/egypt_gameia_17_10_01.html.

[21] Ayatullah Shaykh Muhammad 'Ali Taskhiri, Director of the International Relations Department of the I.P.O., at the International Conference on Terrorism called by the Organization of the Islamic Conference, Geneva, June 22–26, 1987, www.al-islam.org/al-tawhid/definition-terrorism.htm.

[22] ibid.

FAILURE OF LAW ENFORCEMENT

The Council of American-Islamic Relations, the American Muslim Council, and the Muslim Public Affairs Council are all in the grip of manipulators who tell the touchy-feely fibs of love and tolerance to the media and politicians, while pursuing their own agenda within the ranks of the initiated. There is nothing new under the democratic sun, especially for those who take an interest in the rise and fall of pro-Soviet communist parties throughout the Western world. The response from the law-enforcement agencies to Islamic aggression in America should be similar: close monitoring, strict supervision, and zero-tolerance for the infringements of the law. It has not been so thus far, with calamitous consequences for all concerned.

Appeasing the Islamic militants living in America is only making it harder for more tolerant Muslims to emerge, the people who have absorbed enough of American values and way of life to realize that the only way they can be accepted in the long run is to give up the psychotic desire to turn everything and everyone into a mirror-image of themselves. This reality is denied by western secularists obsessed with political correctitude. The old liberal-secular antipathy to Christianity has converged with the new PC movement and the therapeutic society to produce a climate wherein it is easy for the Muslims to lie about the true nature of Islam and get away with it. Defense against such lies is difficult, when it is deemed "insensitive" to respond with facts and in plain language. The result was predictable, according to Oliver Revell, former head of the FBI's counter-terrorist investigations, who bewails the fact that "these radical terrorist groups found that the United States, the freest country in the world, was the best place to organize and build up their terrorist movements." The hypocrisy of "mainstream" Muslim leaders is equally predictable, and condoned by the openly situational morality of their creed.

Incomprehensible permissiveness of the abuse of America's hospitality was sometimes justified by "sensitivity," multiculturalism, or a badly skewed notion of human rights. It was rooted in the inability of post-national, secular-liberal host governments to perceive their countries as real communities, rooted in the continuity of shared memories and cultural legacies. They refused to treat their countries as entities that ultimately

275

belong to the majority of people inhabiting them and bearing their name, and not to whatever loud complaining fringe group is making the most strident claims at any given time. The reluctance to read the riot act to the fanatical newcomers who abuse the host-nations' hospitality, starting with the arrests and swift deportations of all illegal and other law-breaking immigrants, extended to both sides of the Atlantic. In America, it had fatal consequences.

Federal agencies had long known of the extremist activities of Muslim activists in America in general, and of the existence of U.S.-based terrorist cells associated with Osama bin Laden in particular. They did not act to break them up and deport the conspirators, however, or even to monitor them effectively enough to prevent the attacks.[23] Already on June 23, 2001, airline industry officials received a detailed warning about a threat from Bin Laden's network to use airliners to attack Americans. Citing a report from the Arabic-language MBC satellite television channel, the *AirlineBiz.com* news service reported a plot to destroy 12 U.S. airliners in Asia. An MBC reporter who had met with Bin Laden in Afghanistan two days previously predicted that "a severe blow is expected against U.S. and Israeli interests worldwide":

> There is a major state of mobilization among the Osama bin Laden forces. It seems that there is a race of who will strike first. Will it be the United States or Osama bin Laden?" Despite such detailed advance warnings, Bin Laden won that "race."[24]

The strange case of Zacarias Moussaoui is the clearest example of astonishing indolence. Moussaoui, a French citizen of Moroccan descent (once described as a "Frenchman" on NPR!), was arraigned January 3, 2002, on six counts of conspiracy to commit murder and terrorism in the September 11 attacks. He was originally arrested in Minnesota for immigration violations three weeks before the attacks after officials of a flight school, the Pan Am International Flight Academy in Eagan, a suburb of Minneapolis, tipped off the FBI that he was seeking flight training on a Boeing 747 jumbo jet. He was belligerent, evasive about his personal background, and he paid the $6,300 fee in cash. He did not want to learn

---

[23] "Bin Laden Link Cited,"*The New York Times,* September 13, 2001.
[24] William Norman Grigg: "Did We Know What Was Coming?" *The New American,* Vol. 18, No. 5, March 11, 2002.

how to take off or land, only how to steer the jet while it was in the air. The instructor and a vice president of the flight school repeatedly tried to get the FBI to take an interest in Moussaoui's conduct.[25] The instructor became so frustrated by the lack of response that he gave a prescient warning to the FBI that a 747 loaded with fuel can be used as a bomb.

Eventually local FBI investigators in Minneapolis sought authorization for a surveillance warrant to search the hard drive of his home computer. Officials in Washington, however, who said there was insufficient evidence to justify the warrant, rejected this request. FBI agents tracked Moussaoui's movements to the Airman Flight School in Norman, Oklahoma, where he logged 57 hours of flight time earlier in 2001 but was never allowed to fly on his own because of his poor skills. This alone should have set off alarm bells, since a confessed Al-Qaeda operative, Abdul Hakim Murad, had trained at the same school as part of preparations for a suicide hijack attack on CIA headquarters. Murad testified about these plans in the 1996 trial of Ramzi Ahmed Yusef, the principal organizer of the 1993 WTC bombing.

On August 26, 2001, the FBI was notified by French intelligence that Moussaoui had ties to the Al-Qaeda and Bin Laden. Even this report did not spur the agency to action. A special counterterrorism panel reviewed the information but concluded there was insufficient evidence that he represented any threat; he was not even moved from INS detention to FBI custody until after September 11. The French warning arrived on the day after the first two suicide hijackers purchased their one-way, first class tickets for flights on September 11. More tickets were purchased on August 26, 27, 28, and 29, while the FBI was refusing to pursue a more intensive investigation into Moussaoui or search his computer. The notion of flying a plane into a building or using it as a bomb was never considered as a serious threat by the Bureau: it was a straight hijacking scenario that they were worried about.[26]

Moussaoui was not the only member of the conspiracy known to the federal authorities. On the morning of September 11, "two people already identified by the government as suspected terrorists boarded separate American Airlines flights from Boston using their own names."[27] Federal

---

[25] *New York Times,* December 22.

[26] *The Washington Post*, January 2, 2002.

[27] *New York Times*, December 30, 2001.

officials were also aware of a third hijacker, Hani Hanjour, who had come to the attention of the Federal Aviation Administration (FAA) while learning to fly at the Pan Am International Flight Academy in Phoenix. When officials at the school expressed concerns to the FAA about Hanjour's inability to speak English, the agency stepped in to provide assistance—to Hanjour. An FAA representative sat in on a class to observe him and discussed with school officials finding an Arabic-speaking person to help him with his English. Hanjour continued his program, which enabled him to fly American Airlines Flight 77 into the Pentagon.

A reflection of the disarray in monitoring and law enforcement was the fact that Huffman Aviation International flight school in Venice, Florida, received delayed visa approvals by the INS for two suicide pilots, Mohamed Atta and Marwan Al-Shehhi, on March 9, 2002—almost six months after the attacks! Atta and Al-Shehhi filed requests in September 2000 to change their non-immigrant status from visitor to student. Atta's application was approved July 17, 2001, and Al-Shehhi's was approved August 9, 2001. Notices to students were automatically generated on approval, the statement said, adding that a secondary notification to the school occurs later, after data is manually entered at an INS contract facility.

A Justice Department investigation found that all nineteen hijackers involved in the September 11 attacks had legally entered the country on tourist, business, or student visas. Three of the air pirates had overstayed their visas, according to the Department, although sixteen others were in the country legally when they hijacked and piloted four jetliners.

Senior intelligence officers outside the FBI complained that such grotesque failures were possible because they received very little cooperation from the Feds.[28] Several of the September 11 hijackers, including Mohammed Atta, the ringleader, were under direct surveillance by U.S. agencies as suspected terrorists during 2000 and 2001, yet they were given visa upgrades that allowed them to travel freely into and out of the country, which enabled them to carry out their plans. The conclusion is clear:

> Though administrators of federal law enforcement and intelligence agencies would prefer to cloak the issue in self-

---

[28] *Newsweek*, December 21, 2001.

serving euphemisms, Black Tuesday was—at best—a singular intelligence failure, for which those officials must be held responsible. And if, as one of the above-quoted former FBI counterterrorism agents suggests, efforts to prevent that attack were compromised because of covert "agendas" in Washington, Congress must be prepared to take even more serious action.[29]

Belatedly, months after the attacks, the FBI started conducting more than 150 separate investigations into Islamic groups and individuals with possible ties to Osama bin Laden. The domestic targets included dozens of people who were under electronic surveillance through national security warrants, and others who were being watched by undercover agents. The large number of cases suggests the FBI's efforts against the terrorist network have gone well beyond the widely publicized dragnet and suggests the Al-Qaeda presence is far broader than previously known. Most of the suspects are active members of, or have been sponsored by "mainstream" Muslim organizations in the United States. Some have traveled lecturing at mosques and Islamic centers filled to the capacity. They rely on quasi-legitimate civil rights Islamic groups, such as the Council of American-Islamic Relations, the American Muslim Council, and the Muslim Public Affairs Council (MPAC) that operate as fronts of the fundamentalist movement.

UNHOLY ALLIANCE: ISLAM AND LIBERALISM

The American nation's mental unpreparedness for the horror of September 2001 was perhaps to be expected in view of the politicians' assurances—notably President Clinton's announcement almost exactly three years before the attacks, on September 21, 1998—that Islam is as American as apple pie. Addressing the General Assembly of the United Nations, Mr. Clinton derided those who "say there is an inevitable clash between Western civilization and Western values, and Islamic civilizations and values":

---

[29] William Norman Grigg, "Did We Know What Was Coming?" *The New American,* Vol. 18, No. 5, March 11, 2002.

I believe this wrong. False prophets may use and abuse any religion to justify whatever political objectives they have—even cold-blooded murder. Some may have the world believe that almighty God himself, the merciful, grants a license to kill. But that is not our understanding of Islam. . . . There are over 1,200 mosques and Islamic centers in the United States, and the number is rapidly increasing. The six million Americans who worship there will tell you there is no inherent clash between Islam and America. Americans respect and honor Islam.

True to his ideological assumptions, Mr. Clinton took the alleged fact that "six million Americans" believe in Islam as proof that their ideals include religious tolerance and aversion to violence. He did not explain what gave him the right to advance his "understanding of Islam" as the authentic one, in contravention of what most Muslims say, do, and believe, and have done for over thirteen centuries.

The Sufis, the darlings of many Western Islamophiles, admittedly focus on spirituality and disdain political activism, and their rituals contain elements of folklore and their teachings smack of mysticism. To "real" Islam, that is, to orthodox scholars and mainstream umma, Sufism is unwelcome and suspicious, if not outright heretical. Both Ibn Arabi and the New Age circus that surrounds such contemporary Sufis as Sheikh Nazim al-Qubrusi do not belong to the Islamic mainstream any more than the deep-Appalachian snake-handling belongs to the Church of Rome. Nevertheless, there are all too many Westerners prone to the magnetic appeal of "Eastern" mysticism who regularly quote Sufism as an example of "benign" Islam. To them, it is both "interesting" in what it has to say— as opposed to the arid wastelands of Mohammedan orthodoxy—and emotionally appealing, thanks to its semi-coherent, foggy mysticism, to the dopey New Age mindset.

There are many lessons of September 11. The most important one, as yet unknown to most Westerners, is that just like the unicorn, "tolerant Islam" can be defined and visualized, but it cannot be made real. "Let's get this straight," says *The Guardian's* Julie Burchill, one of the few voices of sanity in Britain's depressingly uniform media scene. The terrorist attacks,

> were a tragedy for the people who died or were injured, and for their families and friends. For the rest of us, they were a wake-up

call as to what type of lunatics we are dealing with. And sleepwalking our way back into ill-sorted, dewy-eyed people-are-people personal politics is the last thing we need to set us up for the fight ahead. Come on, you liberals; don't give me the morbid pleasure of saying "I told you so" again.[30]

But the sleep-walking has continued on both sides of the Atlantic. While any attempt to recognize traditional teachings in American public schools results in howls of protest over violation of separation of church and state, the Kuran is now required reading in one California public school district as part of course work introducing students to Islam. The course requires seventh-graders not only to learn the tenets of Islam and study the important figures of the faith, but also to wear a robe, adopt a Muslim name, memorize Kuranic verses, to pray "in the name of Allah, the Compassionate, the Merciful," and to chant, "Praise to Allah, Lord of Creation." As an outraged teacher commented,

> Can you imagine the barrage of lawsuits and problems we would have from the ACLU if Christianity were taught in the public schools, and if we tried to teach about the contributions of Matthew, Mark, Luke, John, and the Apostle Paul? But when it comes to furthering the Islamic religion in the public schools, there is not one word from the ACLU, People for the American Way, or anybody else. This is hypocrisy.[31]

Nancy Castro, principal of Intermediate-Excelsior School of Byron, says that the course "is not religion, but ancient culture and history." The textbook, adopted by the California school system, presents Islam adoringly, while the limited references to Christianity focus on the Inquisition and the Salem witch hunts highlighted in bold, black type.

People like Ms. Castro do not take Islam seriously. They trust the combined efforts of television, the Big Mac, and the public education system to make every little Muhammad from Peshawar and Azra from Algiers into carbon copies of Johnny and Chelsea. The Californian example is a symptom of an alliance no longer in the making but in full swing, and the partners' common ground is considerable. Now that Marx has failed—

---

[30] *The Guardian*, October 20, 2001.
[31] www.worldnetdaily.com/news/article.asp?ARTICLE_ID=25997.

and that's a fact reluctantly conceded even at Berkeley—Islam offers a helping hand to those who want to subvert the tradition of the West.

The mainstream conservatives, while ostensibly in power, are not taking notice. "Muslims make an incredibly valuable contribution to our country," President Bush declared shortly after September 11. But those same mild-mannered "moms and dads" who pay their bills on time sometimes end up becoming terrorists, because "wherever there is Islamic extremism there's a nexus to the potential of violence. . . . Anybody who subscribes to the tenets of militant Islamic fundamentalism is capable of violence."[32]

The Muslim population within North America and the rest of the West is not like any other, for it is the only immigrant group that harbors a substantial segment of individuals who share the key objectives with the terrorists, even if they do not all approve of their methods. It would be idle even for ardent Islamic apologists to pretend that many Muslim immigrants do not despise the West in general and the United States in particular, its institutions and all it stands for. To them their host country is a mine to be stripped, used and converted or destroyed. This was not what other newcomers to America had in mind as they flocked here to enjoy the unique opportunities of freedom. It was not what African Americans fought for as they justly demanded their rights under the Constitution during the civil rights movement. As is evident in the actions and words of many American Muslims a sizeable minority of them wishes to transform their host country into a Muslim country—by whatever means, violent or otherwise, justified by the supposed sanctity of the goal and a corresponding Kuranic injunction.

THE THIRD CONQUEST OF EUROPE

Exactly the same problem is present in each and every Western country that has carelessly opened the floodgates to mass immigration from the Muslim world. An early sign of what was about to hit England came almost 20 years ago in a document published by the Islamic Foundation in the industrial city of Leicester, 100 miles north of London: the Islamic

---

[32] "Don't ask for me by name" by Linda Frum, *National Post* (Toronto), October 20, 2002.

Movement is "an organized struggle to change the existing society into an Islamic society based on the Qur'an and the Sunna and make Islam, which is a code for entire life, supreme and dominant, especially in the socio-political spheres." This demands clear acceptance "that the ultimate objective of the Islamic movement shall not be realized unless the struggle is made by locals. For it is only they who have the power to change the society into an Islamic society."

Since then Jihad has never had it so good. The Muslim population of the world has been exploding, not only in Asia and Africa but also in Europe and the United States. China and India try to control the birth rate in order to raise living standards, but most Muslim countries regard demography as a political weapon. They will gladly export their surplus population to Europe and America, aware that the bigger the diaspora, the greater the political influence it will exert, and the more concessions the Islamic world will be able to extort from the West. Maintaining the loyalty of the dispersed Muslim diaspora has been a top priority. Islamic religious instruction in the newly planted Muslim communities on both sides of the Atlantic has been carried out by immigrant imams who have a clear agenda aimed at inculcating their Western-born wards with disdain and even hatred for their surroundings.

Countries long spared the consequences of Islamic immigration suddenly find themselves on the front line. A bomb blast that damaged parked cars and shattered windows near the Interior Ministry in downtown Rome in February 2002 was preceded only days earlier by the discovery of a tunnel that suspected Muslim terrorists were digging in the vicinity of the U.S. embassy, apparently intending to carry out a chemical attack. A year earlier, the embassy was closed for several days following the information that an attack was imminent.

When four Moroccans were arrested in Rome on February 21, 2002, and found to be in possession of maps showing the city water supply grid and a substance containing cyanide, the *Romani* were thrown into panic. Many people realized that Muslim terrorism is not something that happens only to others and wondered how many similar threats to their lives may remain uncovered. Leaked reports to the press said the Moroccans were linked to Al-Qaeda's European network, four of whose members were due to be sentenced in Milan the following day.

On February 22, the Milanese court convicted the four. Essid Sami Ben Khemais, 33-year-old known among his associates as "the Sabre" and suspected of heading Osama bin Laden's European logistics, pled guilty to charges that included criminal conspiracy to obtain and transport arms, explosives, and chemicals and was sentenced to five years in prison. Three other Tunisians who were tried with him—Belgacem Mohamed Ben Aouadi, Bouchoucha Mokhtar, and Charaabi Tarek—were convicted on the same charges and sentenced to prison terms of up to five years. They also fabricated false documents that allowed Al-Qaeda operatives to travel in Europe and elsewhere. The Tunisians requested and received a fast-track trial, reducing the maximum sentence of nine years to six. The prosecutor, Stefano Dambruoso, said that, since 11 September, "it is the first verdict in Europe that recognizes the existence on European territory of a cell strongly linked to the center in Afghanistan."

"UK mosques prey to terror" warned a headline in the London *Times* in the aftermath of 9-11, and the article explained that this was partly due to the British Home Office routinely approving priority entry into the country to Muslim clerics from countries such as Pakistan who speak no English and do not want to control extremists who took over their mosques.[33] A prime example is the notorious mosque in the north London suburb of Finsbury Park, which has evolved into a nerve center of international Islamic terrorist network, notably Algeria's murderous GIA, the *Groupe Islamique Armé,* connected to Bin Laden's network. One of its preachers, Afghan war veteran Abu Hamza al-Masri, has helped organize military training for Muslims from Britain. He condemned the September 11 attacks, but only because he claims they were carried out by the Israeli Mossad.

The British security services, like the government, have long been in a state of denial regarding the Islamist threat. There has been no serious effort to develop and enhance intelligence coverage and analysis capability; nor was the recruitment of Arabic speakers made a priority. Time and again, the British courts have interpreted the criminal, asylum, and terrorism laws in the manner damaging to the security of the Realm and favorable to the Islamic underground. British police have repeatedly ignored warnings that the recruiting agents for extremist groups prey on

---

[33] *The Times*, December 27, 2001.

mosques, universities, and community centers. There are now over three hundred after-hours schools run by militant groups all over Britain in which the children are indoctrinated, Taliban style.

"We will remodel this country in an Islamic image," gloats Syrian-born Sheikh Omar bin Bakri, a foremost Islamic leader in Britain, who is active in "the struggle against racism and discrimination" to which the Muslims in Britain are supposedly subjected. At the same time, he belongs to The International Islamic Front for Jihad against Jews and Crusaders, founded by Bin Laden, and boasts: "We collect funds to be able to carry on the struggle; we recruit militiamen; and sometimes we take care of these groups' propaganda requirements in Europe."[34] Bakri also heads the London branch of Hizb Al-Tahrir (Islamic Revolutionary Party), which has some 50 branches all over Western Europe. When the Afghan war started in October 2001, Bakri declared:

> We will replace the Bible with the Kuran. . . . Christians have to learn that they cannot do this to Islam. We will not allow our brothers to be colonized. If they try it, Britain will turn into Bosnia.[35]

Remarkably, this same Mr. Bakri, who does not care that the Bible has long been replaced in Great Britain by Mr. Blair's therapeutic state, was expelled from Saudi Arabia in 1985 as a dangerous agitator for creating Al-Muhajirun, a branch of the Islamic Revolutionary Party. He has lived in London since 1986, drawing $500 a week in welfare and calling on young Muslims to take up arms against the "opponents of Islam"—meaning everyone who is not Muslim, or who does not subscribe to his vision of Islam. While living in Britain at its taxpayers' expense, he denounces it as "the spearhead of blasphemy that seeks to overthrow Muslims and the Islamic caliphate." As early as 1991, during the Gulf War, according to the *Mail on Sunday*, Bakri said that then-Prime Minister John Major "is a legitimate target. If anyone gets the opportunity to assassinate him, I don't think they should save it. It is our Islamic duty, and we will celebrate his death."

---

[34] *Il Giornale* (Milan), October 14, 2000.
[35] *The Observer* (London), October 27, 2001.

We can only guess how many thousands of Bakris operate freely in Boston, Michigan, or New Jersey, or—for that matter—in Paris, Berlin, Toronto, Amsterdam, or Milan. If we conservatively assume that 10 percent of adult male Muslims in Britain are regularly hearing incitements to jihad, and 10 percent of that audience might, in some circumstances, be driven to act upon those ideas, "this would mean that, conceivably, Britain has a core of at least 3,000 or 4,000 potential jihad fighters, more than enough to levy a devastating guerrilla war against British society"—and unlike ETA or the IRA, the British mujaheddin would be driven by an ideology that extolled suicide attacks.[36]

All of these people take full advantage of the host-countries' laws and often operate under the guise of charities. A notable example was the International Development Foundation (IDF), with offices in London's Curzon Street, which was named in a French parliamentary report in 2001 as a financial front for Al-Qaeda. Its trustees were four brothers belonging to the wealthy Bin Mahfouz family, one of Saudi Arabia's most powerful, with a fortune estimated at over 4 billion dollars. The British Charity Commission says that the IDF was connected to Khalid bin Mahfouz, a Saudi businessman and Irish citizen who had hosted Bin Laden at his mansion in Buckinghamshire and who is under investigation for his links to Al-Qaeda. The Mahfouz brothers and IDF trustees denied any knowledge of Kahlid when first approached by British investigators, but it was then discovered that he is also their brother.[37] In addition, Kahlid had connections to BCCI, the British bank used by the CIA to pay Bin Laden during the Afghan war with the former Soviet Union.

"Our own legal framework stops us from dealing with extremist religion," concludes a Pakistani-born British Anglican who grew up as a Muslim. Islam has never learned to live as a minority and cannot reconstruct itself in Western societies:

> My own feeling is that what will happen in the British society—I am waiting to see whether it will happen in the U.S.—is Muslim societies will emerge within Western countries where they will develop their own patterns of social Shari'a. In Britain today,

---

[36] Philip Jenkins, "Nor Shall My Sword Sleep in My Hand," *Chronicles*, March 2002.
[37] "UK assets of Islamic charity are frozen" by James Doran, *The Times*, January 16, 2002.

where Islam controls the inner cities, we have major social exclusion and the development of Shari'a. We have had churches burned, Christians attacked, and a mission center destroyed. The media has deliberately kept everything off the air.[38]

By allowing a vast and so far unsupervised subculture of intrinsically hostile immigrants to emerge within their societies, the developed nations have permitted the emergence of an alternative social and political structure in their midst in which terrorists can operate virtually undetected. Even after September 11, the British government has been less concerned by the Islamist threat than by the possibility of an anti-Muslim backlash. A rare occasion when a British minister showed genuine anger in his pronouncements did not concern the activities of the Islamic fifth column in London, Leicester, or Leeds; it came when a Home Office official swore to root out "the cancer of Islamophobia" from British society.[39]

By seeking to appease Islam, the host-countries only prompt demands for more. Examples abound. In Germany, the highest court in the land ruled in January 2002 that Muslim butchers should be allowed to slaughter animals according to Islamic practice, by slitting their throats and letting them bleed to death, and without stunning them first in any way. German law says animals cannot be slaughtered without first being stunned, but the constitutional court has now overturned it. The head of Germany's Islamic Council, Hasan Oezdogan, declared that this will be "an important step in the integration of Muslims in Germany."[40] If and when the Constitutional Court allows clitoridectomy for Germany's Muslim girls, presumably another important step will be made; "integration" will be complete only when Pakistanis in Britain, Algerians in France, and Turks in Germany turn the host country into an Islamic society by compelling it to adapt to their way of life.

A delayed devastating consequence of the second round of European fratricide in 1939–1945 was a reduced workforce in its aftermath, which opened the door for millions of Muslim immigrants. Where France initially looked to its North African colonies, Germany entered into recruitment agreements with Turkey in 1961, Morocco in 1963, and Tunisia in 1965.

---

[38] *The Washington Times*, January 16, 2002.
[39] Philip Jenkins, "Nor Shall My Sword Sleep in My Hand," *Chronicles*, March 2002.
[40] Reuters, 15 January, 2002.

Bosnian Muslims are the second-largest immigrant group in Germany, and it maintains close ties with the Turkish community.[41] Already a decade ago, with the number of Muslim residents approaching 3 million and the number of mosque associations exceeding 2,000, the writing was on the German wall:

> The Turks in Berlin constitute a social problem without a solution. There are entire sections of the city closed in on themselves that support a parallel and hostile culture, with no kind of symbiosis with the German culture. And the Magrebins have done the same thing in Marseilles [France]. The very opposite of integration, their objective is to organize society according to the Kuran. Islam is a way of life that annuls any separation between the religious, civil, and political reality.[42]

Also in 1991, in Australia, a Muslim scholar suggested that polygamy should be legalized and rape in marriage abolished as an impossibility: "a woman should not be able to charge her husband with rape."[43] The shape of things to come in Britain—already apparent during the Rushdie affair when Muslim immigrant leaders openly supported calls for the writer's murder—was visible in the nominally "English" city of Oldham in 2000, when the local council removed dozens of old-fashioned traffic bollards because they had moldings of the town's owl mascot on them and so were liable to "offend" local Muslims who objected both to the concept of "totemic" imagery and to the heraldic symbolism of the old, mono-cultural and racist past.

On the other side of the Channel, where five million Muslims live and create one-third of all newborn "French" babies, an early campaign of Islamic terror was initiated by a Tunisian named Fouad Salah, who was convicted in 1992 of setting off bombs that killed thirteen Frenchmen in a terrorist campaign during 1985–1986. He told the judge: "I do not renounce my fight against the West. . . . We Muslims should kill every last one of you." Imam Abdelali Hamdoune urges the faithful: "Do not permit your children to follow the example of the French. They should comport

---

[41] www.csis.org/europe/frm990412.html.

[42] Vittorio Messori in *Avvenire*, Rome, November 18, 1992.

[43] *The Sun-Herald*, Sydney, April 28, 1991, p. 21.

themselves in a totally different manner than the French. Here in France we have to impose ourselves, and impose Islam."[44]

Accordingly, in France and all over Western Europe, demands are presented for businesses employing Muslims to observe the Islamic calendar, or for state schools to be segregated by sex and include the tenets of Islam in the curriculum. Everywhere they demand that their daughters be allowed to wear the traditional headscarf, or hijab, claiming that it is more a cultural than a religious symbol. In France, they have already prevailed.

Spain is next. A Moroccan girl, Fatima el Hadi, only months after arriving in Madrid, caused a controversy for refusing to wear a uniform in a semiprivate Roman Catholic school in Madrid and insisting on the hijab. Her father is now suing the Spanish state for discrimination.[45] "Why should she stop wearing a scarf when the Christian girls wear little crosses?" asks Tomas Calvo, head of the Migration and Racism Study Center at Madrid University.[46] Gaspar Llamazares, leader of the United Left coalition, described the issue as "racist" and "another example of the government's intolerance."

At the same time, and contrary to the media-promoted stereotypes of the community of "law-abiding citizens," Muslim immigrants account for a disproportionate number of serious crimes in all West European countries. An Algerian Islamic group carried out the only anti-Jewish terrorist attack in Europe in 1995, the attempted bombing of a Jewish school near Lyons. Since then, from Birmingham to Berlin, anti-Semitism has become primarily a Muslim phenomenon in today's Europe. Muslim immigrants on both sides of the Atlantic are the most vibrant contributors to Jew-hatred, boldly using the terms of crude anti-Semitic propaganda unheard since Streicher.

In Denmark, where predominantly Muslim immigrants account for 68 percent of rapes, Islamic "community leaders" went out of their way to describe rape as "un-Islamic."[47] Perhaps they have not read the Kuran. In the Netherlands police had difficulty controlling joyous demonstrations by young Moroccans celebrating the attacks of September 11.

---

[44] *L'Express*, Paris, May 16, 1996.
[45] AP, February 16, 2002.
[46] *El Pais,* February 15, 2002.
[47] *The Copenhagen Post*, September 18, 2001.

In Italy, currently home to over 1 million Muslims, Islamic leaders are demanding the destruction of a priceless fifteenth century fresco in Bologna that "offends Islam" by showing—they claim—Muhammad being cast into Hell. The Union of Italian Muslims has written to the Pope, saying the fresco "constitutes an even graver offense to the religion than that caused by Salman Rushdie's *The Satanic Verses*." In Turin last October, prominent imam Bouriki Bouchta, the leader of two of the city's five mosques, defended Bin Laden and called for the "end of the West."

In *The Flying Inn*, Chesterton depicts a decadent England falling under a Nietzschean version of Islam. Only a drunken, half-mad Irishman, who moves an inn-sign from place to place and defies the de-Christianization of his country, defeats the enemies of life. But, as Thomas Fleming has asked, where, in these sober and progressive times, are we going to find a drunken Irishman who keeps the Faith? Not at the Vatican, if history is to repeat itself: The doors of Spain were opened to the Muslims in the eighth century by the Archbishop of Seville, Oppas. The spirit of the Second Vatican Council keeps the legacy of Oppas alive and well. When Cardinal Giacomo Biffi, Archbishop of Bologna, declared that there should be "no more entry visas for Muslims" and that "Christian Europe" was in danger of being overwhelmed by a "Muslim invasion," the voices from within the Catholic Church were the shrillest in their outrage. Perhaps today's Catholics would be well advised to revisit *The Catholic Encyclopaedia*'s verdict from 1908, which stands as firmly today as it did almost a century ago:

> In matters political, Islam is a system of despotism at home and aggression abroad. . . . The rights of non-Moslem subjects are of the vaguest and most limited kind, and a religious war is a sacred duty whenever there is a chance of success against the "Infidel." Medieval and modern Mohammedan, especially Turkish, persecutions of both Jews and Christians are perhaps the best illustration of this fanatical religious and political spirit.

AVOIDING THE CAMP OF SAINTS

The open-ended population explosion in every predominantly Muslim country in the world and the demographic collapse in Europe provide the context of immigration trends, prompting the conviction among many

Muslims that tomorrow belongs to Islam. It is wrong to conclude that Muslims have simply "replaced" communists as the main threat to the West; they are but two faces of the same menace of the closed society and the closed mind. The totalitarian nature of Islam, akin to Communism and Nazism, makes the threat different in degree to that faced during the Cold War, but not in kind. It demands a similar response. Perhaps only one in a hundred communists living in the West was an active Soviet spy; maybe not one in a hundred Muslim immigrants is an active Bin Laden asset. Nevertheless, managing the communist risk 50 years ago entailed denying entry visas (let alone permanent residences, training or passports!) to self-avowed Party members. Doing the same now, with Bin Laden's potential recruits, is the key to any meaningful anti-terrorist strategy on both sides of the Atlantic.

It is time to pay attention to the fact well known to INS officials: that all too often the attitudes of Muslims who want to live in the United States change rapidly once their status in America is secure. When applying for admission and while awaiting green cards, in interviews with U.S. officials they complain about the lack of freedom in their native country, citing specific instances in the area of human rights and politics. But as soon as they gain permanent residence, let alone citizenship, they suddenly turn against their host nation and begin to praise the virtues of an Islamic state, forgetting their pleadings with immigration officials to accept their application. A thorough and systematic background check of each applicant, coupled with psychological tests and one-on-one in-depth interviews with specialists qualified to detect such "dual personality" traits in potential immigrants, need to be introduced for all newcomers from the countries at risk, as well as for Muslims from non-Muslim countries, like the "Frenchman" Zacarias Moussaoui and the "Briton" Richard Reid.

The alternative is a non-targeted, sweepingly general, clampdown on civil liberties that will be as ineffective in curbing Islamic extremism as it will be undoubtedly successful in making life less pleasant and less dignified for the peoples of the West. It is a matter of balance based on clearly defined strategy: those infringements of civil rights that are essential to anti-terrorist strategy should be open to scrutiny and considered a painful sacrifice or a purely tactical retreat, not as the mere brushing aside of irritating legal technicalities. Everything is wrong with risking liberties that have developed over centuries and not developing a comprehensive defense strategy.

A coherent long-term counterterrorist strategy, therefore, must entail denying Islam the foothold inside the West. As the British writer David Pryce-Jones put it, "Democracy sometimes appears paralyzed by those who take advantage of its freedoms in order to abuse them for undemocratic ends." Muslims themselves are the first who need to be rescued from their own leaders' intent on taking us all, and them, into the abyss.

Like Communism, Islam relies on a domestic fifth column—the Allah-worshiping Rosenbergs, Philbys, Blunts, and Hisses—to subvert the civilized world. It also relies on an army of fellow-travelers, the latter-day Sartres and Shaws in the ivory towers, on "liberal academics and opinion-makers [who] sympathize with Islam partly because it is a leading historical rival of the Western civilization they hate" and partly because they long for a romanticized and sanitized Muslim past that substitutes for the authentic Western and Christian roots they have rejected.[48] Those roots must be defended, in the full knowledge that "those who subscribe to Islam and its civilization are aliens, regardless of their clothes, their professions or their places of residence."[49] They sense Western weakness and expect that if Islam supplies the only old religious tradition left standing 50 years hence, it may attract mass conversion. That would indeed be the end of the West, its final surrender to the spirit masterfully depicted by Jean Raspail in the preface to the 1985 French edition of his *Camp of Saints*:

> The West is empty, even if it has not yet become really aware of it. An extraordinarily inventive civilization, surely the only one capable of meeting the challenges of the third millennium, the West has no soul left. At every level—nations, race, cultures as well as individuals—it is always the soul that wins the decisive battles.

The story that Raspail tells is rooted in a "monstrous cancer implanted in the Western conscience." Its roots are in the loss of Faith, and in the arrogant doctrine—rampant in "the West" for three centuries now—that man can solve the dilemma of his existence by his unaided intellect alone.

---

[48] Philip Jenkins in *Chronicles*, September 2001.
[49] www.vdare.com/francis/specter.htm.

If that loss is not reversed, the game is over anyway—proving yet again that where God retreats, Allah advances.

CONCLUSION

WHAT TO DO?

Before 1914, both the West and the Muslim world could define themselves against each other in a cultural sense. What secularism has done, since replacing Christianity as the guiding light of "the West," is to cast aside any idea of a Christian social, geographic, and cultural space that should be protected. Islam, "extreme" or "moderate," has not softened, however. The consequences will be very serious unless Muslims are either "westernized"—that is to say, made as willing as Christians to see their religion first relativized, then mocked, and its commandments misrepresented or ignored—or else Christianized, which of course cannot happen unless there is a belated, massive, and unexpected recovery of Western spiritual and moral strength.

If neither of those scenarios work, the West faces two clear alternatives: defense, or submission and acceptance of sacred Arab places as its own.[1] Western political leaders have every right to pay compliments to Muslim piety and good works, but they should be as wary of believing their own theological reassurances as they would be of facile insults. Islamic populations and individuals draw very different things from their religion, its scripture and traditions, but anti-infidel violence is a hardy perennial. The challenge remains—how to prevent theocratic intransigence from winning support, and how to prevent it sheltering behind secular-liberal toleration.

While it is proper for democratic government to refrain from legislating the practice of religion in any way, Islam is a special case because it is, on its own admission, much more than "just a religion." It needs to be understood and subjected to the same supervision and legal restrains that apply to other cults prone to violence, and to violent political hate groups whose avowed aim is the destruction of our order of life.

The collective striving embodied in "We the People" makes no sense unless there is a definable "people" to support it. Most Muslim immigrants have no kinship with the striving and no connection to that "people,"

---

[1] V.S. Naipaul (1998).

295

except for the unsurprising desire to partake in its wealth. But their deep disdain for the democratic institutions of the host-countries notwithstanding (and just like the members of communist parties before them), Muslim activists in non-Muslim countries invoke those institutions when they clamor for every kind of indulgence for their own beliefs and customs. They demand full democratic privileges to organize and propagate their views, while acknowledging to each other that, given the power to do so, they would impose their own beliefs and customs, and eliminate all others. Once it is accepted that "true Islam" does not recognize a priori the right of any other religion or world outlook to exist—least of all the atheistic secular humanism of the ruling establishment—a serious anti-terrorist strategy will finally become possible.

The current terrorist threat to the United States comes almost exclusively from the members of the Muslim community. Critical to reducing the chance of an attack in the future are an immediate moratorium on all immigration from the risk-nations, an expansion of the Border Patrol to the point of zero-porosity, a radical reduction of visas issued to nationals of states that harbor or produce terrorists, abandonment of amnesty debate and the swift deportation of all illegal aliens from rogue nations that threaten America.

We are being indoctrinated into the dogma that the trend is inevitable, that economically motivated, unceasing immigration on a vast scale is unstoppable because it is due to inexorable global market forces. This is not true. Free citizens must not submit their destiny, and that of their progeny, to a historicist fallacy. Immigration from Islamic nations can, and should, be subject to the democratic will of the American people. They have every right to defend themselves and their way of life.

The struggle against terrorism starts with knowing thy enemy. A new paradigm on Islam, immigration, and Western identity are needed. Then, and only then, will human intelligence assets be usefully deployed to identify, target, and then destroy the individuals and their networks dedicated to our destruction. All will be in vain unless murderous Islamic extremism, manifested on September 11, spells the end of another kind of extremism: the stubborn insistence of the ruling liberal establishment on treating each and every newcomer as equally meltable in the pot.

Reducing and gradually ending unnecessary and harmful dependence on Middle Eastern oil is probably the easiest to achieve of all prerequisites for the policy of survival. Greed has always blinded power-wielders to danger, however, and it still does:

> The greed of the business tycoons promoting globalism is far greater in scale and its impact on humanity than any greed history has known—and just as blind. It has nurtured an enemy who cares more about land than about money and has a profound religious urge to prove his superiority to the infidel. The message of history is that the United States will be unable to stem the tide of Islam in the twenty-first century unless it abandons globalism and begins to treat Moslem states as potential enemies whose strategic assets and importance must be reduced before it is too late.[2]

From September 11 on, designating "threats to national security" should finally start to follow some clear determination of America's national interests. In longer-term strategy, a wider paradigm shift is needed, based on the need for a genuine Northern Alliance of Russia, Europe, and North America. The prerequisite is to revise Samuel Huntington, who mistakenly puts Orthodoxy in the same league with Islam *vis-à-vis* "the West." Far from being treated as a threat, Russia should be helped on the road to recovery. In the short term, its recovery may help it develop democratic institutions that would make its aggressive comeback unlikely. In the longer term, Russia needs our help so that it can become the West's bulwark against the real threat to our common security stretching along the West's vulnerable eastern flank from the Caucasus to the Pacific as we enter the century that is certain to see a renewed assault of militant Islam on an enfeebled Europe.

The alternative is to open the gates and turn the Remnant into a reeking Camp of Saints. In the functionally nihilistic Western world, the temptation to give up will only grow stronger in the aftermath of America's Black September, and Islam's proselytizers know how to play the game. Ostensibly rejecting the act itself, but not the goals of its perpetrators, they act as if Islam were just another competitor in the marketplace of ideas and lifestyles. They enter the new millennium with a strong hand. For starters, Islam is "non-white," non-European, and non-Christian, which makes it a

---

[2] Ramati, op.cit.

297

natural ally of the ruling Western elites. At the same time, it has an inherent advantage over the tepid ideology of multicultural mediocrity in that it offers Allah in the place of nothing. It also has an advantage over most established Christian denominations, since the latter do not offer God as an alternative. All too happy to abandon their ancient sanctuaries to any mosqueless newcomer who asks politely, they are, at best, the Social Workers at Therapy.

A surge in conversions to Islam in the Western world after September 11, especially among affluent, young whites, attests that the strategy of reliance on the spiritual Death of the West is sound. It also fits a pattern set by recent history; similar surges followed the outbreak of the Gulf War, the Bosnian conflict, and the fatwa against Salman Rushdie. Perhaps there is, after all, no such thing as bad publicity. The "Green Brigades" of the not-too-distant future will be increasingly composed of Johnny Walker Lindh clones. To a self-hating nihilist, Bin Laden is willy-nilly an admirable figure: a man with a cause for which educated people are ready to die. "Why grapple with mental puzzles such as the Holy Trinity and Original Sin, they ask, when the alternative proved to them so much more satisfying?"[3] By contrast, Christianity seems cluttered and its meaning obscure, its once powerful symbols wrapped up in ritual and hidden away. The starkness and terror of the Cross have been forgotten.

Islam should not be blamed for being what it is, nor should its adherents be condemned for maintaining their traditions. We should not hate it, nor ban it. We should, however, blame ourselves for refusing to acknowledge the facts of the case and failing to take stock of our options. People did not take *Mein Kampf* seriously, at their own peril.

The Kuran's exhortations to the believers to annihilate the non-believers, to confiscate their land and property, to take their women and enslave their children are equally frank, and the fruits visible through the centuries. In the present state of Western weakness, this firmness may appear attractive to the legions of cynical nihilists and lead further millions to the conclusion that we should all become Muslims, since our goose is cooked anyway, spiritually and demographically. Those of us who do not cherish that prospect should at least demand that our rulers present that

---

[3] "Allah came knocking at my heart" by Giles Whittell, *The Times*, Monday, January 7, 2002.

option fairly and squarely. To pretend, as the ruling elite does, that Islam is "a religion of peace," rather like Episcopalianism, is stupid or deeply dishonest.

A chronic pseudo-war of American secular wealth against Islamic religious poverty is an ominous outcome, the contest presumably desired by the minds behind the atrocities. The American foreign policy establishment wants a "civilization" that includes Saudi Arabia and pays only lip service to the world's largest country, Russia, or the world's largest democratic society, India. Their coalition is too close to what went wrong in Afghanistan. Terrorism was factored into their political equations and their balances of power. They tried to ride the tiger: they are conspicuously unqualified to lead a defense against it.

If the Saudis have the right to travel to Western countries and build mosques, then we should have the right to engage in open missionary activity in Saudi Arabia or anywhere else. We have every right to proclaim our ideas of Western freedom and an open society, whether this offends other countries' rulers or not. We have no obligation to "respect other cultures" and ideas when those cultures and ideas lead to human suffering, misery, and servitude. We have every right to protect our ideas and way of life by openly proclaiming the superiority of our principles.

Our second task after defending ourselves is to help our fellow humans trapped in Islam to become free. The Islamist campaign of violence in Algeria has turned some Muslims, especially Berbers, away from Islam and toward Christianity. The massacres and killings in the name of Islam have prompted converts to declare: "Christianity is life, Islam is death."[4] For their sake, and for that of the yet unknown and unenlightened millions of others, we must reject the absurd notion that we have no right to try and convert Islamic nations and peoples to a more humane, and more rewarding world outlook. The allied nations did not shirk their duty to convert Germany and Japan into democracies after defeating them. In the same way, we have every right to openly evangelize the Islamic nations with not only the gospel of Christianity, but also the "gospel" of secular democratic thought.

---

[4] "Christianity Is Life," *Middle East Quarterly*, Summer 2001, www.mequarterly. org/article.php?id=104.

Some critics may object that this account of Islam in the modern world does not pay much attention to Islamic moderation, to the everyday wish of everyday Muslims for a quiet life. This is not because such moderates are rare, but because they are rarely important. Religions, like political ideologies, are pushed along by money, power, and tiny vocal minorities. Within Islam, the money and the power are all pushing the wrong way. So are the most active minorities. The urgent need is to recognize this. Our problem is not prejudice about Islam, but folly in the face of its violence and cruelty. And in any case, the willingness of moderates to be what are objectively *bad Muslims,* because they reject key teachings of historical Islam, may be laudable in human terms but does nothing to modify Islam as a doctrine.

Islam might have been made much less threatening if the West had not conciliated or sponsored its most threatening exponents. Islam was exposed to a devastating collapse in credibility within the Arab world itself in the middle of the twentieth century. The forces of secularity were very strong indeed. But America opposed them at every turn because they were socialist or communist or simply not "in the national interest." America gave whole-hearted support to the worst fascist nation on earth: Saudi Arabia. As the economies of real states faltered and halted, the Saudi petrodollars were poured into establishing violent fanaticism as the big alternative. Gradually, the people who could moderate Islam have been pushed aside by raving sheiks congratulated by U.S. diplomats. The main reason for hailing Islam as a "religion of peace" is to cover this fact up.

There is a huge problem for all Muslims—the violent message of the Kuran. We cannot solve it for them, and we should not be asked to deem the problem solved by pretending that the Kuran is a pacifist tract. Humans are perfectly capable of reinterpreting scripture when absolutely necessary, but until the petrol dollars support a line of Islamic exegesis that can renounce the ideals of jihad, terror, tax, and subjugation we must have the guts to call a religion of war by its right name. After the Bolshevik revolution, the liberal response was to regret its excess but to allow that its idealism was somehow for the best. If this line had persisted, Communism would have triumphed. America supplied Europe with the stamina it needed to dismiss all the claims of Communism comprehensively. Once this was done, the corner was turned, and the Cold War could not be lost.

"As a man thinketh, so is he." The real problem of the Muslim world is not that of natural resources or political systems. Ernest Renan, who started his study of Islam by praising its ability to manifest "what was divine in human nature," ended it—a quarter of a century and three long tours of the Muslim world later—by concluding that "Muslims are the first victims of Islam" and that, therefore, "to liberate the Muslim from his religion is the best service that one can render him."

Islam is a collective psychosis seeking to become global, and any attempt to compromise with such madness is to become part of the madness oneself. No one who believes that jihad is the right or duty of all Muslims, or who promotes adoption of Shari'a law or reestablishment of the caliphate, should be allowed to settle in any Western country, and every applicant should be asked. The passport of anyone preaching jihad should be revoked. This may be called discrimination but the quarrel is not of our choosing.

Islam, in Muhammad's texts and its codification, discriminates against us. It is extremely offensive. Those who submit to that faith must solve the problem they set themselves. Islam discriminates against all "unbelievers." Until the petrodollars support a Kuranic revisionism that does not, we should go for it with whips and scorpions, hammer and tongs. Secularists and believers of all other faiths must act together before it is too late.

BIOGRAPHICAL NOTES

James Bissett is a distinguished Canadian diplomat and foreign affairs analyst, formerly the head of his country's Immigration Foreign Service and Assistant Under-Secretary for Social Affairs. Mr. Bissett was Canadian Ambassador to Yugoslavia, Bulgaria, and Albania, and, most recently, Director of the International Organization for Migration in Moscow. His comments appear regularly in *The Globe and Mail* and the *National Post* as well as the Canadian Broadcasting Corp. and C-SPAN.

Serge Trifkovic has combined a distinguished career in journalism with occasional forays into the academe that reflect the variety and depth of his interests. A graduate of the University of Sussex in England, he started his working life as a broadcaster and producer with the BBC World Service in London (1980-1986). After a year with the Voice of America in Washington he covered southeast Europe for *U.S. News & World Report* and *The Washington Times* during the early stage of the Yugoslav crisis (1988-1991).

Having obtained his PhD at the University of Southampton, Trifkovic pursued his postdoctoral research on a State Department grant at the Hoover Institute at Stanford (1991-1992). In addition to authoring several books and many refereed articles, over the past decade he has written scores of commentaries for-among others-the *Philadelphia Inquirer*, *The Times of London*, and the *Cleveland Plain Dealer*. He has appeared many times on the BBC World Service, CNN International, MSNBC, and other leading media outlets on both sides of the Atlantic.

As a regular contributor and, since 1998, foreign affairs editor of *Chronicles,* Trifkovic has been an outspoken advocate of the Jacksonian enlightened nationalism in world affairs and a stubborn upholder of the unsurpassed legacy of dead white males at home. This, his latest book reflects his life-long interest in the relationship between ideas and politics, the word and the world.

INDEX

A

Abbasids, 94, 113, 193
Abdullah, Saudi Prince, 244
Abraham, 14, 24, 32, 58, 68, 71, 78
Abu Sufyan, 36, 44, 45, 48
Abu-Bakr, 29, 34, 91, 151
Adam, 32, 60, 68, 78, 145, 146, 176
Afghanistan, 5, 112, 168, 190, 210, 211,
    212, 220, 222, 223, 225, 226, 227,
    229, 230, 231, 232, 233, 236, 237,
    246, 248, 249, 255, 256, 260, 276,
    284, 299
Aisha, 46, 81, 91, 158, 242
Akbar (, 112, 234, 267
Albania, 220, 226, 302
Al-Bukhari, 40, 45, 46, 71, 75, 145, 150,
    152, 163
Algeria, 137, 240, 249, 255, 259, 284,
    299
Ali, 29, 34, 35, 38, 46, 76, 91, 92, 93, 94,
    120, 136, 160, 161, 163, 169, 183,
    244, 266, 274
Allah, 3, 4, 22, 23, 24, 25, 28, 29, 30, 31,
    32, 36, 39, 40, 41, 43, 44, 46, 47, 49,
    50, 51, 55, 56, 57, 58, 59, 60, 61, 62,
    63, 65, 66, 67, 68, 69, 71, 72, 73, 74,
    75, 76, 77, 78, 79, 80, 81, 82, 83, 84,
    85, 87, 88, 90, 104, 107, 113, 122,
    130, 138, 143, 144, 145, 146, 147,
    149, 151, 152, 155, 156, 157, 158,
    161, 164, 168, 180, 194, 206, 207,
    212, 234, 253, 266, 271, 274, 281,
    293, 298
Almohads, 108, 183
Almoravids, 108
Al-Qaeda, 5, 211, 220, 222, 223, 225,
    226, 227, 230, 231, 243, 248, 266,
    270, 277, 279, 283, 284, 286
Amnesty International, 168, 169, 177,
    213, 215
Antioch, 96, 97, 99, 100, 101, 126

Arabia, 5, 12, 13, 14, 15, 16, 19, 20, 22,
    23, 26, 31, 37, 41, 42, 45, 49, 50, 89,
    91, 95, 113, 114, 126, 132, 135, 136,
    137, 138, 139, 140, 151, 154, 166,
    168, 173, 175, 186, 196, 203, 222,
    242, 243, 244, 245, 246, 247, 248,
    249, 250, 252, 254, 256, 261, 262,
    266, 285, 286, 299, 300
Arianism, 95
Aristotle, 193, 194, 197, 198
Armenia, 19, 95, 97, 107, 122, 137, 172,
    213
Armenians, 99, 113, 122, 124, 129, 133,
    238
Asia Minor, 96, 97, 98, 99, 101, 114,
    120, 124, 125, 127, 206, 238
Assad, 269
Attaturk, 124
Attaturk, Mustafa Kemal, 231, 240, 241,
    269

B

Badr, Battle of, 36, 37, 38, 40, 46, 88,
    171, 186
Baghdad, 11, 66, 94, 113, 173, 182, 183,
    184, 193, 200
Balkans, 49, 97, 114, 119, 120, 122, 133,
    174, 186, 213, 219, 220, 221, 223,
    227, 228, 237, 238, 262
Banu Nadir, 42
Banu Qurayza, 42, 44
Barbary Coast, 175
Bat Ye'or, 108, 129, 183
Bedouin, 13, 50, 64
Beirut, 160
Berbers, 299
Bible, 74, 83, 212, 217, 285
Bin Laden, Osama (Usama), 4, 5, 102,
    165, 220, 222, 224, 225, 226, 246,
    250, 257, 276, 277, 284, 285, 286,
    290, 291, 298

C

D

E

F

SELECT BIBLIOGRAPHY

Dr. Abdul Aziz Al-Fawzan, *The Evil Sin of Homosexuality*, www.islamweb.net/english/family/sociaffair/socaff-84.html

Africa Watch Report: *Mauritania Slavery Alive and Well, 10 Years after the Last Abolition*, 1990.

Tor Andrae, *Mohammed, the Man and His Faith*, New York, 1955.

W.N. Arafat, "New light on the story of Banu Qurayza and the Jews of Medina," *Journal of the Royal Asiatic Society of Great Britain and Ireland*, 1976.

Fr. Hugh Barbour, O. Praem, "A Latin's Lamentation Over Gennadios Scholarios," The Lord Byron Foundation's conference, "Overcoming the Schism," Chicago, May 9, 1998.

Bat Ye'or, The Dhimmi: *Jews and Christians under Islam, London*, 1985.

____, Myths and Politics: Origin or the Myth of a Tolerant Pluralistic Islamic Society, Paper delivered at the annual conference of The Lord Byron Foundation, Chicago, August 1995.

____, The Decline of Eastern Christianity under Islam: From Jihad to Dhimmitude, www.cmep.com/by.htm

Dan Cohn-Sherbok (ed.), *Islam in a World of Diverse Faiths*, New York, St. Martin's Press, 1991.

Patricia Crone and M. Cook, *Hagarism: The Making of the Muslim World*, Cambridge, 1977.

John Docker, "Arabesques of the Cosmopolitan and International," Paper delivered at the symposium: Visions of a Republic, The Powerhouse Museum, Sydney, 6 April, 2001.

Bruce Dunne, "Power and Sexuality in the Middle East," *Middle East Report*, Spring 1998.

Oriana Fallaci, "Anger and Pride," *Corriere della* Sera, September 29, 2001 (translated from the Italian by Chris and Paola Newman).

____, "An Interview with Khomeini," *The New York Times Magazine*, 7 October 1979, p. 31.

Thomas Fleming, "East is East, and West is Wuss," *Chronicles*, February 1999.

Franklin Foer, "Blind Faith," *The New Republic*, October 22, 2001.

Francois Gautier, *Rewriting Indian History*, New Delhi, Vikas Publishing, 1996.

Norman Geisler and Abdul Saleeb, *Answering Islam*, Baker Books, 1993.

Jamie Glazov, "The Sexual Rage Behind Islamic Terror," www.frontpagemag.com/columnists/glazov/glazov10-04-01.htm

Ignaz Goldziher, *Introduction to Islamic Theology and Law*, Princeton, 1981.

Alfred Guillaume, *Islam*, London, 1954.

Hadith:

—Sahih Al-Bukhari, www.usc.edu/dept/MSA/fundamentals/hadithsunnah/bukhari.

—Sahih Muslim, www.usc.edu/dept/MSA/fundamentals/hadithsunnah/muslim.

George Horton, *The Blight of Asia*, Indianapolis, 1926.

Albert Hourani, *A History of the Arab Peoples*, New York,1991.

T.P. Hughes, *A Dictionary of Islam* (1st ed.), London, 1935.

Samuel Huntington, "The Clash of Civilizations," *Foreign Affairs*, Summer 1993, Vol. 72, no. 3.

Ibn Ishaq, *The Life of Muhammad* (translated by A. Guillaume), New York, OUP, 1980.

Ibn Kammuna, *Examination of the Three Faiths*, Berkeley and Los Angeles, 1971.

Ibn Warraq (Ed.), *The Quest for the Historical Muhammad*, New York, 2000.

___, Why I Am Not a Muslim, New York,1995.

James Jatras, "Pravoslavophobia," *Chronicles*, February 1997, p. 43.

____, "Insurgent Islam and American Collaboration," *Chronicles*, February 1999.

Arthur Jeffery (ed.), *Islam: Muhammed and His Religion*, New York, 1958.

Philip Jenkins, "Empires of Faith: Islam and the Academy," *Chronicles*, September 2001.

Paul Johnson, *Modern Times*, London, Phoenix, 1996.

Koran, [1] Translated by J.M. Rodwell, reprinted 1992; [2] Translated by Dawood, London, 1956; [3] Translated by Palmer, London, 1949; [4] Translated by M. Pickthall, London, 1948; [7] Translated by Yusuf Ali, Lahore, 1934.

M. Kramer, "Islam vs. Democracy," *Commentary*, January 1993.

Peter Kreeft, "Ecumenical Jihad," in *Reclaiming the Great Tradition*, InterVarsity Press, 1997.

Bernard Lewis, *Race and Slavery in the Middle East*, OUP, 1994.

____, *What Went Wrong? Western Impact and Middle Eastern Response*, OUP, 2002.

Thomas F. Madden, "Crusade Propaganda: Abuse of Christianity's Holy War," *National Review Online*, November 2, 2001.

D.S. Margoliuth, *Mohammed and the Rise of Islam*, London, 1905.

A.E. Mayer, *Islam and Human Rights*, Boulder, 1991.

John Mercer, *Anti-Slavery Society Report of 1982.*

Robert Morey, *The Islamic Invasion*, Eugene, 1992.

Sir William Muir, *The Life of Muhammad*, Edinburgh, 1923.

____, *The Kuran in "Sacred Books of the East,"* I, Oxford, 1880.

V.S. Naipaul, *Beyond Belief: Islamic Excursions Among the Converted Peoples*, New York, Random House, 1998.

Ronald L. Nettler, *Past Trials and Present Tribulations: A Muslim Fundamentalist's View of the Jews*, Pergamon Press, 1987.

T. Noldeke, "Arabs (Ancient)," *Encyclopaedia of Religion and Ethics*, Vol. 8, pp. 11–12.

Daniel Pipes, "You Need Beethoven to Modernize," *Middle East Quarterly*, September 1998.

____, "There Are No Moderates: Dealing with Fundamentalist Islam," *National Interest*, Fall 1995.

____, "Are Today's Islamic Movements Compatible with Democracy?" *Insight*, August 14, 2000.

Yohanan Ramati, *The Islamic Danger to Western Civilization*, www.westerndefense.org/special/TwinTowers2001.htm.

BIBLIOGRAPHY

Ahmed Rashid, *Taliban: Militant Islam, Oil and Fundamentalism in Central Asia*, Middle East Studies, 2000.

Joseph Ratzinger, *Introduction to Christianity*, New York, 1979.

Maurice Roumani, *The Case of the Jews from Arab Countries: A Neglected Issue*, Tel Aviv, World Organization of Jews from Arab Countries, 1977.

Joseph Schacht, "A Revaluation of Islamic Tradition," *Journal of the Royal Asiatic Society*, 1949.

Abd El Schafi, *Behind the Veil*, Pioneer Books, 1996.

Ronald Segal, *Islam's Black Slaves: The Other Black Diaspora*, Farrar, Straus & Giroux, 2001.

Andre Servier, *Islam and the Psychology of the Musulman*, New York, 1924.

Lt.Col. John E. Sray, *Selling the Bosnia Myth to America: Buyer Beware*, U.S. Army Foreign Military Studies Office, Fort Leavenworth, KS, October 1995.

Michael Stenton, "Frankish Blinkers," Unpublished paper presented at The Lord Byron Foundation's conference, "Overcoming the Schism," Chicago, May 1998.

____, "The Trap of Victory: Middle Eastern Policy After Afghanistan," *Byronica*, April 2002.

N.A. Stillman, *The Jews of Arab Lands*, Philadelphia, 1979.

W. St. Clair Tisdall, *The Original Sources of the Qur'an*, London, 1905.

John Wansbrough, *Kuranic Studies*, Oxford, 1977.

W. Montgomery Watt, *Introduction to the Quran*, Edinburgh, 1977.

____, *Islamic Philosophy and Theology*, Edinburgh, 1979.

____, *Muslim-Christian Encounters*, London, 1991.

Samuel Zwemer, *Islam: A Challenge to Faith*, New York, 1908.

____, *The Moslem Doctrines of God*. New York, 1905.